MICROSCOPY OF ASTROLOGY

MICROSCOPY OF ASTROLOGY

(ASTROLOGY SIMPLIFIED)

BALDEV BHATIA
(CONSULTANT ASTROLOGY)
INDIA

PARTRIDGE
A Penguin Random House Company

To order additional copies of this book, contact
Partridge India
000 800 10062 62
www.partridgepublishing.com/india
orders.india@partridgepublishing.com

CONTENTS

MICROSCOPY OF ASTROLOGY

(ASTROLOGY SIMPLIFIED)

Astrology has stood the test of times ever since it revealed the mystery and the mastery of the ancient wisdom of forecasting the influence of the stars on human bodies.

The author Baldev Bhatia has penned this mysterious subject into a simple book that reveals the true perception of knowing oneself and the art of prediction.

Professionally the author has put his entire life experience in promoting Astrology in various fields with a view to serve the millions of curious readers of this mystic science with the intension of imparting them the real knowledge of astrology through this marvelous scripture.

The Astrologer has been associated with Astrology for the past 45 years and have been practicing Astrology in various forms.

His predictions have been very useful, purposeful, and a pin point to the service of Mankind.

His aim is to impart immense knowledge of astrology and is working hard for maintaining Peace, Harmony, Prosperity and Happiness of the mankind, along with the lasting peace of the World. He wishes his readers all the success"

Sd/-
(Author)
(Baldev Bhatia)

PREFACE

A thought of penning down the wonders of the mystic science of Astrology has lured the astrologer to bring it to the knowledge of the millions of readers who have been striving hard to get the Real Knowledge to know about themselves and their Zodiac Signs.

The time in which they have been born with references to their Character tics; Appearance; Personality; Profession and Career; Business and Finances; Their Matching with other Zodiac signs; Romance and Marriage, their Weakness and finally their Health and Disease while gathering the immense knowledge of Astrology.

Endeavoring the placement of the planetary position in one's chart at the time of birth has enlightened the author to impact this interesting subject into a manuscript.

It is hoped that this book would be a guide to their destiny and would assist them in all walks of lives.

The knowledge gathered through this book will be a moral booster to each and every one that nothing is in their hands except to work hard and harder.

That one's life is pre-destined and gathered to move in the direction where the planets are positioned and their movement carry specific influence on their lives.

This book will definitely be an assets in ascertaining the real facts of life and the destiny as to what is stored for them in future.

Various chapters have been covered and maximum emphasis have been paid to cover the Subjects pertaining to the Significance of Different House in one chart; Different Zodiac Signs, Planets and their placements in different houses and signs affliction of planets with the interpretation of the major period and the meaning of the Birth Constellation Star.

The influence of Gems and Stones in one's life, the Remedial Measures of the planets with the Compatibility of the individual zodiac signs with the other signs and the effect of various planets on them.

It is hoped that this book would work and guide the readers to achieve their personal goals and would assist them to over come All the crises, Speed Breakers and the unforeseen negatives forces, in their lives, and which would assist them in achieving their targets with a aim to reach to the destined goal of their financial prosperity, maximum happiness and progress in life.

It is often said that Man is governed by his own destiny and destiny consists of two parts. The first is his hard work or the Effort that he makes to achieve his aims and goals and the second is the Time, when he is doing his action.

When the time is good everything is good and when the time is bad everything seems to go wrong and bad.

To know the time whether it is a good time or bad, one usually goes to an astrologer to seek his blessing and advice, to know the exact favorable time of his actions and deeds. Time is therefore the essence of astrology and it is this time that is governing the planets to favor him, or harm the individuals.

To simply this meaning of the good or bad time the author has put all his heart and soul to materialize his hope of getting closer to the heart of readers, with a view to impart the basic knowledge of astrology to them.

Hope the author has satisfied his readers with the utmost need of Knowing and understanding Astrology in brief. The readers have gained Good experience going through this useful and purposeful book.

I would definitely like to express my sincere thanks to MS. Alpa Shah Director travel company of UK, for encouraging me to pen down this book in the interest of the beginners of astrology.

I am also grateful and thankful to A Partridge India A PENGUIN RANDOM HOUSE COMPANY for publishing my book.

BALDEV BHATIA

INTRODUCTION

MICROSCOPY OF ASTROLOGY (ASTROLOGY SIMPIFIED)

Having entered the 21ˢᵗ Century that implies the greater trust on modern technology and a newer life style our lives are almost determined what the super computers will have to say about us.

Not withstanding that what is stored for us in future and being at the mercury of these designed gadgets which could be controlling our lives the desire to know the in depth the planetary influence on human life would still remain to be a Mistry.

Astrology being a combination of Science and Metaphysics enables us the construct a birth chart of ourselves, to know about ourselves in depth and to know what exactly will be the impact of the heavenly bodies on our lives with the passage of time need to be study in detail.

Since this science is itself seems to be a deep in depth, going into it for an extensive study can be a pretty though and a uphill task to voch for its microscopy study.

The Zodiac consists of a Arc having having 360 degrees comprising of Planets and Signs which are further divided into Constellations Stars. The combination of these planets with Zodiac Signs and placement of them in different divisional parts termed as "Houses" do indicate the power of their influence on human bodies. These constellation divisons come into a handy compellation while analyzing its result thorough their microscopic study.

The need to know and study these complication combinations of Planets, Houses and Zodiac signs has compelled the author to go in for a comprehensive study of the authencity of the planetary configuration and varous combination thorough its microscopy study.

Experts in this field can clearly indicate and say that if your birth chart has been drawn perfectly, analyzed accurately and interpreted correctly can reveal as to what would be your basic characteristics your profession job and career, your health and disease your likes and dislikes your future in store for you and the matters of your love life with emphasis on your legal cases.

The prediction made can be a guiding factor and can bring back one confessed and distress person to his normal behavior and pleasing life. "Microscopy of this astrology has made us to feel secure sound and has encouraged us to face our destiny with immense strength and has also given us the power to face the challenges of this universe with utter confidence zeal and power".

BALDEV BHATIA

DATED 27-12-2013

"MICROSCOPY OF ASTROLOGY"

WITH THE BLESSISNG OF LORD SHIVA

OMKAR

CHAPTER 1

"MICROSCOPY OF ASTROLOGY"

WITH THE BLESSING OF GOD GANESHA

WITH THE BLESSINGS OF GOD SHIVA AND GODESS PARVATI

"OM NAMAH SHIVAY"

SIGNIFICANCE OF DIFFERENT HOUSES

SIGNS, PLANETS AND THEIR PLACEMENT.

In Astrology it is understood that at any point of time. The native is governed by a planet and the position of that planet at the time of birth, in the horoscope, determines how the native will feel or behave. In Astrology the following represents a horoscope:

1. HOUSES
2. SIGNS
3. PLANETS IN DIFFERENT HOUSES
4. PLANETS IN DIFFERENT SIGNS

DIFFERENT HOUSES

SIGNIFICANCE OF DIFFERENT HOUSES

FIGURE NO.1

RELATIONSHIP RULED BY VARIOUS HOUSES

FIGURE NO.2

HOUSES WHICH REPRESENTS BODY PARTS

FIGURE NO. 3

HOUSES REPRENTED BY SIGNS

FIGURE NO. 4

HOUSES

1st house is called Ascendant. It is the most important of all the houses and determines the Longevity, Health, Character, Physical appearance and the nature of the native. It specifically signifies the head and to some extent mind of the native. It also denotes head, hair, forehead and brain.

2nd house: This house is also called the house of Income. It deals with Money Matters, Deposits, Income tax matters, Customs related affairs, and Computers. It represents Joint Family, Face, including right eye, nose, cheeks, teeth and tongue and also Speech, Food, Eating Habits.

3rd house: It is called the house of Relatives, Friends and in particular the Brother's and Sisters house. It signifies courage, boldness, short journeys, throat shoulders, windpipe, right arm and ears. One is made singer by this house in addition to the second house.

4th house: It represents Mother, Motherland, House, Vehicles, Mental Peace, and Education. It represents Chest, the Lungs, particularly the Heart, Breast and Rips. It is also called the house of Mother, House of Public affairs, House of Happiness.

5th house: This house is called as the house of Children. House of Mental Faculty and it represents Children, Intelligence, Speculation and Love Affairs. It indicates Abdominal and its parts like stomach, navel, and the small intestine.

6th house: This house is called the house of Disease or Illness. It is also called the house of Enemies. It governs lower abdomen, large intestine, Digestive System, Hips and Back, apart from Quarrels, Court Cases and Litigations.

7th house: It is called the house of Partner, whether Life Partner or Business Partner, it represents Wife, Marriage, Business or Employment in a private firm. It governs sexual organs, the upper part of generative organs, kidneys and uterus.

8th house: It is known as the house of longevity or the Age house and it represents Death, Reasons of Death, Hidden wealth, Accidents, Parental Property, and it also denotes, reproductive organs, prostrate glands and the excretory organs apart from the Anus.

9th house: It is called the House of Fortune or house of Luck and Religion; it represents Pilgrimage, Higher studies, Long Journeys, Foreign Travel. It also indicates Grand Parents and Mental Aptitude towards Religious Acts and Deeds. It governs the Thighs the Hips and the nervous system.

10th house: It is called the house of profession/job/service and it represents the father of the native. It is also known as the house of routine works. It deals with the knees, joints and the flesh.

11th house. It is house of Gains or Lottery and Speculation. It represents sources of income through speculative games, Elder Brothers and Sisters. It also represents the calves, left ear apart from the legs.

12th house: It is the house of Expenditure the house of Losses and Expenses and covers Bad Habits, Hospitalisation, Jail, long Distant journeys or Journeys to foreign land. It also indicates business of Export and Import. It represents the feet, heals and the left eye.

CHAPTER 2

ZODIAC SIGNS IN BRIEF

ARIES-MESHA

Persons born in Aries will have a certain amount of independent thinking and reasoning faculty. Aries will be capable. Aries may not be strict followers of convention. They are lovers of scientific thought and philosophy; have their own ideas of right and wrong and are strongly bent upon educational pursuits. Aries are rather stubborn but often frank, impulsive and courageous. Aries are more gossipers than practical men. They sometimes require a certain amount of cajolery and sycophancy to raise them to action. Aries become pioneers.

As Mars is the lord of Aries, they will be martial in spirit. Their constitution will be hot, and they are occasionally subject to hot complaints, piles and the like, and must avoid enterprises obviously involving any serious risks. Aries love beauty, art and elegance.

The diseases Aries suffer from will be mostly those of the head and unpleasant sightseeing may often lead to mental affliction and derangement of brain. Their build will be slender and females generally possess fairly perfect contours. One peculiarity is craning the neck.

TAURUS

The stature of the persons born in Taurus will be medium or short and often inclined towards corpulence, lips thick, complexion swarthy, square face, well-shaped lips and dark hair are prominent features. Women in Taurus are generally handsome. They generally resemble the bull in their behavior toward new people if they are not listened to properly. They have their own principles and ways. Often they have a piercing intellect. They shine well as authors, book dealers and journalists. They are not bound by sentimentality but appreciate truth. They are remarkable for their ability to commit to memory. Physical and mental endurance of Taurus are note-worthy. They have much business knack and good intuition. They often think they are born to exercise authority over others and in a sense they are right. They are sensitive to physical influences. They are often liable to extremes, zealous and easily accessible to adulteration. They are sensitive to suffer from nervous complaints after their fiftieth year but their memory and powers of imagination will never deceive them. They are slow to anger, but when provoked, furious like the bull. Taurus are passionate and may become preys to sexual diseases in their old age unless they moderate their pleasures and learn to exercise self-control.

GEMINI

Persons when born in Gemini is rising have a wavering mind, often tall and straight in nature and active in motion, forehead broad, eyes clear and nose, a bit snub. Gemini is active and become experts in mathematical sciences; and mechanical sciences provided Saturn has some strong influence over them.

They will be "jack of all trades but master of none". Gemini are vivacious, but liable to be inconstant. They will have sudden nervous breakdowns and must exercise a certain amount of caution in moving with the opposite sex; a habit of self-control must be cultivated. Mind of Gemini will be often conscious of their own faults. Gemini is liable to fraud and deceit will characterize their nature.

If evil planets are found in Gemini, trickery and deceit will characterize their nature. Many of these traits can be corrected by training.

CANCER

Persons born under Cancer have a middle-sized body, face full, nose snubbed to some extent and complexion white. They often have a double chin. They are very intelligent, bright and frugal and equally industrious. Their frugality often takes the form of miserliness. They are sympathetic but moral cowardice will be present. They will be much attached to their children and family. Their extreme sensitiveness renders them nervous and queer. Their minds will be bent upon schemes of trade and manufacture. They often meet with disappointments in marriage and love affairs. They are very talkative, self-reliant, honest and unbending. Cancer has reputation for love of justice and fair play. Saturn's situation in the ascendant is not desirable.

LEO

Persons born under Leo will be majestic in appearance, broad shoulders, and bilious constitution and bold and respectful in appearance. They possess the knack to adapt them to any condition of life. They are rather ambitious and sometimes avaricious too. They are independent thinkers. They stick up to orthodox principles in religion but are perfectly tolerant towards to others precepts and practices. Leo is lovers of fine arts and literature and possesses a certain amount of philosophical knowledge. They are voracious readers. If the ascendant or the tenth house is afflicted, they may not succeed in life as much as they expect. They put forth much struggle. Their ambitions remain unfulfilled to some extent unless the horoscope has certain definite Raja-Yogas. They are capable of non-attachment and contentment.

As Saturn happens to be lord of the 7th, Leo must resist the temptation of yielding much to their wives or husbands if domestic happiness is to prevail.

VIRGO

People born when Virgo is rising will exhibit their intelligence and memory when quite young. They will be middle-sized persons and exhibit taste in art and literature.

Their chest will be prominent and when afflicted, very weak also. They are discriminating and emotional and are carried away by impulses. Virgo love music and fine arts and acquire much power and influence over other people. They are liable to suffer from nervous breakdowns and paralysis when the sign is afflicted. Other combinations warranting Virgo can become great philosophers or writers. They are generally lucky in respect of their wives or husbands.

LIBRA

The complexion of persons born in Libra sign will be fair, their stature middle-sized, face broad, eyes fine, chest broad and light, appearance handsome, constitution rather phlegmatic, sensual disposition and keen observation. They have keen foresight and reason out things from the standpoint of their own views. Firm in conviction and unmoved by mean motives they are somewhat susceptible to the feelings of others' minds. They are more idealists than realists or practical men and often contemplate upon schemes like building castles in the air. Libra is not sensitive to what others say to them. But as political leaders and religious reformers they exert tremendous influence over masses and sometimes their zeal and enthusiasm goes to such a high pitch that they force their views upon others of opposite thoughts not realizing the baneful after-effects of such procedure. They love excitement and have the power of intuition upon which they often rely for their own guidance. They are not amenable to reason. Libra are great lovers of music. Libra have a special liking for truth and honesty and do not hesitate to sacrifice even their lives at the alters of freedom and fair play. Domestic life of Libra may be crossed by frequent tensions.

SCORPIO

Those born under Scorpio sign have youthful appearance, a generous disposition and fierce eyes. Scorpio are fickle minded and love much excitement. Scorpio is inclined to sensual things in reality while they will not hesitate to philosophies upon the merits of controlling sensual pleasures. Even females born in Scorpio sign will have more of masculine tendencies. They are good correspondents and invite from among people throughout the world. They can become expert musicians if they care to practice the art.

They are proficient in fine arts, dancing and the like and no doubt they have a philosophic disposition. They set at naught conventional habits and customs. They vehemently uphold their own views but nevertheless will not clash with those holding opposite ones. Constitution of Scorpio will be hot and they are liable to suffer from piles after their 30th year. They are silent and dignified and never speak before weighing each and every word. Scorpio is a good conversationalist as well as writers and often rely too much on their own intelligence. Married life of Scorpio may not be quite happy not only due to temperamental differences but also due to illness affecting the generative system of the partner, unless there are other compensating combinations.

SAGITTARIUS

Jupiter rules this sign and persons born under this sign will generally be inclined towards corpulence. Sagittarius possesses almond eyes and their hair is brown. They are of a phlegmatic temperament. Sagittarius are somewhat conventional and sometimes business like also. They are prompt and uphold conservative views. They will be attracted towards the study of occult philosophy and sciences. In these departments of knowledge Sagittarius can acquire mastery. They are too callous and enthusiastic. They hate all external show. Sagittarius is God-fearing, honest, humble and free from hypocrisy. They never think of schemes, which are calculated to disturb the progress of others. Sagittarius generally exercise control over their food and drinks but in regard to their relationship with the opposite sex restraint is called for. They are brilliant, their manners affable, winning and hearts, pure.

Sagittarius is prone to be misunderstood unintentionally by others on account of their hastiness in conversation. In their later years they must be careful about their lungs as they are liable to suffer from rheumatic pains and the like. Combinations for political power warranting, persons born in Sagittarius sign will exercise power with firmness and justice and without yielding to corruptive influences.

CAPRICORN

Persons born in Capricorn sign will be tall, reddish brown in colour with prominent hair on the eyebrows and the chest. Women born in Capricorn will be handsome and youngish in appearance. Capricorn has large teeth and sometimes protruding outside the lips and presenting an uncouth appearance if the second house is afflicted. The lips of Capricorn are fleshy and ladies have an inviting appearance. They have the knack of adopting themselves to circumstances and environments. They have great aspirations in life and cannot economies funds even if they were to be under the influence of adversity. They are modest, liberal and gentlemanly in business transactions. Capricorn is noted for their perseverance and strong mindedness. In fact they are stoical to the miseries of life. They are possessed of sympathy, generosity and philanthropy and take great interest in literature, science and education. Sometimes they are vindictive. When Saturn is badly posited, Capricorn is possessed of bigotry. God-fearing and humble they make good husbands or wives. Depending upon the disposition of the 9th house Capricorn can become philosophically minded or develop social consciousness.

AQUARIUS

Those born under Aquarius sign will be tall, lean, fairly handsome, manners winning, appearance attractive, and disposition elegant. Lips of Aquarius are fleshy, cheeks broad with prominent temples and buttocks. They are highly intelligent and make friends of others very soon. They are peevish and when provoked, rise like a bulldog but their anger is very soon subsided. They are pure in heart and always inclined to help others. They shine very well as writers and good spokesman. They are at times timid. Aquarius feel shy to exhibit their talents but their conversation will be most interesting and highly instructive.

They will specialize in subjects like astrology, psychology and healing arts, etc. Literacy greatness of Aquarius will come before the world when they are quite young and they themselves will not be able to estimate their capacities well, while others find in them something remarkable and extraordinary. They are intuitive and good judges of character. Aquarius have no organizing capacity and are devoted to their husbands or wives and never betray the interests of even their enemies, when trust is placed in them. Aquarius are liable to suffer from colic troubles and must take special precautions to safeguard themselves against diseases incidental to exposure to cold weather. On the whole Aquarius people have something subtle in them, which endears them to all they come in contact with.

PISCES

Persons born in Pisces sign will be fair, stout and moderately tall. Pisces are reserved in their manners and are liable to draw premature conclusions on any matter. They are God-fearing. Pisces are generally superstitious and religious, rigid in the observance of orthodox principles and can forego anything but their orthodoxy; or they can be exactly the opposite. They are somewhat stubborn, rather timid, and ambitious to exercise authority over others. They are true friends and are proud of their educational and other attainments. If the lord of the 7th is badly afflicted, Pisces will have double marriage. They are restless and fond of history, antiquarian talks and mythological masterpieces. Pisces are frugal in spending money and though generally dependent upon others thorough out their life still bear a mark of independence. Pisces are just in their dealings and fear to transgress the laws of truth. With all this, they lack self-confidence.

CHAPTER 3

MICROSCOPY OF ASTROLOGY

Planets in Different HOUSES

SUN	MOON	MARS
RAHU	JUPITER	SATURN
MERCURY	KETU	VENUS

SUN

In the First house.—Righteous-minded, healthy, bilious, eye-disease, intelligence, good morals, political success, stately appearance, humanitarian instincts, lazy in work, fond of daring deeds, hot constitution, careless of reputation, string will, caprice, generosity, neglect of personal credit or respect, good work, not combative or impetuous and pioneering.

Second house.—Diseased face, ugly, losses from prosecution good earnings, inclined to waste, bright speech, enquiring, well-educated, scientific, stubborn and peevish temper, and danger in the 25th year, will stammer.

Third house.—Courageous, liberal, adventurous, famous, intelligent, wealthy, successful and restless.

Fourth house.—Mental worry, meditative defective organs, success in foreign countries, hatred of relations, keen-minded, sensitive, good reputation, success after middle age, quarrels without causes, weak constitution, introspective, unhappy, philosophical, squanders paternal property.

Fifth house.—Intelligent, poor, few children, paternal danger, corpulent, danger to father early, unhappy, disturbed in mind, lover of fine arts, and tactful in decision.

Sixth house.—Defer of customs and castes, good administrative ability, few cousins and few enemies, bold a successful, war-like, licentious, wealthy, gain from enemies, clever in planning, terror to enemies, executive ability, colic troubles.

Seventh house.—Late marriage and rather troubled, loose morals and irreligious, hatred by the fair sex, fond of traveling, submissive to wife, wealth through female agency, fond of foreign things, discontented, wife's character questionable, subservient to women and risk of dishonor and disgrace through them.

Eighth house.—Well read in solar sciences, attracted by sublime phenomena, charitable, godly, lucky and successful, devoted, ordinary health, little patrimony, dutiful sons, a man of action and thought, self-acquired property, many lands, philosophical, glandular disease, lover of poetry and music, successful agriculturist, learned in esoteric and occult subjects, ambitious and enterprising.

Ninth house.—Well read in solar sciences, attracted by sublime phenomena, charitable, godly, lucky and successful, devoted, ordinary health, little patrimony, dutiful sons, a man of action and thought, self-acquired property, many lands, philosophical, glandular disease, lover of poetry and music, successful agriculturist, learned in esoteric and occult subjects, ambitious and enterprising.

Tenth house.—Bold, courageous, well known, famous, clever in acquiring wealth, superior knack, healthy, learned, adventurous, educated, quick decision, fond of music, founder of institutions, high position, dutiful sons, much personal influence, successful military or political career.

Eleventh house.—Learned, wealthy, stately and persevering, success without much effort, famous, many enemies, wealth through fair means, good reputation, profound insight, capacity to befriend, many political enemies, man of principles, great sagacity, great success and position.

Twelfth house.—Sinful, poor, fallen, thieving nature, unsuccessful, adulterous, neglected, long limbs, ceremonial minded and lover of esoteric and occult knowledge, no happiness from children.

Planets in Different HOUSES

MOON

In the Ascendant.—Fanciful and romantic, moderate eater, an attractive appearance, inclined to corpulence, windy temperament, much travelling, disease in private organs and ears, capricious, licentious, sociable, easy going, educated, warring, loved by the opposite sex, shy, modest, stubborn, proud, fickle-minded and eccentric.

Second house.—Wealthy, handsome, attractive, generous, highly intelligent, breaks in education, charming, poetical, great respect, sweet speech, persuasive, squint eyes and much admired.

Third house.—Sickly, dyspeptic and later on piles, mild, lean, disappointments, impious, many brothers, cruel, educated, consumption, famous, sisters, intelligent, unscrupulous, purposeless, miserly, fond of travelling and active-minded.

Fourth house.—Sickly mother, quarrels, unhappy home life, danger to father, domestic quarrels and conveyances, uncomfortable, coarse, brutal, tyrannical, vulgar.

Fifth house.—Subtle, handsome wife, shrewd, showy, many daughters, intelligent, gains through quadrupeds, interrupted education, high political office.

Sixth house.—Submissive to the opposite sex, indolent, imperious, short-tempered, intelligent, lazy, slender body, weak sexual connection, widow-hunter, poor, drunkard, refined, tender, pilfering habits stomach troubles, many foes, worried by cousins.

Seventh house.—Passionate, fond of women, handsome wife, mother short-lived, narrow-minded, good family, pains in he loins, social, successful, jealous and energetic in several matters.

Eighth house.—Unhealthy, legacy, capricious, mother short-lived, few children, bilious, slender bad sight, Kinney disease, unsteady, easy acquisitions.

Ninth house.—Popular, educated, intelligent, well read, lover of fiction, builder of charitable institutions, wealthy, active, inclined to travel, godly, good children, immoveable property, religious, mystical, righteous, agricultural success, devotional, successful and good reputation.

Tenth house.—Persuasive, passionate, charitable, shrewd, adulterous, bold, tactful, ambitious, great position, active, trustee of religious institutions, obliging to good people, many friends, easy success, popular and able, wealthy, comfortable and long life.

Eleventh house.—Many children, powerful, philanthropic, polite, literary an artistic taste, helpful, influential, cultured, charitable, many friends, great position, reputation, good lands, easy success, liked and helped by the fair sex, giver of donations, man of principles.

Twelfth house.—Obstructed, deformed, narrow-minded, cruel, unhappy, obscure, powerless, deceived, solitary, and miserable.

Planets in Different HOUSES

MARS

In the First house.—Hot constitution, scars in the body, pilfering habits, big navel, early danger to father, reddish complexion, active, adventurous, powerful and low-minded.

Second house.—Quarrelsome, extravagant, harsh speech, adulterous, short-tempered, wasteful, sharp-tongued, broken education, satirical, large patrimony, bad-tempered, aggressive, unpopular and awkward.

Third house.—Pioneering, few brothers, sex-morals weak, courageous, intelligent, reckless, adventurous, short-tempered, unprincipled, easy morals, unpopular.

Fourth house.—Sickly mother, quarrels, unhappy home life, danger to father, domestic quarrels and conveyances, uncomfortable, coarse, brutal, tyrannical, vulgar.

Fifth house.—Unpopular, no issues, ambitious, intelligent persevering, unhappy, bold, unprincipled, decisive.

Sixth house.—Successful, good lands, rich success over enemies, intelligent, political success, powerful, worry from near relations.

Seventh house.—Two wives or friction with wife, dropsy, rash speculations, unsuccessful, intelligent, tactless, stubborn idiosyncratic, peevish, passionate, tension in married life.

Eighth house.—Short life, few children, danger to maternal uncles, widower later, and hater of relations, bad sight, and extra marital relations.

Ninth house.—Unkind worldly, successful trader, loss from agriculture, sickly father, naval merchant, dependent life, self-seeking, acute, stubborn, impetuous, logical.

Tenth house.—Founder of institutions and towns, energetic, adventurous, wealthy, active, healthy, famous, self made man, good agriculturist, good profits, clever, successful loved by relations, decisive.

Eleventh house.—Learned, educated, wealthy, influential property, crafty, happy, commanding.

Twelfth house.—Unsuccessful, poor, rotten body, unpopular, incendiary diseases, suffering, stumbling, active, fruitless, liable to fraud and deception, dishonest, unseen, impediments, deformed eyes.

Planets in Different HOUSES

DRAGON'S HEAD (RAHU)

In the Ascendant.—Obliging, sympathetic, abortion, courageous, sickly wife or husband.

Second house.—Poor and more than one wife if afflicted, dark complexion, diseased face, peevish, luxurious dinners.

Third house.—Few children, wealthy, bold, adventurous, courageous, good gymnastic, many relations.

Fourth house.—Liaison with women of easy virtue, subordinate, proficient in European languages.

Fifth house.—Childless, flatulent, tyrannical, polite, narrow-minded and hard-hearted.

Sixth house.—Enjoyment, venereal complaints, no enemies, many cousins.

Seventh house.—Wife suffering from menstrual disorders, widow or divorcee connection, diabetes, luxurious food, unhappy.

Eighth house.—Vicious, degraded, quarrelsome, narrow-mined, immoral, adulterous.

Ninth house.—A puppet in the hands of the wife, impolite, uncharitable, emaciated waist, loose morals.

Tenth house.—Intimacy with widows, taste in poetry and literature, good artist, traveller, learned.

Eleventh house.—Wealthy, influential among lower castes, many children, and good agriculturist.

Twelfth house.—Deformed, few children, defective sight, very many losses, saintly.

Planets in Different HOUSES

JUPITER

In the first house.—Magnetic personality, good grammarian, majestic appearance, highly educated, many children, learned, dexterous, long-lived, respected by rulers, philologist political success, sagacious, stout body, able, influential leader.

Second house.—Wealthy, intelligent, dignified, attractive, happy, fluent speaker, aristocratic, tasteful, winning manners, accumulated fortune, witty, good wife and family, eloquent, humorous, and dexterous.

Third house.—Famous, many brothers, ancestors, devoted to the family, miserly, obliging, polite, unscrupulous, good agriculturist, thrifty, good success, energetic, bold, taste for fine arts and literature, lived by relatives.

Fourth house.—Good conveyances, educated, happy, intelligent, wealthy, founder of charitable institutions, comfortable, good inheritance, good mother, well read, contented life.

Fifth house.—Broad eyes, handsome, states manly ability good insight, high position, intelligent, skilful in trade, obedient children, pure-hearted, a leader.

Sixth house.—Obscure, unlucky, troubled, many cousins and grandsons, dyspeptic, much jocularity, witty, unsuccessful, intelligent.

Seventh house.—Educated, proud, good wife and gains through her, diplomatic ability, speculative mind, very sensitive, success in agriculture, virtuous wife, pilgrimage to distant places.

Eighth house.—Unhappy, earnings by undignified means, obscure, long life, mean, degraded, thrown with widows, colic pains, pretending to be charitable, dirty habits.

Ninth house.—Charitable, many children, devoted, religious, merciful, pure, ceremonial-minded, humanitarian principles, principled, conservative, generous, long-lived father, benevolent, God-fearing, highly cultured, famous, high position.

Tenth house.—Virtuous, learned, clever in acquisition of wealth, conveyances, children, determined, highly principled, accumulated wealth, founder of institutions, good agriculturist, non-violent, ambitious, scrupulous.

Eleventh house.—Lover of music, very wealthy, states manly ability, good deeds, accumulated funds, God-fearing, charitable, somewhat dependent, influential, many friends, philanthropic.

Twelfth house.—Sadistic, poor, few children, unsteady character, unlucky, life lascivious later life inclined to asceticism, artistic taste, pious in after-life.

Planets in Different HOUSES

SATURN

In the first house.—Foreign customs and habits, perverted mind, bad thoughts, evil-natured, tyrannical, unscrupulous, well-built thighs, strong-minded, cunning, thrifty, unclean, passionate, aspiring, curious, deformed, sickly, exploring, flatulence, licentious, addicted to low-class women.

Second house.—More than one marriage, diseased face, unpopular, broken education, weak sight, unsocial, harsh speech, stammering, addicted to wine.

Third house.—Intelligent, wealthy, wicked, loss of brothers, polite, adventurous, bold, eccentric, cruel, courageous, obliging, agriculturist.

Fourth house.—Danger to mother if with the Moon, unhappy, sudden lodes, colic pains, narrow-minded, crafty, estates encumbered, good thinker, success in foreign countries, political disfavour, licentious, interrupted education.

Fifth house.—Narrow-minded, mediocre life no children, perverted views, taleteller, government displeasure, troubled life, clear-minded.

Sixth house.—Obstinate, sickly, deaf, few children, quarrelsome, sex diseases, clever, active, indebted.

Seventh house.—More than one wife, enterprising, sickly, colic pains, deafness, diplomatic, stable marriage, ambitious, political success, travelling, dissimulator, foreign honours, deputation.

Eighth house.—Seeking disappointments, big belly, few issues, corpulent, inclined to drinking, friendship with women of other castes, colic pains, defect in sight, seductive, clever, well-informed, impious, danger by poisons, asthma, consumption, dishonest, ungrateful children, cruel, long life.

Ninth house.—Legal success, founder of charitable institutions, very miserly, thrifty in domestic life, scientific, irreligious, logical, ceremonial-mined.

Tenth house.—Visits to sacred rivers and shrines, great worker, bilious, good farmer, sudden elevations and depressions, residence in foreign countries uncertain, later on in life an ascetic.

Eleventh house.—Learned, feared and respected, very wealthy, much landed property, broken education, conveyances, political success, influential, political respect.

Twelfth house.—Deformed, squint eyes, losses in trade, learned in occult science, poor, spendthrift, many enemies, dexterous, unpopular, attracted towards yoga in later life.

Planets in Different HOUSES

MERCURY

In the First house.—Cheerful, humorous, well read, clever, many enemies, learned, fond of occult studies and astronomy, witty, influential, intellectual, respected, long-lived, love of literature and poetry.

Second house.—Learned in religious and philosophical lore, sweet speech, good conversationalist, humorous, clever many children, determined, fine manners, captivating look, self-acquisition, wealthy, careful, thrifty, and clever in earning money.

Third house.—Daughter, happy mother, clever, cruel, loved by fair sex, tactful, diplomatic, discretion, bold, sensible.

Fourth house.—Learned, agriculturist, good mother, unhappy, skilled in conjuring tricks, obliging, cultured, affectionate, popular, inclined to pursue literary activities.

Fifth house.—Showy, learned, quarrelsome, danger to maternal uncles, parents sickly, good administrative capacity, fond of good furniture and dress, respect from moneyed men, ministerial office, executive ability, speculative, scholar, vain, danger to father, combative.

Sixth house.—Respected, interrupted education, subordinate officer, executive capacity, quarrelsome, showy, dissimulation, losses in money peevish, bigoted, troubles in the feet and toes.

Seventh house.—Diplomatic, interesting literary ability early in life and success through it, early marriage, wife handsome, dutiful and short-tempered, breaks in education, learned in astrology, astronomy and mathematics, success in trade, successful, dashing, gay, skilful, religious, charitable, strong body.

Eighth house.—Long life, landed estate, easy access to anything desired, grief through domestics, obliging, few issues, many lands, famous, respected, ill-health.

Ninth house.—Highly educated, musician, many children, obliging, licentious, philosophical, lover of literature, creative mind, inquisitive, scientific-minded, popular, well known.

Tenth house.—Determined, fortunate, enjoyments in life, intelligent, bad sight, active, cheerful, charitable, able, philanthropic.

Eleventh house.—Wealthy, happy, mathematical faculty, good astrologer, many friends among famous men, many lands, logical and scientific, success in trade.

Twelfth house.—Philosophical, intelligent, worried, adulterous, obliging, capricious, wayward, narrow-minded, gifted, despondent, passionate, few children, lacking in opportunities, danger to mother.

Planets in Different HOUSES

DRAGON'S TAIL (KETU)

In the first house.—Emaciated figure, weak constitution, much perspiration, weak-hearted, slender, piles, and sexual indulgence, diplomatic.

Second house.—Bad speaker, quiet, quick in perception, peevish, hard-hearted, thrifty and economical.

Third house.—Adventurous, strong, artistic, wealthy, popular.

Fourth house.—Quarrelsome, licentious, weak, fear of poisons.

Fifth house.—Liberal, loss of children, sinful, immoral if afflicted.

Sixth house.—Fond of adultery, good conversationalist, licentious, venereal complaints, learned.

Seventh house.—Passionate, sinful, connections with widows, sickly wife.

Eighth house.—Senseless, obscure, dull, sanguine complexion, piles and similar troubles.

Ninth house.—Shortsighted, sinful, untruthful, thrifty, many children, good wife.

Tenth house.—Fertile brain, happy, religious, pilgrimages to sacred rivers and places, fond of scriptures.

Eleventh house.—Humorous, witty, licentious, intelligent, wealthy.

Twelfth house.—Capricious, unsettled mind, foreign residence, attracted to servile classes, much travelling, licentious, spiritual knowledge

Planets in Different HOUSES

VENUS

In the Ascendant.—Expert mathematician, very fortunate, ambitious, bold, long life, pioneering, fond of wife, strenuous, skilled in sexual science, successful, practical, scents, flowers, women skilled in fine arts, pleasing, vivacious, astrologer, much magnetic power, leader of people.

Second house.—Large family, happy, delicious drinks, luxurious meals, handsome, large fair eyes, charming wife, witty, brilliant, polite, educated, hating women, obliging, rapid in mind, clever in speech, agreeable, creative author, conservative, composer, economical, wealthy, logical, able.

Third house.—Lover of fine arts, prosperity to mother wealthy, miserly, obliging, well placed, travelling, original.

Fourth house.—Intelligent, happy, affectionate, learned, affectionate mother, agriculturist, educated, scientific methods, peaceful life, protector of cattle, endeared by relations, fond of milk, famous, literary, successful, popular.

Fifth house.—Clever, intelligent, states manly ability, good counsel, danger to mother, commander, educated, able, sociable, kind-hearted, affable, good-natured, many daughters and few sons, affable manners.

Sixth house.—Licentious, loose habits, anger, low minded, well informed, destruction to enemies, fond of other women.

Seventh house.—Passionate, unhealthy habits, happy marriage, sensual, inclined towards sex pleasure.

Eighth house.—Danger to mother, happy, given to bad habits, short-lived, famous, celebrated, unexpected legacies, trouble in mind, disappointment in love affairs, pious later in life.

Ninth house.—Selfish, religious, respect for preceptors, able, successful, commander, lover of fine arts, generous.

Tenth house.—Respect for divine people and parents, carriage, broken education, successful as a lawyer, popular, social, moderate eater.

Eleventh house.—Influential, learned, wealthy, good conveyances, successful, many friends, much popularity.

Twelfth house.—Mean-minded, find of low women, miserly, obscure, licentious, unprincipled, weak eyes, fond of sexual pleasures, clever, liar, pretentious, unhappy love affairs.

Chapter 4

ASTROLOGICAL HINTS MICROSCOPY OF ASTROLOGY

Planets in Different Signs

SUN	MOON	MARS
JUPITER	SATURN	MERCURY
VENUS		

Sun

In Aries.—Active, intelligent, famous, traveller, wealthy, warrior, variable fortune, ambitious, phlegmatic, powerful, marked personality, impulsive, irritable, pioneering, initiative.

Taurus.—Clever, reflective, attracted by perfumes and dealer in them, hated by women, slow to action, musician, self-confident, delicious drinks, happy meals, tactful, original, sociable, intelligent, prominent nose.

Gemini.—Learned, astronomer, scholarly, grammarian, polite, wealthy, critical, assimilative, good conversationalist, shy, reserved, lacking in originality.

Cancer.—Somewhat harsh, indolent, wealthy, unhappy, constipation, sickly, travelling, independent, expert astrologer.

Leo.—Stubborn, fixed views, strong, cruel, independent, organizing capacity and talents for propaganda, humanitarian, frequenting solitary places, generous, famous.

Virgo.—Linguist, poet, mathematician, taste for literature, well read, scholarly, artistic, good memory, reasoning faculty, effeminate body, frank, lucid comprehension, learned in religious lore, reserved, wanting adulation.

Libra.—Manufacture of liquors, popular, tactless, base, drunkard, loose morals, arrogant, wicked, frank, submissive, pompous.

Scorpio.—Adventurous, bold, fearing thieves and robbers, reckless, cruel, stubborn, unprincipled, impulsive, idiotic, indolent, surgical skill, dexterous, military ability.

Sagittarius.—Short-tempered, spoils, reliable, rich, obstinate, respected by all, happy, popular, religious, wealthy, musician.

Capricorn.—Mean-minded, stubborn, ignorant, miserly, unhappy, boring, active, meddlesome, obliging, humorous, witty, affable, prudent, firm.

Aquarius.—Poor, unhappy, unlucky, unsuccessful, medium height, rare faculties, self-esteem.

Pisces.—Pearl merchant, peaceful, wealthy, uneventful, religious, prodigal, loved by women

Planets in Different Signs

MOON

In Aries.—Round eyes, impulsive, fond of travel, irritable, fond of women, vegetable diet, quick to decide and act, haughty, inflexible, sores in the head, dexterous, fickle-minded, war-like, enterprising, good position, self-respect, valiant, ambitious, liable to hydrophobia if the Moon is afflicted, large thighs, popular, restless, idiosyncratic, versatile.

Taurus.—Liberal, powerful, happy, ability to command, intelligent, handsome, influential, fond of fair sex, happy in middle life and old age, great strides in life, beautiful gait, large thighs and hips, phlegmatic afflictions, rich patience, respected, love-intrigues, inconsistent, wavering mind, sound judgment, voracious eater and reader, lucky, popular, influenced by women, passionate, indolent.

Gemini.—Well read, creative, fond of women, learned in scriptures, able, persuasive, curly hair, powerful speaker, clever, witty, dexterous, fond of music, elevated nose, thought reader, subtle, long life.

Cancer.—Wise, powerful, charming, influenced by women, wealthy, kind, good, a bit stout, sensitive; impetuous, unprofitable voyages, meditative, much immovable property, scientist, middle stature, prudent, frugal, piercing, conventional.

Leo.—Bold, irritable, large cheeks, blonde, broad face, brown eyes, repugnant to women, likes meat, frequenting forests and hills, colic troubles, inclined to be unhappy, haughty, mental anxiety, liberal, generous, deformed body, steady, aristocratic, settled views, proud, ambitious.

Virgo.—Lovely complexion, almond eyes, modest, sunken shoulders and arms, charming, attractive, principled, affluent, comfortable, soft body, sweet speech, honest; truthful, modest, virtuous, intelligent, phlegmatic, fond of women, acute insight, conceited in self-estimation, pensive, conversationalist, many daughters, loquacious, astrologer and clairvoyant or attracted towards them, skilled in arts like music and dancing, few sons.

Libra.—Reverence and respect for learned and holy people, saints and gods; tall, raised nose, thin, deformed limbs, sickly constitution, rejected by kinsmen, intelligent, principled, wealthy, business-like, obliging, love for arts, far-seeing idealistic, clever, mutable, amicable, losses through women, loves women, just, not ambitious, aspiring.

Scorpio.—Broad eyes, wide chest, round shanks and thighs, isolation from parents or preceptors, brown complexion, straight-forward, frank, open-minded, cruel, simulator, malicious, sterility, agitated, unhappy, wealthy, impetuous, obstinate.

Sagittarius.—Face broad, teeth large, skilled in fine arts, indistinct shoulders, disfigured nails and arms, deep and inventive intellect, yielding to praise, good speech, upright, help from wife and women, happy marriage, many children, good inheritance, benefactor, patron of arts and literature, ceremonial-minded, showy, unexpected gifts, author, reflective mentality, inflexible to threats.

Capricorn.—Ever attached to wife and children, virtuous, good eyes, slender waist, quick in perception, clever, active, crafty, somewhat selfish, sagacious, strategic, liberal, merciless, unscrupulous, inconsistent, low morals, niggardly and mean.

Aquarius.—Fair-looking, well-formed body, tall, large teeth, belly low, youngish, sensual, sudden elevations and depressions, pure-minded, artistic, intuitional, diplomatic, lonely, peevish artistic taste, energetic, emotional, esoteric, mystical, grateful, healing power.

Pisces.—Fixed, dealer in pearls and fond of wife and children, perfect build, long nose, bright body, annihilating enemies, subservient to opposite sex, handsome, learned, steady, simple, good reputation, loose morals, adventurous, many children, spiritually inclined later in life.

Planets in Different Signs

MARS

In Aries.—Organizing capacity, commanding, rich, social, scars in the body, sensual, dark, mathematician, rich social, scars in the body, sensual, dark, mathematician, active, powerful, inspiring, pioneering able, statesman, frank, generous, careful not economical in domestic dealings, vague imaginations, combative tendencies, hard-hearted.

Taurus.—Influenced by women, timid, rough body, stubborn, sensual, liking for magic and sports, somewhat unprincipled, selfish, tyrannical, not softhearted, and rash, emotional, animal instinct strong sensitive.

Gemini.—Loving family and children, taste in refinement, scientific, middle stature, well built, earned, ambitious, quick, rash, ingenious, skilled in music fearless, tactless, peevish, unhappy, subservient, diplomat, humiliating, detective.

Cancer.—Intelligent, wealthy, rich travels and voyages, wicked perverted, love of agriculture, medical and surgical proficiency, fickle-minded, defective sight, bold, dashing, headlong, speculative unkind, egoistic.

Leo.—Tendency to occultism, astrology astronomy and mathematics, love for parents, regard and respect for elders and preceptors, independent thinking, peevish, liberal, victorious, stomach troubles, worried by mental complaints, generous, noble, author early in life, successful, combative, restless.

Virgo.—Imitable, explosive, trouble in digestive organs, no marital harmony, general love for the fair sex, revengeful, self-confident, conceited, affable, boastful, materialistic, ceremonial-minded, positive, indiscriminative, pretentious, deceptive, scientific enterprises.

Libra.—Tall, body symmetrically built, complexion fair and swarthy, ambitious, self-confident, perceptive faculties, materialistic, live for family, self-earned wealth, affable, warlike, foresight, business-like, deceived by women, sanguine temperament, king, gentle, fond of adulation, easily ruffled, boastful.

Scorpio.—Middle stature, clever, diplomatic, positive tendency, indulgent, tenacious memory, and malicious, aggressive, proud, haughty, great strides in life.

Sagittarius.—Gentlemanly, many foes, famous minister, statesman, open, frank, pleasure loving, few children, liable to extremes, conservative, indifferent, exacting, impatient, severe, quarrelsome, litigation troubles, good citizen.

Capricorn.—Rich, high political position, many sons, brave, generous, love for children, middle stature, industrious, indefatigable, successful, penetrating, bold, tactful, respected, generous, gallant, influential.

Aquarius.—Unhappy, miserable, poor, not truthful, independent, unwise, wandering, impulsive, controversial, combative, well-versed in dialects, free, quick in forgiving and forgetting, conventional, danger on water, morose, meditative.

Pisces.—Fair complexion, troubles in love affairs, few children, passionate, restless, antagonistic, exacting, and uncertainty of feeling, faithful, unclean, colic, indolent, and wilful.

Planets in Different Signs

JUPITER

In Aries.—Love of grandeur, powerful, wealthy, prudent, many children, courteous, generous, firm, sympathetic, happy marriage, patient nature, harmonious, refined, high position.

Taurus.—Stately, elegant, self-importance, liberal, dutiful sons, just, sympathetic, well read, creative ability, despotic, healthy, happy marriage, liked by all, inclination to self gratification.

Gemini.—Oratorical ability, tall, well-built, benevolent, pure-hearted, scholarly, sagacious, diplomatic, linguist or poet, elegant, incentive.

Cancer.—Well read, dignified, wealthy, comfortable intelligent, swarthy complexion, inclined to social gossip mathematician faithful.

Leo.—Commanding appearance, tall, great, easily offended ambitious, active, happy intelligent, wise, prudent, generous broad-minded, literary, harmonious surroundings, likes hills and dales.

Virgo.—Middle stature, ambitious, selfish, stoical, resignation, affectionate, fortunate, stingy, lovable, a beautiful wife, great endurance, learned.

Libra.—Handsome, free, open-minded, hasty, attractive, just, courteous, strong, able, exhaustion from over-activity, religious, competent, unassuming, pleasing.

Scorpio.—Tall, somewhat stooping, elegant manners, serious, exacting, well built, superior air, selfish, imprudent, weak constitution, passionate, conventional, proud, zealous, ceremonious, unhappy life.

Sagittarius.—Pretty, wealthy, influential, handsome, noble, trustworthy, charitable, good executive ability, weak constitution, artistic qualities, poetic, open-minded, good conversationalist.

Aquarius.—Learned, not rich, controversial figure, philosophical, popular, compassionate, sympathetic, amiable, prudent, humanitarian, melancholic, meditative, dreamy, dental troubles.

Pisces.—Good inheritance, stout, medium height, two marriages if with malefic, enterprising, political diplomacy, high position.

Planets in Different Signs

SATURN

In Aries.—Idiotic, wanderer, insincere, peevish, resentful, cruel, fraudulent, immoral, boastful, quarrelsome, gloomy, mischievous, perverse, misunderstanding nature.

Taurus.—Dark complexion, deceitful, successful, powerful, unorthodox, clever, likes solitude, voracious eater, persuasive cool, contagious diseases, many wives, self-restraint, worried nature.

Gemini.—Wandering nature, miserable, untidy, original, thin, subtle, ingenious, strategic, few children, taste for chemical and mechanical sciences, narrow-minded, speculative, logical, desperado.

Cancer.—Poor, weak teeth, pleasure-seeking, few sons, cheeks full, slow, dull, cunning, rich, selfish, deceitful, malicious, stubborn, devoid of motherly care.

Leo.—Middle stature, severe, obstinate, few sons, stubborn, unfortunate, conflicting, hard worker, and good writer evil-minded.

Virgo.—Dark complexion, malicious, poor, quarrelsome, erratic, narrow-minded, rude, conservative, taste for public life, weak health.

Libra.—Famous, founder of institutions and the like, rich, tall, fair, self-conceited, handsome, tactful, powerful, respected, sound judgment, antagonistic, independent, proud, prominent, charitable.

Scorpio.—Rash, indifferent, hard-hearted, adventurous, petty, self-conceited, reserved, unscrupulous, violent, unhappy, danger from poisons, fire and weapons, wasteful, unhealthy.

Sagittarius.—Pushing, artful, cunning, famous, peaceful, faithful, pretentious, apparently generous, troubles with wife, courteous, dutiful children, generally happy.

Capricorn.—Intelligent, harmony and felicity in domestic life, selfish, covetous, peevish, intellectual, learned, suspicious, reflective, revengeful, prudent, melancholy, inheritance from wife's parties.

Aquarius.—Practical, able, diplomatic, ingenious, a bit conceited, prudent, happy, reflective, intellectual, philosophical, vanquished by enemies.

Pisces.—Clever, gifted, polite, happy, good, wife trustworthy, scheming, wealthy, helpful.

Planets in Different Signs

MERCURY

In Aries.—Evil-minded, middle stature, obstinate, clever, social, great endurance, materialistic tendencies, unscrupulous, wavering mind, antagonistic, fond of speculation, impulsive, greedy, dangerous connections, deceitful, swerving from rectitude.

Taurus.—High position, well built, clever, logical, mental harmony, many children, liberal, persevering, opinionative, wealthy, practicable, friends among women of eminence, inclination to sensual pleasures, well read, showy.

Gemini.—Inclination to physical labour, boastful, sweet speech, tall, active, cultured, tactful, dexterous to mothers, indolent, inventive, taste in literature, arts and sciences, winning manners, liable to throat and bronchial troubles, musician, mirthful, studious.

Cancer.—Witty, likes music, disliked by relations, low stature, speculative, diplomatic, discreet, flexible, restless, sensual though religious, liable to consumption, strong parental love, dislike for chastity.

Leo.—Few children, wanderer, idiotic, proud, indolent, not fond of women, boastful, orator, good memory, two mothers, poor, early marriage, independent in thinking, impulsive, positive will, remunerative profession, likes travelling.

Virgo.—Learned, virtuous, liberal, fearless, ingenious, handsome, irritable, refined, subtle, intuitive, sociable, no self-control, morbid imaginations, dyspeptic, difficulties, eloquent, author, priest, astronomer.

Libra.—Fair complexion, sanguine disposition, inclination to excesses, perceptive faculties, material tendencies, frugal, agreeable, courteous, philosophical, faithful, ceremonial-minded, sociable, discreet.

Scorpio.—Short, curly hair, incentive to indulgence, liable to disease of the generative organ, general debility, crafty, malicious, selfish, subtle, indiscreet, bold, reckless.

Sagittarius.—Taste in sciences, respected by polished society, tall, well built, learned, rash, superstitious, vigorous, executive, diplomatic, cunning, just, and capable.

Capricorn.—Selfless, business tendencies, economical, debtor, inconsistent, low stature, cunning, inventive, active, restless, suspicious, drudging.

Aquarius.—Middle stature, licentious, proud, quarrelsome frank, sociable, rapid strides in life, famous, scholar, cowardly, weak constitution.

Pisces.—A dependent, serves others, dexterous, peevish, indolent, petty-minded, respect for goods, and Brahmins.

Planets in Different Signs

VENUS

In Aries.—Extravagant, active, mutable, artistic, dreamy, idealist, proficient in fine arts, licentious, sorrowful, fickle-minded, prudent, unhappy, irreligious, easy going, loss of wealth due to loose life.
Taurus.—Well built, handsome, pleasing countenance, independent, sensual, love of nature, fond of pleasure, elegant, taste in dancing and music, voluptuous.

Gemini.—Rich, gentle, kind, generous, eloquent, proud, respected, gullible, love of fine arts, learned, intelligent, good logician, just, dual marriage, tendencies towards materialism.

Cancer.—Melancholy, emotional, timid, more than one wife, haughty, sorrowful, light character, inconsistent, unhappy, many children, sensitive, learned.

Leo.—Money through women, pretty wife, wayward, conceited, passionate, fair complexion, emotional, zealous, licentious, attracted by the fair sex, premature in conclusions, superior airs, unvanquished by enemies.

Virgo.—Petty-minded, licentious, unscrupulous, unhappy, illicit love, agile, loquacious, rich, learned.

Libra.—Statesman, poet, intelligent, generous, philosophical, handsome, matrimonial felicity, successful marriage, passionate, proud, respected, intuitive, sensual, wide travels.

Scorpio.—Broad features, quarrelsome, medium height, independent, artistic, unjust, proud, disappointed in love, haughty, not rich.

Sagittarius.—Medium height, powerful, wealthy, respected, impertinent, generous, frank, happy domestic life, high position, philosophical.

Capricorn.—Fond of low class women, imprudent, ambitious, unprincipled, licentious, boastful, subtle, learned, weak body.

Aquarius.—Liked by all, middle stature, handsome, affable, persuasive, witty, timid, chaste, calm, helpful and humanitarian.

Pisces.—Witty, tactful, learned, popular, just, ingenious, caricaturist, modest, refined, powerful, exalted, respected, pleasure seeking.

Chapter 5

Astrological Hints Microscopy of Astrology

Affliction of Various Planets

Affliction of Sun

The affliction of sun can lead to headaches, fevers, pain in bones, and lack of energy.

Affliction of Moon

The affliction of moon indicates mental illness, and can be a cause of blood pressure, cough and diseases of chest.

Affliction of Mars

The affliction of Mars can cause boils, blood cancer, bone marrow, as well as menstrual disorder in ladies.

Affliction of Rahu

The affliction of Rahu is responsible for smallpox, sleeplessness, delusions, varicose veins and leprosy.

Affliction of Jupiter

The affliction of Jupiter can be the cause of Diabetes, jaundice, and flatulence.

AFFLICTION OF SATURN

The affliction of Saturn denotes Arthritis, pain in knees and legs as well as diseases like tumours, paralysis and bone fractures.

AFFLICTION OF MERCERY

The affliction of Mercery can cause skin problems, diseases of nerves, epilepsy and leucoderma.

AFFLICTION OF KETU

The affliction of Ketu can lead to situation where surgery becomes imperative. It also indicates the root of wounds caused through accidents and skin eruptions apart from speech defects and phobias.

AFFLICTION OF VENUS

The affliction of Venus can lead to impotency, problem in the ovaries, barrenness and drug abuse or addiction.

CHAPTER 6

ASTROLOGICAL HINTS MICROSCOPY OF ASTROLOGY

MAHA DASHA INTERPRETATION

1. SUN
2. MOON
3. MARS
4. RAHU
5. JUPITER
7. SATURN
8. KETU
9. MERCURY
10. VENUS

DASHA INTERPRETATIONS
SUN MAHA DASHA

General Interpretations

General effects, which are felt during the Maha Dasha of the Sun, are as follows:

- During the Maha Dasha of the Sun wealth is obtained through medicine, weapons, fire, Brahmins, land and royalty.
- There is an increase in spiritualism, yantras and mantras.
- Friendship with government employees will develop and their favourable attitude will help in getting work done.
- Anxiety may prevail during this period.

- There may be enmity with brothers, friends, and separation from spouse, son and father.
- There may be fear due to thieves, fire, enemies and the government.
- There may be ailments of the teeth, eyes and abdomen.
- There may be decrease in the number of the servants and cattle (cows).
- One will migrate and settle abroad.

Specific Interpretations:

Interpretations based on the conditions of the planet in the birth chart and divisional charts is as follows—

- There may be unhappiness caused by the pain of venereal diseases, fever and mental anxiety.
- There maybe hardships in the course of travelling and harm related to one's souse, children, wealth and land.
- Father and paternal relatives may suffer from fear due to death, conflicts and disputes.
- There is a possibility of punishment, fear and sorrow due to state displeasure.
- Health may cause irritation and headaches may cause pain.
- Fame may be attained due to education, one's family and the company of females cause happiness.
- Parents will be happy.
- State honours may be received.
- Physical beauty may increase and one may get opportunities of going on pilgrimages and performing sacrifices.
- Agricultural farming may be profitable, land and vehicles may be acquired.
- Fame, state honors and good clothes may received.
- One will mix with friends and family members, wealth may be acquired from others.
- Progress may be attained through increase in ambitions and valour.
- Success in important work and high authority may be acquired.

- State honour and attainment of wealth bring happiness.
- Friends may cause pain and brothers may be harmed.
- A desire to attain high authority and power may arise.
- Anger increases and gastric problems may cause pain.
- One may be distanced from ones parents and friends.
- Fame and popularity in the world may increase.
- There is a possibility of being defeated and dominated by one's spouse.

Friends may suffer pain and cause pain too.

EFFECTS OF SUB PERIODS

(ANTARDASHA)

Sun-Sun

SUN-SUN

Effect of the Antar Dasha of Sun in the Maha Dasha of Sun

- One may attain some honour from the government/state and government contacts may be beneficial.
- There will be an increase in authority and one may attain a high position.
- One may acquire wealth either through war or by winning in some disputed matter.
- The mind may be restless and one may travel abroad or take a holiday trip to some jungles.
- Good effects like acquisition of wealth and grains, etc., are derived.
- Adverse results will be experienced.

Medium effects will be realized.

Sun-Moon

SUN-MOON

Effect of the Antar Dasha of Moon in the Maha Dasha of Sun

- Authority, respect, honour and happiness may increase.
- One may gain from the rich, business may be profitable and one may acquire all worldly comforts.
- Wealth may be acquired from friends and family members. One may also attain clothes and ornaments.
- Those in the opposition will be destroyed and enemies may be defeated.
- Functions like marriage, etc., gain of wealth and property, acquisition of a house, of land, cattle and conveyances, etc
- There will be marriage of the native, birth of children, beneficence of and favour from kings (the government) and fulfilment of all ambitions.
- Distress of wife and children, failures in ventures, disputes with others, loss of servants, antagonism with the king (government), and destruction's of wealth and grains.
- Effects like danger from water, mental agony, imprisonment, danger from diseases, loss of position, journeys to difficult places, disputes with coparceners, bad food, trouble from thieves, etc., displeasure of the king (government), urinary troubles, pains in the body will be experienced
- Luxuries, comforts, pleasures, dawn of fortune (Bhagyodaya), increase in the enjoyment from wife and children, acquisition of kingdom, performance of marriage and religious functions, gain of garments, land, and conveyance, and birth of children and grand children will be the auspicious effects.

Unpalatable food or course food, exile to outside places, etc.

Sun-Mars

SUN-MARS

Effect of the Antar Dasha of Mars in the Maha Dasha of Sun

- One may attain gains and respect from the state. One's status also increases.
- Gold, jewels and garments are acquired and wealth increases.
- Auspicious events take place at home and one is blessed with brothers.
- One may be opposed to family members and acidity and other ailments may cause distress.
- Auspicious effects like acquisition of land, gain of wealth and grains, acquisition of a house, etc.
- All round gains, attainment of the position of a commander of the army, destruction of enemies, peace of mind, family comforts, and increase in the number of co-borns.
- Brutality, mental ailment, imprisonment, loss of kinsmen, disputes with brothers, and failure in ventures.
- Destruction of wealth by the displeasure of the king (government).

Diseases of the mind and body will result.

Sun-Rahu

SUN-RAHU

Effect of the Antar Dasha of Rahu in the Maha Dasha of Sun

- There will be business related tension and physical pain.
- Enemies and family members may cause pain, one may lose one's position, or be demoted and the person may be unhappy.
- There is a fear of adverse work, loss of public image, loss of wealth and fear of poison.

- In the first two months there will be loss of wealth, danger from thieves, snakes, infliction of wounds, and distress to wife and children.
- After 2 months inauspicious effects will disappear and enjoyment and comforts, sound health, satisfaction, favour from the king and government, etc., will be the favourable effect.
- Recognition from the king (government), good fortune, name and fame, some distress to wife and children, birth of a son, happiness in the family, etc., will be derived.

Imprisonment, loss of position, danger from thieves and snakes, inflection of wounds, happiness to wife and children, destruction of cattle, house, and agricultural fields, diseases, consumption (Gulma: enlargement of the skin,) dysentery, etc., will be the result.

Sun-Jupiter

SUN-JUPITER

Effect of the Antar Dasha of Jupiter in the Maha Dasha of Sun

- Get respect from government and there will be promotion.
- Acquire fame in education, have good friends and increase in knowledge.
- One may be inclined towards good deeds, there is faith in gods and Brahmins and religious pilgrimages are undertaken.
- One may be desirous of accumulating wealth, good clothes, gold and ornaments.
- One may be blessed with a son and the son may acquire wealth and destroy enemies.
- Marriage of the native, favours by the king (government) gain of wealth and grains, birth of a son, fulfilment of the ambitions by the beneficence of the sovereign and gain of clothes, will be the auspicious effects.
- Acquisition of a kingdom (attainment of a high position in government), comforts of conveyance like palanquin (motor car in the present times,), gain of position, etc.

- Better fortune, charities, religious inclinations, worship of deities, devotion to preceptor, and fulfilment of ambition.

Distress to wife and children, pains in the body, displeasure of the king (government), non-achievement of desired goals, loss of wealth due to sinful deeds, mental worries, etc.

Sun-Saturn

SUN-SATURN

Effect of the Antar Dasha of Saturn in the Maha Dasha of Sun

- The mind is agitated, there is defame in education and obstacles at work.
- One may be inimical towards people, friends may oppose and one's wife and children may suffer pain.

One may fear the king and thieves. Laziness may increase.

- One may suffer due to pain and due to a lowly means of earning one's living.
- Destruction of foes, full enjoyment, some gain of grains, auspicious functions like marriage, etc., at home.
- Well-being, acquisition of more property, recognition by the king (government), achievement of renown in the country, gain of wealth from many sources.
- Rheumatism, pains, fever, dysentery-like disease, imprisonment, loss in ventures, loss of wealth, quarrels, disputes with coparceners, claimants, etc.

There will be loss of friends at the commencement, good effects during the middle part and distress at the end of the Dasha. In addition to other evil effects, there will be separation from parents and wandering.

Sun-Mercury

SUN-MERCURY

Effect of the Antar Dasha of Mercury in the Maha Dasha of Sun

- The mind is restless; there is a lack of enthusiasm.
- Friends may cause pain and expenditure may increase.
- Happiness is limited and people may be supportive.
- One may suffer from skin ailments, itching and occasionally leprosy also.
- Acquisition of a kingdom (attainment of a high position in government), enthusiasm and vivacity, happiness from wife and children, acquisition of conveyance through the beneficence of the Sovereign, gain of clothes, ornaments, pilgrimage to holy places, acquisition of a cow, etc.
- Mercury becomes very beneficial because of association with the lord of Dharm Bhava.
- Reverence from and popularity amongst people, performance of pious deeds and religious rites, devotion to the preceptor and deities, increase in wealth and grains, and birth of a son.
- Marriage, offering of oblations, charity, performance of religious rites, name and fame, becoming famous by assuming another name, good food, becoming happy like Indra by acquiring wealth, robes and ornaments.
- Body distress, disturbance of peace of mind, distress to wife and children.
- There will be evil effects at the commencement of the Antar Dasha, some good effects in the middle part of the Antar Dasha and the possibility of displeasure of the king and exile to a foreign country at the end of the Dasha.

There will be pain in the body and attacks of fever.

Sun-Ketu

SUN-KETU

Effect of the Antar Dasha of Ketu in the Maha Dasha of Sun

- There may be problems related to business and the government.
- There will be mental tension, physical pain and eye ailments.
- If Ketu is associated with the lord of Lagna, distress in the middle part of the Antar Dasha, fear from enemies, loss of wealth.
- Body Pains, mental agony, danger from the king (government), quarrels with the kinsmen, will be the effects of the Antar Dasha of Ketu in the Dasha of Sun.
- Body Pain, mental agony, loss of wealth, danger from the king (government), quarrels with the kinsmen.
- There will be some happiness at the commencement, distress in the middle part, and receipt of the news of death at the end of the Antar Dasha.
- Disease of teeth or cheeks, urinary troubles, loss of position, loss of friends and wealth, death of father, foreign journey, and troubles from enemies.

Beneficial effects like happiness from wife and children, satisfaction, increase of friends, gain of clothes, etc., and renown.

Sun-Venus

SUN-VENUS

Effect of the Antar Dasha of Venus in the Maha Dasha of Sun

- Worldly comforts may be adversely affected.
- One may acquire things produced by the sea.

- One may seek the company of women, migrate, indulge in useless discussions, spend money for luxurious pleasures and conflicts in the house may take place.
- Physical pain due to fever, headaches, earaches and other ailments are possible.
- Marriage and happiness as desired from wife, gain of property, travels to other places, meeting with Brahmins and the king (government officials), acquisition of kingdom (attainment of a high position in government).
- Riches, magnanimity and majesty, auspicious function at the home, availability of sweet preparations, acquisition of pearls and other jewels, clothes, cattle, wealth, grains and conveyances, enthusiasm, good reputation, etc.
- Displeasure of the king mental agony and distress to wife and children.
- The effects of the Antar Dasha would be moderate at its commencement, good during the middle portion and evil effects like disrepute, loss of position, inimical relations with kinsmen and loss of comforts, will be derived at the end.

There will be pains in the body and the possibility of suffering from diseases.

DASHA INTERPRETATIONS

MOON MAHA DASHA

General Interpretations

General effects which are felt during the Maha Dasha of the Moon are as follows:

- Interest in mantras and Vedas will increase and there may be faith in elders, teachers and gods.
- Happiness and a good position may be attained due to the favour of those in authority.

- One may enjoy the pleasing company of young females and the joy of acquiring wealth, land, flowers, incense and ornaments.
- One may attain skill at many arts.
- Status and fame in society may increase
- Modesty, benevolence and other good habits will increase.
- The mind may be lively and restless.
- The birth of a daughter is possible.
- Water related work, gardening and agriculture will be profitable.
- One may wish to travel.
- If the Moon is weak, then physical pain may be caused by cough and gastric ailments.
- Laziness may increase and one may be a loss of wealth.
- There may be quarrels and arguments with dear ones.
- The mind may not be interested in good deeds.

Specific Interpretations:

Interpretations based on the condition of the planet and other influences in the birth chart and divisional charts are as follows:

- There may be a decrease in the acquisition of clothes and ornaments during the Maha Dasha of the Moon.
- There may be migration, service of lowly persons and harm to friends.
- Benevolent deeds may be performed, fame may be attained.
- One's wishes will be fulfilled.
- Honours will be received from the state and the mind will be overjoyed due to the attainment of water borne products.
- During the Maha Dasha of the Moon, education causes fame, happiness, victory and monetary gains are attained.
- The number of children and servants increase.
- Spouse and children bring bliss.
- Business will be profitable.
- Mental happiness may prevail.
- Carpets and a comfortable bed may be acquired.

- Venereal and urinary ailments may cause suffering.
- During the Maha Dasha of the Moon, the person may gain financially from water borne products.
- Spouse and children bring happiness.
- Enemies will be destroyed and prudence may increase.
- A lot of money will be spent on good deeds.

EFFECTS OF SUB PERIODS *(ANTARDASHA)*

Moon-Moon

Effects of Antar Dasha of Moon in the Maha Dasha of Moon
There may be physical ailments and love for music and education.

- Superior clothes, ornaments and company of good people may be attained.
- A high position in the government may be attained.
- One may go on to pilgrimages with one's family and benefits may be gained.
- There will be good fame, attainment of land, cows (dairy products) and vehicles and increase of wealth.
- Occasionally one may suffer from ailments.
- Acquisition of horses, elephants, and clothes, devotion to deities and preceptor, recitation of religious sons in praise of God, acquisition of a kingdom (attainment of a high position in government), extreme happiness and enjoyment and name and fame.

Loss of wealth loss of position, lethargy, agony, antagonism towards the king and ministers, distress to mother, imprisonment and loss of kinsmen.

Moon-Mars

Effects of Antar Dasha of Mars in the Maha Dasha of Moon

- Accumulated wealth may be lost and one may have to leave one's native place.

- There may be conflicts with brothers and friends and parents may cause pain.
- Many ailments may arise and there may be a fear of fire, acidity, blood ailments and stomach problems.
- Enthusiasm may increase and one may acquire land.
- Advancement of fortune, recognition by the government, gain of clothes and ornaments, success in all efforts, increase in agricultural production and prosperity at home, and profits in business.
- Great happiness and enjoyment of comforts.
- Distress to the body, losses at home and in agricultural production, losses in business dealings, antagonism, or adverse relations with servants (employees) and the king (government), separation from kinsmen and hot temperament.

Moon-Rahu

Effects of Antar Dasha of Rahu in the Maha Dasha of Moon

- Lack of enthusiasm, mental agony and pain due to enemies and diseases may prevail.—Friends may be lost, money may be spent, there may be defame and business losses.
- There may be obstacles in attainment of happiness and fever due to consumption of contaminated food.
- There will be some auspicious results at the commencement.
- Later there will be danger from the king (government), thieves, and snakes, distress to cattle, loss of kinsmen and friends, loss of reputation and mental agony.
- Success in all ventures, gain of conveyances, garments, etc., from the king (government), etc., in the South West direction.
- Loss of position, mental agony, distress to wife and children, danger of diseases, danger from the king (government), scorpions, and snakes, etc.,
- Pilgrimage to holy places, visit to sacred shrines, beneficence, inclination towards charitable deeds, etc.
- There will be body troubles (physical afflictions.)

MOON-JUPITER

Effects of Antar Dasha of Jupiter in the Maha Dasha of Moon

- Religious inclinations may increase and wealth and food grains may be attained.
- Elephants, horses, vehicles, clothes, ornaments and comforts of life will enhance happiness.
- One may receive honors from the king, efforts may be successful and one may celebrate the birth of a child.
- Fame may be attained through education, wishes may be fulfilled and physical happiness may be attained.
- Acquisition of a kingdom (attainment of a high position in government), auspicious celebrations at home, gains of clothes and ornaments, recognition from the king (government) beneficence of the Isht lord ('Isht Devata'), gains of wealth, land, conveyances, and success in all ventures by the beneficence of the king (government).
- Destruction of preceptor (and father, etc.) and children, loss of position, mental agony, quarrels, destruction of a house, conveyances and agricultural land.
- Gains of cattle, grains, clothes and happiness from brothers, acquisition of property, valour, patience, oblations, celebrations like marriage, etc., gain of a kingdom (attainment of a high position in government), etc.
- Effects like unpalatable food, journeys to place away from the homeland.
- There will be good effects at the commencement of the Antar Dasha and distress at its end.

MOON-SATURN

Effects of Antar Dasha of Saturn in the Maha Dasha of Moon

- One may be unhappy due to mother's sufferings.
- Work may be delayed; unhappiness may be caused by harm, fear, mourning and suspicion.
- One may have bad addictions and pain due to gastric problem.

- Fear due to fire, theft, harsh speech, and conflicts with opponents and insult may prevail.
- One's wife, child or brother may be ailing and their pain may cause unhappiness.
- Effects like birth of a son, friendship, gain of wealth and property, profits in business with the help of Sudras, increase in agricultural production, gain from son, riches and glory by the beneficence of the king (government).
- Effects like visits to holy places, bathing in holy rivers, etc., the creation of troubles by many people and distress from enemies.
- Effects like visits to holy places, bathing in holy rivers, etc., the creation of troubles by many people and distress from enemies.
- Effects like enjoyments, and gains of wealth some times.
- Opposition or quarrels with wife and children at other times.
- There will be physical distress.

MOON-MERCURY

Effects of Antar Dasha of Mercury in the Maha Dasha of Moon

- One may acquire education & intelligence, enjoy the company of scholars, progress in business or attain a high position.
- One may attain wealth from one's maternal relatives, acquire land, vehicles and increase one's wealth
- One may become famous due to one's liberal nature.
- Effects like acquisition of wealth, recognition by the king (government), gain of clothes etc., discussions on Shastras Vedic scriptures), gain of knowledge from society with learned and holy people, enjoyments, birth of children, satisfaction, profits in business, acquisition of conveyance and ornaments, etc.
- Effects like marriage, oblations ('Yagya'), charities, performance of religious rites, close relations with the king (government), social contacts with men of learning, acquisition of pearls, corals, Mani (jewels), conveyances, clothes, ornaments, good

health, affections, enjoyments, drinking of Soma Rasa, and other tasty syrups. Etc.
- Pains in the body, loss in agricultural ventures imprisonment, distress to wife and children.

There will be fear of fever

MOON-KETU

Effects of Antar Dasha of Ketu in the Maha Dasha of Moon

- There may be loss of wealth and people
- There may be pain due to stomach ailments; destruction of family and his wife may be ailing.
- Sudden danger may arise and mental unrest and liveliness' may prevail.
- Effects like gain of wealth, enjoyment, happiness of wife and children, religious inclination, etc.
- There will be some loss of wealth at the commencement of the Antar Dasha.
- Later all will be well.
- Gain of wealth, cattle, etc.
- There will be loss of wealth at the end of the Antar Dasha
- There will be obstacles in ventures due to interference by enemies and quarrels.
- There will be danger of affliction of the body with diseases.

MOON-VENUS

Effects of Antar Dasha of Venus in the Maha Dasha of Moon

- Wealth and food may be attained and wealth may be gained through one's wife.
- Worldly comforts, pleasure due to female company and an excellent wife may be attained.
- Business may be favourable and one may possess clothes, ornaments and water related products.

- One may suffer from an ailment, which has been passed on by one's mother.
- Effects like acquisition of a kingdom (attainment of a high position in government), gaining of clothes, ornaments, cattle, conveyances, etc., happiness to wife and children, construction of a new house, availability of sweet preparations every day, use of perfumes, affairs with beautiful women, sound health, etc.
- Physical soundness, good reputation, acquisition of more land and houses.
- There will be loss of landed property, children, wife and cattle, and opposition from government.
- Acquisition of an underground hidden treasure, gain of land, enjoyment, birth of a son, etc.
- Advancement of good fortune, fulfilments of ambitions with the beneficence of the king (government), devotion to deities and Brahmins, gain of jewels like pearls, etc.
- Acquisition of more house property and agricultural land, and gain of wealth and enjoyment.

Deportation to foreign lands, sorrows, death and danger from thieves and snakes will be the results.

MOON-SUN

Effects of Antar Dasha of Sun in the Maha Dasha of Moon

- One may attain wealth and fame from the king and acquire the authority of a king.
- Wealth may be earned through work and business and influence and valour may increase.
- Enemies may be destroyed, disputes may subdue, and freedom from ailments and progress may be attained.
- Recovery of a lost kingdom (high position in government0 and wealth, happiness in the family, acquisition of villages and land with then kind assistance of one's friends and the king (government), birth of a son, beneficence of Goddness Lakshmi.
- At the end of the Antar Dasha, there is the likelihood of attacks of fever and lethargy.

- Danger from the government, thieves, and snakes, affliction with fever and troubles in foreign journey.
- Suffering from fever in his Antar Dasha.

Worship of Lord Shiva is the remedial measure to obtain relief from the above evil effects.

DASHA INTERPRETATIONS

MARS MAHA DASHA

General Interpretations

General effects which are felt during the Maha Dasha of the Mars are as follows:

- There may be fear from those in authority, domestic quarrels, and enmity with spouse, children, and relatives is possible.
- One may have to consume contaminated food.
- There may be problems from thieves, fire, bondage, etc.
- There may be pain due to acidity, blood infection and fever resulting in unconsciousness.

Specific Interpretations:

Interpretations based on the condition of the planet and other influences in the birth chart and divisional charts are as follows:

- During this period, pain may be caused due to conflicts with enemies and unhappiness due to mourning, fire and poison.
- Pain in the eyes, kidneys and urinary organs may occur.
- During this period one may suffer from pain, imprisonment and loss of wealth.
- Extreme pain and suffering are foreseen.
- One may have to move away from one's motherland due to some state displeasure and will be separated from spouse and friends.

- During this period, enemies may surface suddenly, however they are defeated in the end.
- Financial instability persists.
- Fame in courageous deeds may be attained.
- Some maternal relative may meet with an accident or may be in pain.
- During the Maha Dasha of Mars, one's behaviour may not be up to the mark.

Worry due to expenditure, anxiety because of children and mental restlessness may prevail.

EFFECTS OF SUB PERIODS (ANTARDASHA)

Mars-Mars

Effects of Antar Dasha of Mars in the Maha Dasha of Mars

- There may be differences with brothers and brothers may suffer pain.
- There may be conflicts with enemies, destruction of enemies, increase of courage and valour.
- Fear of king and obstacles in work may be possible.
- Physical heat may increase and there may be pain due to vrana ailment and ailments caused by the blood acidity and burning sensation.
- Effects like gains or wealth by the beneficence of the king (government), beneficence of Goddess Lakshmi, recovery of a lost kingdom (reinstatement in a high position) and have wealth, birth of a son.
- Fulfilment of ambitions by the beneficence of the king (government) and acquisition of a house, land cow, buffalo, etc.
- Urinary troubles, wound danger from snakes and the king (government) will be the results.

There will be mental agony and body pains.

Mars-Rahu

Effects of Antar Dasha of Rahu in the Maha Dasha of Mars

- There may be fear from the king, thieves, fire, weapons and enemies.
- Wealth and food may be destroyed, elders and friends may be harmed and these may multiply problems.
- There may be physical pain and ill deeds may be accomplished.
- Effects like recognition from government, gain of house, land, etc., happiness from son, extraordinary profits in business, bathing in holy rivers like Ganges, and foreign journeys.
- Danger from snakes, wounds, destruction of cattle, danger from animals, diseases due to imbalance of bile and wind, imprisonment, etc.

There will be loss of wealth.

Mars-Jupiter

Effects of Antar Dasha of Jupiter in the Maha Dasha of Mars

- Wealth and land may be attained by the king and Brahmins.
- Illness may prevail; enlightenment, strength and valour may increase.
- There may be enthusiasm in performing good deeds, faith and devotion in gods and interest in pilgrimages.
- There may be bliss due to sons, friends and vehicles. Victory will be attained and respect and honors will be received from the people.
- There may be a fear of ailments to the kidneys.
- Effects like good reputation and renown, honors by government, increase in wealth and grains, happiness at home, gain of property, happiness from wife and children, etc.
- Acquisition of a house, land, well being, gain of property, sound health, good reputation, gains of cattle, success in

business, happiness to wife and children, reverence from government, gain of wealth etc.,

Danger from thieves, snakes, wrath of the king (government), bilious diseases, oppression by goblins ('Prot'), loss of servants and co-borns.

Mars-Saturn

Effects of Antar Dasha of Saturn in the Maha Dasha of Mars

- Pain may be caused by wife, son and relatives and physical hardships may persist till death.
- There may be obstacles related to wealth, loss in business, a lowly position in service and hardships due to transfers.
- There may be fear due to enemies, thieves, kings, loss of wealth and problems related to domestic life.
- Ailments may cause pain, anxiety and one may return to one's native place.
- Effects like recognition from the king (government), increase in reputation, gain of wealth and grains, happiness from children and grand children, increase in the number of cows, etc.
- Results will generally fructify on Saturday s in the month of Saturn
- Danger from Yavana king (foreign dignitaries), loss of wealth, imprisonment, possibility of affliction with diseases, loss in agricultural production.
- Effect like great danger, loss of life, wrath of king (government), mental agony, danger from thieves and fire, punishment by the king (government), loss of co-borns, dissensions amongst members of the family, loss of cattle, fear of death, distress to wife and children, imprisonment, etc.
- There will be journeys to foreign lands, loss of reputation, violent actions, loss from sale of agricultural lands, loss of position, agony, defeat in battle, urinary troubles, etc.

Effects like death, danger from the king (government) and thieves, rheumatism, pain, danger from the enemy and members of the family.

Mars-Mercury

Effects of Antar Dasha of Mercury in the Maha Dasha of Mars

- Wealth may be acquired from business and from vaishyas.
- There may be happiness due to festivities, increase of houses, cows and grains.
- There may be fear due to enemies, thieves, and king's mental agony and separation from wife, son and friends.
- Relatives may be insulting and some wicked person may cause mental agony.
- Effects like association with pious and holy persons, performance of Ajaya Japa, charities, observance of religious rites, gain of reputation, inclination towards diplomacy, availability of sweetish preparations, acquisition of conveyances, clothes and cattle, etc., conferment of authority in government), success in agricultural projects, etc.
- Diseases of heart, imprisonment, loss of kinsmen, distress to wife and children, destruction of wealth and cattle, etc. will result
- There will be journeys to foreign lands, increase in the number of enemies, affliction with many kind of ailments, antagonism with the king (government), quarrels with kinsmen etc.,
- Fulfilment of all ambitions, gain of wealth and grains, recognition by the king (government), acquisition of a kingdom (attainment of a high position in government), gain of clothes and ornaments, attachment to many kind of musical instruments, attainment of the position of a commander of an army, discussions on Shastras and Puranas (Vedic scripts), gain of riches to wife and children, and beneficence of Goddess Lakshmi.
- Effects like defamation, sinful thinking, harsh speech, danger from thieves, fire, and the king (government), quarrels without reason, fear of attack by thieves and dacoits (armed rubber bands) during travel.

There will be a possibility of critical illness.

Mars-Ketu

Effects of Antar Dasha of Ketu in the Maha Dasha of Mars

- Business may be negative and there may be loss of wealth.
- Friends and brothers may cause pain, wife and children may suffer hardships & there may be enmity towards wicked people.
- There may be agony due to stomach ailments and sudden pain due to fire or weapons.
- Beneficence of the king (government), gain of wealth, little gains of land at the commencement of the Dasha and substantial later, birth of a son, conferment of authority by government, gain of cattle, etc.
- Birth of a son, increase in reputation, beneficence of Goddess Lakshmi, gains of wealth from employees, attainment of the position of a commander of an army, friendship with the king (cordial relations with high government officials), performance of oblations, gains of clothes and ornaments.
- Effects like quarrels, tooth trouble, distress from thieves and tigers, fever, dysentery leprosy, and distress to wife and children, etc.
- Diseases, disgrace, agony and loss of wealth

Mars-Venus

Effects of Antar Dasha of Venus in the Maha Dasha of Mars

- One may be inclined to do many types of business.
- Wealth may be attained from friends and happiness may prevail.
- Wife will be endowed with clothes, ornaments and vehicles.
- Money may be spent excessively and migration.
- Effects like acquisition of a kingdom (attainment of a high position in government), great enjoyment and comfort of luxuries, gain of elephants, horses, clothes, etc.
- Happiness of wife and children, opulence and glory, and increased good fortune.

- Gain of property, celebrations on the birth of a son, gain of wealth from the employer, acquisition of a house, land, villages, etc. b the beneficence of the sovereign.
- In the last part of the Dasha there will be functions of songs and dances and bathing in holy water.
- Construction of wells, reservoirs, etc, and performance of religious, charitable and pious deeds.
- There will be sorrows, physical distress, loss of wealth, danger from thieves, and the king (government), dissensions in the family, distress to wife and children and destruction of cattle.
- Pains in the body in his Antar Dasha.

For regaining good health, the remedial measure to be adopted is giving a cow or female buffalo in charity.

Mars-Sun

Effects of Antar Dasha of Sun in the Maha Dasha of Mars

- Victory and honour will be received from the state.
- Valour and influences increase and there may be success in debates.
- Wealth may be gained and there may be desire to roam around.
- Father may suffer pain, there may be enmity towards paternal relatives and dear ones may cause sufferings.
- Effects like acquisition of conveyances, gain of reputation, birth of a son, growth of wealth, amicable atmosphere in the family, sound health, potency, recognition by the king (government), extraordinary profits in business, and audience with the king (meeting with high officials of the government), etc.
- Distress to the body, agony, failure in ventures, possibilities of suffering from troubles in the forehead, fever, dysentery, etc.

There will be attacks of fever, danger from snakes and poison and distress to son.

Mars-Moon

Effects of Antar Dasha of Moon in the Maha Dasha of Mars

- A high position and state honour may be received.
- Ornaments, wealth and jewels may be gained.
- One will meet friends and receive help and worldly comforts from them.
- Desire will be fulfilled and there may be auspicious events everyday.
- Laziness and cough ailment may afflict the body.
- Acquisition of more kingdom (promotion to a higher position in government)
- Gain of perfumes, clothes, construction of reservoirs, shelters for cows, etc.
- Celebrations of auspicious functions like marriage, etc. happiness to wife and children, good relations with parents.
- Acquisition of property by the beneficence of the sovereign, success in the desired projects.
- Since the Moon is waxing, the good effects will be realized in full.
- Since the Moon is waning, the impact of the effects are reduced to some extent.

The effects like death, distress to wife and children loss of lands, wealth and cattle, and danger of a war, etc.

DASHA INTERPRETATIONS

RAHU MAHA DASHA

General Interpretations

General effects which are felt during the Maha Dasha of the Rahu are as follows:

- There may be unhappiness due to various reasons; physical hardships and a state of mindlessness may prevail.

- There may be fear from thieves, powerful persons, poison and weapons.
- Children may suffer and separation from children and dear ones may cause unhappiness.
- One may fear insult and defame from lowly people.
- Some ill deed may cause defame.
- There may be a change of job, and residence abroad is possible.
- Diseases may cause pain and one may be inclined towards quarrelling.
- Rahu will give excellent results.
- During the excellent Maha Dasha of Rahu, one may attain wealth and there will be an advent of money and religious inclinations.
- Pious deeds are performed.
- The dasha of Rahu normally last for 18 years.
- The 6th and 8th years are the most painful ones.
- Rahu is exalted in Taurus, Gemini (according to a different viewpoint), and a Mool Trikona in Cancer, Aquarius and a friendly planet in Aries.

Specific Interpretations:

Interpretations based on the condition of the planet and other influences in the birth chart and divisional charts are as follows:

- One may suffer due to weakness, venereal diseases, cough, asthma and urinary ailments.
- There may be fear due to the powerful, cheating by thieves and destruction of one's family.
- During this period one may have to earn a living by having a lowly job or business.
- Good food may not be available and one's spouse and son may behave wickedly.
- Fear of those in authority, upheavals in business and loss of job is possible.
- There may be fear of fire, thieves, ailments and harm to religion and work.

- There may be physical weakness, conflicts in the community, fear of those in high places, enemies and thieves.
- Ailments due to cough and urinary problems may arise.
- Mental agony, enmity with relatives and cheating by friends is possible.
- There may be disagreement with family members; one's spouse and children may be ailing.
- One's mother may suffer pain.
- Fear and anger of those in high places, problems due to immovable assets and anxiety related to house and land are possible.
- There may be loss of wealth and injury or fall from a vehicle.
- A high position may be attained and one may be honored in parliament or in huge gatherings and become famous.
- One may be endowed with children, spouse and vehicles.
- There may be occasional hurdles and problems in progress.

EFFECTS OF SUB PERIODS *(ANTARDASHA)*

Rahu-Rahu

Effects of Antar Dasha of Rahu in the Maha Dasha of Rahu

- The mind may be misled and mental tension increases.
- Family members like father and brothers may be harmed, wife may be ailing and conflicts are possible.
- Loss of wealth, sorrow, ailments, poison and fear of poisonous being prevails, wicked people may cause agony.
- Good fortune is possible, away from ones native place and one may have to travel far.
- Effects like acquisition of a kingdom (attainment of a high position in government), enthusiasm, and cordial relations with the king (government), happiness from wife and children, and increase in property.
- There will be danger from thieves, distress from wounds, antagonism with government officials, destruction of kinsmen, distress to wife and children.
- There will be distress and diseases.

- To obtain relief from the above evil effects Rahu should be worshipped (by recitation of his mantras) and by giving in charity things connected with or ruled by Rahu.

Rahu-Jupiter

Effects of Antar Dasha of Jupiter in the Maha Dasha of Rahu

- Interest in worshipping God and in superior shastras arise.
- One may undertake religious pilgrimages, seek the company of sages and perform pious, religious deeds.
- Fame may be attained in knowledge; friendship with officials, bliss of children and sufficient wealth may be attained.
- Ailments and enemies may be overcome, good health and enthusiasm prevails.
- Effects like gain of position, patience, destruction or foes, enjoyment, cordial relations with the king (government), regular increase in wealth and property like the growth of Moon of the bright half of the month (Shukla Paksh), gain of conveyance and cows.
- Audience with the king (high government officials) by performing journey to the West or South East, success in the desired ventures, return to one's homeland, doing good for Brahmins, visit to holy places.
- Gain of a village, devotion to deities and Brahmins, happiness from wife, children, and grand children, availability of sweetish preparations daily.
- Loss of wealth, obstacles in work defamation, distress to wife and children, heart disease, entrustment of governmental authority, etc.
- There will be gains of land, good food, gains of cattle, etc., inclinations towards charitable and religious work.
- Loss of wealth, and distress to body.
- There will be danger of premature death.
- The person will get relief from the above evil effects and enjoy good health by the beneficence of the lord Shiva if he worships his idol made of gold.

Rahu-Saturn

Effects of Antar Dasha of Saturn in the Maha Dasha of Rahu

- Imprudent acts may cause losses. There is a possibility of loss of position and incurring the anger of the state.
- Quarrels with dear ones, unhappiness for friends and residing in far off lands is possible.
- One may suffer injury on some part of the body and there may be ailments due to gastric and blood infection.
- Effects like pleasure of the king for devotion in his service, auspicious functions like celebration of marriage, etc at home, construction of a garden, reservoir, etc., gain of wealth and cattle from well to do persons belonging to the Sudra class, loss of wealth caused by the king 9government officials) during journey to the West, reduction in income due to lethargy, return to homeland.
- Danger from menials, the king, and enemies, distress to wife and children, distress to kinsmen, disputes with the coparceners, disputes in dealings with others, but sudden gain of ornaments.
- There will be heart disease, defamation, quarrels, danger from enemies, foreign journeys, affliction with Gulma (enlargement of the skin), unpalatable food, and sorrows, etc.

Rahu-Mercury

Effects of Antar Dasha of Mercury in the Maha Dasha of Rahu

- Good health, intelligence and prudence increases.
- Love for brothers and friends increases and help is attained from friends.
- Worldly comforts are increased, wealth and progress in business is attained.
- Auspicious effects like Raj Yog, well being in the family, profits and gain of wealth in business, comforts of conveyances, marriage and other auspicious functions, increase in the number of cattle, gain of perfumes, comforts of bed, women.

- Good results like Raj Yog, beneficence of the king, and gain of wealth and reputation, will be realized particularly on Wednesday in the month of Mercury.
- Sound health, Isht Siddhi, attending discourse on Puranas and ancient history, marriage, offering of oblations, charities, religious inclination, and sympathetic attitude towards others.
- There will be opprobrium (Ninda) of deities and Brahmins by the native, loss of fortune, speaking lies, unwise actions, and fear from snakes, thieves, and the government, quarrels, distress to wife and children.

Rahu-Ketu

Effects of Antar Dasha of Ketu in the Maha Dasha of Rahu

- There is a possibility of state displeasure and loss of wealth and fame.
- Wife and son may suffer hardships, animals may die and one may be assaulted by many problems.
- There may be pain due to ailments caused by fever etc., fear of thieves, fire, weapons and poison and by conflicts.
- One may have to wander, incur state displeasure, suffer from ailments caused by gas and fever and there may be loss of animals.
- There will be distress to the body and mental tension.
- Enjoyment, gain wealth, recognition by the king (government), acquisition gold etc.
- There will be Isht Siddhi.
- There will definitely be gain of wealth.
- Effects like danger from thieves and snakes, distress from wounds, separation from parents, antagonistic relations with kinsmen, mental agony, etc.
- There will be distress to the body.

Rahu-Venus

Effects of Antar Dasha of Venus in the Maha Dasha of Rahu

- Very little money may be earned in work and business inspite of immense struggle.
- Bliss of wife and gain of wealth through her is possible.
- Friends may cause agony and fear of opposition with the family prevails.
- One may go abroad and prosper there.
- Ailments related to urinary organs may occur.
- Effects like gains of wealth through Brahmins, increase in the number of cattle, celebrations for the birth of a son, well being, recognition from government, acquisition of a kingdom, attainment of a high position in government, great enjoyment and comforts, etc.
- Construction of a new house, availability of sweet preparations, happiness from wife and children, association with friends, giving of grains etc., in charity, beneficence of the king (government), gain of conveyances and clothes extraordinary profits in business, celebration of Upasayan ceremony of wearing the sacred thread ('Janou')
- There will be diseases, quarrels, separation from one's son or father, distress to kinsmen, disputes with coparceners, danger of death to oneself or to one's employer, unhappiness to wife and children, pain in the stomach, etc.
- Enjoyments from perfumes, bed, music, etc., gain of a desired object, fulfilment of desires will be the results.
- Effects like danger from the wrath of Brahmins, snakes, and the king (government) possibility of a affliction with diseases like stoppage of urine, diabetes, pollution of blood, anaemia, availability of only coarse food, nervous disorder, imprisonment, loss of wealth as a result of penalties or fines imposed by government.
- There will be distress to wife and children.

Rahu-Sun

Effects of Antar Dasha of Sun in the Maha Dasha of Rahu

- Many upheavals may be quieted down.
- Wealth and prosperity and interest in charity and religion increase.
- Enemies may cause agony and fear of king, poison, fire and weapons prevails.
- There is a possibility of pain due to eye, heart and infections disease.
- Effect like cordial relations with the king (government), increase in wealth and grains, some popularity /respect, some possibility of becoming head of a village, etc.
- There will be good reputation and encouragement and assistance by government, journeys to foreign countries, acquisition of the sovereignty of the country, gains of elephants, horse, clothes, ornaments, fulfilments of ambitions, happiness to children.
- Fevers, dysentery, other diseases, quarrels, antagonism with the king (government), travels, danger from foes, thieves, fire.
- Well being in every way and recognition from kings (high dignitaries) in foreign countries.
- There will be danger of critical illness.

Rahu-Moon

Effects of Antar Dasha of Moon in the Maha Dasha of Rahu

- Circumstances causing anxiety may arise.
- There may be a conflict with the dear ones, opposition with friends and increase in the number of enemies.
- Money may come in with difficulty and food may be attained.
- Daughter in law may expire, fear of water prevails and conflicts cause unhappiness.
- Effects like acquisition of a kingdom (attainment of high position in government), respect from the king (high officials of government).

- Gains of wealth, sound health, gains of garments and ornaments, happiness from children, comforts of conveyances, increase in house and landed property.
- Beneficence of the Goddess Lakshmi, all round success, increases in wealth and grains, good reputation, and worship of deities.
- There will be the creation of disturbances at home and in the agricultural activities by evil spirits, leopards, and other wild animals, danger from thieves during journeys, and stomach disorders.

Rahu-Mars

Effects of Antar Dasha of Mars in the Maha Dasha of Rahu

-Many upheavals and movements may arise.

-Physical pain, lack of enthusiasm and loss of memory are possible.

-Position may be lost and fear of king, thieves, fire and weapons prevail.

-Public opinion, residing in one's native land, wife and son may be disturbed or harmed.

-Effects like the recovery of a lost kingdom (reinstatement in a high position in government) and recovery of lost wealth, property at home, and increase in agricultural production, gain of wealth, blessings by the household deity (Isht Dev), happiness from children, enjoyment of good food, etc.

-There will be acquisition of red coloured garments, journeys, audience with the king (meeting with high governmental officials), well being of children and employer, attainment of the position of a commander of the army, enthusiasm, and gain of wealth through kinsmen.

-Distress of wife, children, and co-borns, loss of position, antagonistic relations with children, wife, and other close relations, danger from thieves, wounds and pain in the body.

DASHA INTERPRETATIONS

JUPITER MAHA DASHA

General Interpretations

General effects which are felt during the Maha Dasha of the Jupiter are as follows:

- During the Maha Dasha of Jupiter, the desired fruits are attained from those in positions of authority.
- Interest in worship of god, religion, study of Veda, Puranas, Shastras and performing yagyas, etc. prevails.
- One may keep the company of good people, saints, be devoted to elders and may perform pious deeds.
- Respect in the community and leadership is attained.
- One may be skilled in the knowledge of the past and future
- One may be endowed with land, clothes and vehicles.
- Wealth may be acquired.
- During the Maha Dasha of Jupiter, some very good job or position involving authority and domination may be acquired.
- In the end, wealth, honour from the king and opportunities for undertaking long travels may be attained.
- However, mental anxiety may cause physical pain.
- Moderate amount of wealth, some fame, some patience and bliss may be attained during the Maha Dasha of Jupiter.
- Thieves may cause loss of wealth.
- There may be friendship with those in high places and success in arguments.
- Happiness from good friends, good clothes, spouse, children, and wealth. This Maha Dasha is very auspicious. It brings respect from friends and possession of vehicles.
- Yagyas and weddings and other auspicious events bring happiness.
- Wealth and kingdom may be attained.
- Friendship with rich and powerful people is possible.
- Job and vehicle may be attained.

- Bliss from spouse, children and friends is possible.
- Birth of a child is foreseen.
- High position, service, respect and authority are attained during the Maha Dasha of Jupiter.
- Friendship with big people, name and leadership in the family are foreseen.
- Gain, prosperity and happiness are attained from those in high places.

EFFECTS OF SUB PERIODS *(ANTARDASHA)*:

Jupiter-Jupiter

Effects of Antar Dasha of Jupiter in the Maha Dasha of Jupiter

- Enthusiasm and physical enlightenment will prevail.
- Educational and scientific knowledge will be attained. Fame and position will be acquired through education.
- One will enjoy the king's favour, prosperity, respect, good habits and good fortune.
- All work will be successfully accomplished, bliss of children will prevail and there will be monetary gains of many types.
- Sovereignty over many kings, very well endowed with riches, reversed by the king, gains of cattle, clothes ornaments, conveyances.
- Construction of a new house, and a decent mansion, opulence and glory, dawn of fortune, success in ventures, meetings with Brahmins and the king, extraordinary profits from the employer and happiness of wife and children.
- Association with the menials, great distress, slander by coparceners, wrath of the employer, separation from wife and children, and loss of wealth and grains.
- There will be pains in the body.

Jupiter-Saturn

Effects of Antar Dasha of Saturn in the Maha Dasha of Jupiter

- There is a possibility of physical weakness, a jealous mentality and internal unhappiness.
- Work and business may suffer; wealth, religion and fame will be harmful. Bed addictions may develop and one may have illicit relations with other women.
- There may be pain due to fever and excessive expenditure.
- Effects like acquisition of a kingdom (attainment of a high position in government), gain of clothes, ornaments, wealth, grains, conveyances, cattle, and position, happiness from son and friends, etc., gains specially of a blue coloured horse, journey to the West, audience with the king, and receipt of wealth from him.
- Loss of wealth, affliction with fever, mental agony, infliction of wounds to wife and children, inauspicious events at home, loss of cattle and employment, antagonism with kinsmen, etc.
- There will be gain of land, house, son, and cattle, acquisition of riches and property through the enemy etc.
- Effects like loss of wealth, antagonistic relations with kinsmen, obstacles in industrial ventures, pains in the body, danger from the members of the family, etc., will be realised

Jupiter-Mercury

Effects of Antar Dasha of Mercury the Maha Dasha of Jupiter

- Faith in God and acquiring knowledge of the yogas is predicted.
- One may be honored by scholars and interest in good deeds may arise, work efficiency increases.
- Happiness increases due to the king's favor and wealth may be attained through business and because of one's wife.
- One may be endowed with vehicles, temples may be built and the bliss of friends, wife and son prevails.

- Long journeys may be undertaken and the mind may be energetic. Headaches and fear of restlessness may prevail.
- Effects like gains of wealth, bodily felicity, acquisition of a kingdom (attainment of a high position in the government), gain of conveyances, clothes, and cattle etc.
- There will be loss of wealth, journeys to foreign countries, danger from thieves while travelling, wounds, burning sensations, eye troubles, wanderings in foreign lands.
- Distress without reason, anger, loss of cattle, loss in business.
- There will be enjoyment, gains of wealth conveyances and clothes at the commencement of the Antar Dasha.
- At the end of the Dasha, however, there will be loss of wealth and bodily distress.
- There will be loss of wealth, journeys to foreign countries, danger from thieves while traveling, wounds, burning sensations, eye troubles, wandering in foreign lands.

Jupiter-Ketu

Effects of Antar Dasha of Ketu the Maha Dasha of Jupiter

- There is a possibility of loss of position, wandering and instability.
- There may be disagreement with relatives, sons and brothers may suffer and public opinion may be opposing.
- Elders may suffer due to conflicts; the king's anger and loss of wealth and ailments may prevail.
- There may be fear of injury, harm due to servants and mental agony.
- Moderate enjoyment, moderate gain of wealth, coarse food or food given by others food given at the time of death ceremonies and acquisition of wealth though undesirable means.
- Effects like loss of wealth by the wrath of the king, imprisonment, diseases, loss of physical strength, antagonism with father and brother and mental agony.
- Acquisition of a palanquin (motor car), elephants, etc. beneficence of the king success in the desired spheres, profit

in business, increase in the number of cattle, gain of wealth, clothes etc., from a Yavana King (Muslim dignitary).

- There will be physical distress.

Jupiter-Venus

Effects of Antar Dasha of Venus the Maha Dasha of Jupiter

- One may be inclined towards religious deeds and service of good people.
- Happiness due to excellent education and the company of scholars may prevail.
- The government will be favourable and wealth, vehicles and royal symbols are attained.
- Women may cause pain and loss of wealth, there may be enmity with people, separation from friends and one may be addicted to bad habits.
- Gastric ailments, conflicts and mental anxiety are possible.
- Effects like acquisition of conveyances like palanquin, elephants, etc., gain of wealth by the beneficence of the king (govt.) enjoyment, gain of blue and red articles, extraordinary income from journeys to the East, well being in the family, happiness from parents, devotion to deities, construction of reservoirs, charities, etc.
- Evil effects like quarrels, antagonism with kinsmen, distress to wife and children.
- There will be quarrels, danger from the king (government), antagonism with the wife, disputes with the father in law and with brothers, loss of wealth, etc.,
- There will be gain of wealth, happiness from wife, meeting with the king (high governmental officials), increase in the number of children, conveyances and cattle, enjoyment of music, society with men of learning, availability of sweetish preparation, giving help and assistance to kinsmen, etc.
- Loss of wealth, antagonism with wife, etc.

Jupiter-Sun

Effects of Antar Dasha of Sun Maha Dasha of Jupiter

- Authority and respect may be attained from the king. Some respectable title may also be fortunately received.
- Friendship with good people, increase of enlightenment and valour and domination over the nation and public are possible.
- Bliss of children, progress of children, journeys to religious places and increase in fame are possible.
- Happiness increase, enthusiasm prevails and wealth and many things are attained.
- Enemies will be won over and good health prevails.
- Gain of wealth, reverence, happiness and acquisition of conveyances, clothes, ornaments, etc., birth of children, cordial relations with the king (government), success in ventures, etc.
- Effect like nervous disorder, fever, laziness or reluctance in the performance of good deeds, indulgence in sin, antagonistic attitude towards all, separation from kinsmen, and distress without reason.
- There will be physical distress.

Jupiter-Moon

Effects of Antar Dasha of Moon Maha Dasha of Jupiter

- Some royal symbol may be acquired and the king's favor may add to the happiness.
- Friendship with king and high officials and frame and status are acquired.
- Bliss of women, wealth due to women, ornaments and good clothes will be attained.
- Wealth and fame are enhanced due to superior knowledge.
- Good fortune of possessing land, property house and vehicles prevails.
- Effects like reverence from the king (government), opulence and glory, happiness from wife and children, availability of good food, gain of reputation by performance of good

deeds, increase in the number of children and grand children, comforts by the beneficence of the king (government), religious and charitable inclinations.

- There will be loss of wealth and kinsmen, wanderings in foreign lands, dander from the king (government) thieves, quarrels with co-parceners, separation from a maternal uncle, distress to mother, etc.
- Physical distress will be experienced

Jupiter-Mars

Effects of Antar Dasha of Mars Maha Dasha of Jupiter

- Valour increases and success in arguments and disputes is attained.
- Fame may be attained in the work-sphere and wife and son may bring happiness.
- Physical strength wanes, there is a lack of enthusiasm, pain due to fever and fear due to enemies and venereal diseases may be caused.
- Effects like the celebration of functions such as marriage, etc., gain of land or villages, growth of strength and valour, and success in all ventures.
- There will be gain of wealth and grains, availability of good sweetish preparations, pleasure of the king (government), happiness from wife and children and other auspicious effects.
- Loss of wealth and house, eye trouble and other inauspicious effects will be the results.
- The effects will be particularly adverse at the commencement of the Antar Dasha.
- There will be some mitigation of evil effects later.
- There will be physical distress and mental agony.

Jupiter-Rahu

Effects of Antar Dasha of Rahu Maha Dasha of Jupiter

- There may be unnecessary enmity and opposition with friends and brothers.
- There is a fear of many types of conflict and upheavals.
- There may be pain to children & long journeys.
- Wealth may decrease and there is fear of death or its equivalent.
- Effects like attachment to Yog, gain of wealth and grains during the first five months, sovereignty over a village or country, meeting with a foreign king (high dignitary).
- Well being in family, journeys to distant lands, bathing in holy places.
- Danger from thieves, snakes, the king (government), wounds, troubles in domestic affairs, antagonism with co-borns, and coparceners, bad dreams, quarrels without reason, danger from diseases, etc.
- There will be physical distress.

SATURN MAHA DASHA

General Interpretations

General effects which are felt during the Maha Dasha of the Saturn are as follows:

- During the Maha Dasha of Saturn, some sort of authority in the city, village or society may be acquired.
- One may become the leader of a lowly community.
- Modesty, intelligence and knowledge is enhanced, inclination towards charity and skilled in arts and crafts.
- Happiness may be gained from the acquisition of some ancient place.
- One may be endowed with vehicles, clothes, gold and wealth.
- Faith in God and interest in the construction of temples may prevail.
- One may bring name and fame to the family.
- Bliss of the family, increase of valour prevails and journeys are undertaken.
- There may be gains from animals, camels, Asses, goats, birds, old ladies and coarse grains.

Specific Interpretations:

Interpretations based on the condition of the planet and other influences in the birth chart and divisional charts are as follows:

- During the Maha Dasha of Saturn, one may acquire the leadership of villages, cities and countries.
- One's father may be harmed or may expire and there may be enmity with friends.
- During the Maha Dasha of Saturn, wealth, spouse, children, siblings and servants maybe harmed.
- Bad feed maybe consumed and one may be defamed.
- When Saturn is strong:
- During the Maha Dasha of Saturn, there is an increase in happiness and fame.
- Land may be lost and there may be opposition with servants, spouse, children and siblings.
- There may be fear of demotion or suspension and imprisonment by the government.
- When Saturn is cruel, 'drashkanastha', then
- During the Maha Dasha of Saturn, there may be restlessness and fear of the powerful, thieves, fire and poison.
- There may be opposition from relatives, domestic crisis and disagreement with workers.
- There may be loss of wealth, fear from those in high places, mental unrest and ailments related to eyes and kidney may happen.
- The spouse may suffer and elders in the family may be in pain.
- State authority, honour and progress at work are foreseen.
- Immovable assets, jewels, ornaments and wealth will be attained.
- Vehicles, servants and objects of comfort will be attained.
- Vehicles, servants and objects of comfort will be attained.
- Sympathy in the mind is aroused.

EFFECTS OF SUB PERIODS *(ANTARDASHA)*

Saturn-Saturn

Effects of Antar Dasha of Saturn Maha Dasha of Saturn

- Physical lethargy and lack of enthusiasm prevails.
- Obstacles at work, shortage of money, migration and indebtedness may occur.
- Gastric problems, ailments and anger caused by price and jealousy are possible.
- Kings and thieves may be responsible for destruction of wealth & prosperity.
- One may become imprudent due to ones wife, there may be conflicts with children and many problems and hardships may prevail.
- Effects like acquisition of a kingdom (attainment of a high position in government), happiness from wife and children, acquisition of conveyances like elephants, gain of clothes, attainment of the position of a commander of the army by the beneficence of the king, acquisition of cattle, villages, and land, etc.
- Fear or danger from the king (government), getting inflicted with injuries with some weapon, bleeding gums, dysentery, etc., will be the evil effects at the commencement of the Dasha.
- There will be danger from thieves etc., going away from the homeland, mental agony, etc., in the middle portion of the Dasha. The last part of the Dasha will yield beneficial result.

Saturn-Mercury

Effects of Antar Dasha of Mercury Maha Dasha of Saturn

- Status is attained in the royal court and promotion is attained.
- Success in business & trade, and gain of wealth is possible.
- One may derive pleasure from the company of scholars, interest in pious deeds increases and friends are beneficial.

- Wife and sons cause happiness, vehicles, fame and name are attained, and good fortune is enhanced.
- Cough and cold may cause physical pain.
- Effects like reverence from the people, good reputation, gain of wealth, comforts of conveyances, etc.
- Inclination towards performance of religious sacrifices (Yagya's), Raj Yog, bodily felicity, enthusiasm, well being in the family, pilgrimage to holy places, performance of religious rites, listening to Puranas (Vedic scriptures), charities, availability of sweetish preparations, etc.
- Acquisition of a kingdom (attainment of a high position in Government), gain of wealth, and headship of a village will be the effects at the commencement of the Dasha.
- Affliction with diseases, failure in all ventures, anxiety and feeling of danger, etc. will be experienced in the middle portion and in the last part of the Dasha.
- There will be physical distress.

Saturn-Ketu

Effects of Antar Dasha of Ketu Maha Dasha of Saturn

- Fear of imprisonment prevails and unhappy circumstances may arise.
- Conflict with lowly and wicked people and separation from wife and son are possible.
- Loss of wealth, bad dreams and fear of ailments caused by gas etc., are possible.
- Evil effects like loss of position, dangers, poverty, distress, foreign journeys, etc.
- There will be gain of wealth and enjoyment and bathing in holy places and visit to a sacred shrine at the commencement of the Antar Dasha.
- Gain of physical strength and courage, religious thoughts, audience with the king (high dignitaries of government like: president, prime minister, governor, ministers), and all kinds of enjoyments.

- Fear of coarse food, cold fever, dysentery, wounds, danger from thieves, separation from wife and children etc.
- There will be physical distress.

Saturn-Venus

Effects of Antar Dasha of Venus Maha Dasha of Saturn

- Both auspicious and inauspicious fruits are attained.
- Fame in the village or country, wife, children, ornaments and wealth are attained.
- Happiness from agriculture, affection towards friends and love for the people, bliss from son, destruction of enemies and enlightenment due to fame is possible.
- Effects like marriage, birth of a son, gain of wealth, sound health, and well being in the family.
- Acquisition of a kingdom (attainment of high position in government), enjoyment by the beneficence of the king (government), honours.
- Gain of clothes, ornaments, conveyance and other desired objects.
- If during the period of Antar Dasha of Venus, Jupiter is favourable in transit, there will be dawn fortune and growth of property.
- If Saturn is favourable in transit, there will be Raj Yog effect or the accomplishment of Yog rites ('Yog Triya Siddhi').
- Distress of wife, loss of position, mental agony, quarrels with close relations, etc.
- Fulfilment of ambitions by the beneficence of the king, charities, performance of religious rites, creation of interest in the study of Shastras, composition of poems, interest in Vedanta, etc., listening to Puranas, happiness from wife and children.
- There will be eye trouble, fevers, loss of good conduct, dental problems, heart disease, pain in arms, danger from drowning or falling from at tree, antagonism towards relations, with the officials of government and brothers.
- There will be physical distress

Saturn-Sun

Effects of Antar Dasha of Sun Maha Dasha of Saturn

- There is possibility of physical pain and mental agony
- Indefinite circumstances, sudden events, public criticism and defame are possible.
- There may be pain to wife, son and friends, enemies may be created and one may have to wander uselessly.
- There may be a loss of wealth, pain due to thieves and king and ailments related to appetite, heart and eyes.
- Effects like good relations with one's employer, well-being in the family, happiness from children, gain of conveyances and cattle, etc.
- There will be heart disease, defamation, loss of position, mental agony, separation from close relatives, obstacles in industrial ventures, fevers, fears loss of kinsmen, loss of articles dear to the person.
- There will be physical distress

Saturn-Moon

Effects of Antar Dasha of Moon Maha Dasha of Saturn

- Lack of enthusiasm, mental agony, anger and outrage may increase.
- There may be disagreements with friends, constant conflicts, hardships due to children and harm caused by hidden enemies.
- Wife may expire or separate or may suffer pain equivalent to death. Happiness may be disturbed.
- Gastric problems or venereal diseases may cause pain.
- Effects like gains of conveyance, garments, ornaments, improvement of fortune and enjoyments, taking care of brothers, happiness in both maternal and paternal homes increase in cattle wealth, etc.
- There will be great distress, wrath, and separation from parents, ill health of children, losses in business, irregular meals, administration of medicines.

- There will, however be good effects and some gain of wealth at the commencement of the Antar Dasha.
- Enjoyment of conveyances and garments, happiness from kinsmen, happiness from parents, wife, employers, etc.
- Effects like sleepiness, lethargy, loss of position, loss of enjoyments, increase in the number of enemies, antagonism with kinsmen, will be experienced.
- There will be lethargy and physical distress.

Saturn-Mars

Effects of Antar Dasha of Mars Maha Dasha of Saturn

- The body may suffer pain due to some serious ailments.
- Brothers may be in pain, friends may be jealous, wife and son may be separated and pain due to children may occur.
- There may be loss of position, demotion, losses in business and work or ordinary gains.
- Fear of many types may prevail and friends and status may be harmed.
- Effects like enjoyments, gain of wealth, reverence from the king (government), gain of conveyances, clothes a ornaments, attainment of the position of a commander of the Army, increase in agricultural and cattle wealth, construction of a new house, happiness of kinsmen, will be derived from the very commencement of the Antar Dasha of Mars in the Dasha Saturn.
- There will be loss of wealth, danger of wounds, danger from thieves, snakes, weapons, gout and other similar disease, distress to father and brothers, quarrels with co-partners, loss of kinsmen, coarse food, going away to foreign lands, unnecessary expenditure etc.
- Great distress, dependence on others and fear.

Saturn-Rahu

Effects of Antar Dasha of Rahu Maha Dasha of Saturn

- Inspite of excessive effort and struggle, gains may be very little.
- There may be shortage of mental enthusiasm and anxiety related to worldly comforts.
- Quarrels with friends, pain due to enemies and unhappiness due to friends may be possible.
- Physical ailments like gastric attacks, fever etc. are possible.
- Effects like quarrels, mental agony, physical distress, agony, antagonism with the sons, danger from diseases, unnecessary expenditure, discord with close relations, danger from the government, foreign journeys, loss of house and agricultural lands.
- Enjoyment, gain of wealth, increase in agricultural production, devotion in deities and Brahmins, pilgrimage to holy places, increase in cattle wealth, well-being in the family will be the results at the commencement of the Antar Dasha.
- There will be cordiality with the king and happiness from friends in the middle portion of the Antar Dasha.
- There will be acquisition of elephants, opulence, and glory, cordial relations with the king (government), gain of valuable clothes.
- There will be physical distress.

Saturn-Jupiter

Effect of the Antar Dasha of Jupiter in the Maha Dasha of Saturn

- Devotion towards God, elders and saints may increase.
- Wealth, land, vehicles and servants may be attained due to the king's favor.
- New work may be started, wealth may be attained and fame may be enhanced.
- Bliss of wife and son prevails; happiness, pleasure and other comforts may be enjoyed.
- Skill at arts and increase in talents and good habits is foreseen.

- Effects like success all round, well being in the family, gain of conveyances, ornaments, and clothes by the beneficence of the king (government), reverence, devotion of deities and the preceptor, association with men of learning, happiness from wife and children, etc.
- Results like death of the near relations, loss of wealth, antagonism with the government officials, failure of projects, journeys to foreign lands, affliction with disease like leprosy, etc.
- There will be opulence and glory, happiness to wife, gains through the king (government), comforts of good food and clothes, religious mindedness, name and fame in the country, interest in Vedas and Vedanta, performance of religious sacrifices, giving grains, etc. in charity.
- Antagonism with kinsmen, mental agony, quarrels loss of position, losses in ventures, loss of wealth as a result of imposition of fines or penalties by government imprisonment distress to wife and son.
- There will be physical distress, agony, death of the native or any member of the family.

DASHA INTERPRETATIONS

MERCURY MAHA DASHA

General Interpretations

General effects which are felt during the Maha Dasha of the Mercury are as follows:

- One may acquire money through contacts with big people, various enterprises, friends and family members.
- Excellence in education, skills in speech and crafts and love for music may prevail.
- Love and respect for teachers, elders and scholars may increase.
- Interest in construction and gain of new clothes and ornaments is possible.
- Money may be attained through trading gold.

- Opportunities for acting as an arbitrator or middleman may arise.
- Life will be passed happily in humour, fun and play.
- Public importance and fame may increase.
- Happiness from spouse and children may be derived.
- Gastric problems may persist.

Specific Interpretations:

Interpretations based on the condition of the planet and other influences in the birth chart and divisional charts are as follows:

- Fear of enemies and those in high places may prevail.
- Hardships for spouse and children is possible. One may attain food through service of those who do not have a family.
- Disinterest in studies may arise.
- Destruction of auspicious deeds and the advent of sorrow and unhappiness are foreseen.
- There may be obstacles in celebrating festivities, opposition with dear ones and lack of enterprise.
- Inclination towards sinful deeds and harm to wealth, land, agriculture and cows may occur.
- Trouble may come in many forms. There is mental unhappiness, enmity with the family and state, and public criticism. Eye ailments are possible.
- Attaining fame and education may enhance state honour, respect and valour.
- Laziness, physical hardships, ailments loss of appetite, ear problems, etc. may prevail during the Maha Dasha of Mercury.
- There may be a possibility of migration or transfer.
- Brothers may be harmed but respect may be attained from those in position of authority.
- During this period enthusiasm in business prevails and wealth through art and poetry is possible.
- Friendship with new people and opposition with old friends is possible.

There is a possibility of residence abroad, and hurdles to happiness, anxiety and worry prevail.

EFFECTS OF SUB PERIODS *(ANTARDASHA)*

Mercury-Mercury

Effect of the Antar Dasha of Mercury in the Maha Dasha of Mercury

- Interest in arts and crafts, increase of education and knowledge is possible.
- One may attain beautiful clothes, attain wealth and worldly comforts.
- Wealth may be attained from friends and Brahmins and all work may be financially profitable.
- One may attain the bliss of children, friends and the affection of relatives.
- Gain of jewels like pearls, etc., learning, increase in happiness and performance of pious deeds, success in the educational sphere, acquisition of name and fame, meeting with new kings (high dignitaries), gain of wealth, and happiness from wife children and parents.
- There will be loss of wealth and cattle, antagonism with kinsmen, diseases like stomach pains, piety in discharging duties as a government officials.
- Distress to wife, death of members of the family, affliction with diseases like rheumatism and stomach pains, etc.

Mercury-Ketu

Effect of the Antar Dasha of Ketu in the Maha Dasha of Mercury

- The mind may be misled, there may be a lack of enthusiasm and many problems may occur.
- Industry and valour may suffer, physical pain and loss of wealth is possible.

- Friends may cause pain, the mind may be heated up, and there may be a loss of happiness, fear of enemies and obstacles at work.
- Effects like physical fitness, little gain of wealth affectionate relations with kinsmen, increase in cattle wealth, income from industries, success in educational sphere, acquisition of name and fame, honours audience with the king, and joining a banquet with him, comforts of clothes etc., will be experienced.
- Fall from a conveyance, distress to son, danger from the king (government), indulgence in sinful deeds, danger from scorpions, etc., quarrels with the menials, sorrow, diseases and association with menials, etc.
- There will be physical distress.

Mercury-Venus

Effect of the Antar Dasha of Venus in the Maha Dasha of Mercury

- There is faith in god and elders, hospitality of scholars and quests.
- One may be inclined towards charity and religion.
- Status and work may yield financial gains due to education.
- One may be endowed with many types of clothes, ornaments, children and increase in fame.
- According to a scholar, there may be pain due to hard work and headaches.
- Effects like inclination to perform religious rites, fulfilment of all ambitions through the help of the king (government) and friends, gains of agricultural lands, and happiness, etc.
- There will be acquisition of a kingdom (attainment of a high position in government), gain of wealth and property, construction of a reservoir, readiness to give charities and to perform religious rites, extraordinary gain of wealth and gains in business.
- Heart diseases, defamation, fevers, dysentery, separation from kinsmen, physical distress and agony.

Mercury-Sun

Effect of the Antar Dasha of Sun in the Maha Dasha of Mercury

- Success in government work and state honors may be attained.
- One may be endowed with horses, elephants, vehicles, ornaments, jewels and clothes.
- Fame, wealth, prosperity and all types of happiness may be attained.
- Birth of a son and interest in religious deeds is possible.
- Ailments, eye problems, transfer or migration may occur.
- Effects like dawn of fortune by the beneficence of the king (high government officials), happiness from friends, etc.
- There will be acquisition of land.
- Comforts of good food, and clothes if such a Sun receives a drishti from Lagan's lord.
- Fear or danger from thieves, fire and weapons, bilious troubles, headache, mental agony, and separation from friends.

Mercury-Moon

Effect of the Antar Dasha of Moon in the Maha Dasha of Mercury

- There is a possibility of physical pain, skin ailments and acidity.
- All work may suffer, many problems may arise and enemies may cause pain.
- Vehicles and four legged animals may cause harm, hardships may be experienced during journeys, children may cause pain or dead child may be born.
- Very beneficial effects will come to pass
- Marriage, birth of a son, and gain of clothes and ornaments.
- Construction of a new house, availability of sweetish preparations, enjoyment of music, study of Shastras journey to the South, gains of clothes from beyond the seas, gain of gems like pearls, etc.
- There will be physical distress.

- At the commencement of the Antar Dasha there will be visits to sacred shrines, patience, enthusiasm, and gains of wealth from foreign countries.
- Danger from the king, fire and thieves, defamation or disgrace and loss of wealth on account of wife, destruction of agricultural lands and cattle, etc.
- There will be physical distress.

Mercury-Mars

Effect of the Antar Dasha of Mars in the Maha Dasha of Mercury

- Pain caused by wife, son and friends.
- There may be obstacles in official work and expenditure maybe excessive.
- There may be mental anguish, fear of injury on wound due to weapons and addiction for bad habits.
- There may be fear of gastric problems, eye ailments, blood infection and venereal diseases.
- Effects like well being and enjoyments in the family by the beneficence of the king (government), increase in property, recovery of a lost kingdom, etc., (reinstatement in a high position in government), birth of a son, satisfaction, acquisition of cattle, conveyances, and agricultural lands, happiness from wife, etc.
- Physical distress, mental agony, obstacles in industrial ventures, loss of wealth, gout, distress from wounds, and danger from weapons and fever, etc.
- There will be gain of wealth, physical felicity, birth of a son, good reputation affectionate relations, etc., with kinsmen, etc.
- Distress, danger from kinsmen, wrath of the king, and fire, antagonism with the son, loss of position, at the commencement of the Antar Dasha.
- Enjoyments and gains of wealth in the middle portion of the Antar Dasha.
- Danger from the king (government) and loss of position at the end of the Antar Dasha.

Mercury-Rahu

Effect of the Antar Dasha of Rahu in the Maha Dasha of Mercury

- One may be mentally upset and there may be a sudden loss of wealth.
- There may be conflicts with dear ones, sudden trouble may be caused and an inclination towards untruthful behaviour may be there.
- There may be cause for occasional defame.
- There may be fear of fire poison, water and pain in the abdomen, eyes and head.
- Effects like reverence from the king (government), good reputation, gain of wealth, visits to sacred shrines, performance of religious sacrifices and oblations, recognition, gain of clothes, etc.
- There will be some evil effects at the commencement of the Antar Dasha, but all will be well later.
- There will be an opportunity to have conversation or a meeting with the king (high dignitaries).
- There will be a visit to a new king (dignitary).
- Pressure of hard work as a government functionary, loss of position, fears, imprisonment, diseases, agony to self and kinsmen, heart disease, loss of reputation and wealth, will be the results.

Mercury-Jupiter

Effect of the Antar Dasha of Jupiter in the Maha Dasha of Mercury

- One may be inclined towards pious deeds, spiritual knowledge may increase.
- There may be gain in status, honors may be received from the state and pious habits like modesty and purity may be enhanced.
- Children and wealth may increase. Wife and son may cause bliss.

- Elders and friends may be troubled. There may be conflicts with parents.
- Effects like physical felicity, gain of wealth, beneficence of the king, celebration of auspicious functions like marriage etc., at home, availability of sweetish preparations, increase in cattle wealth, attending discourses on Puranas (religious scriptures,) etc. devotion to deities and the preceptor, interest in religion, charities, etc., worship of Lord Shiva, etc.
- Discord with king and kinsmen, danger from thieves, etc. death of parents, disgrace punishment from government, loss of wealth, danger from snakes and poison, fever, losses in agricultural production, loss of lands etc.
- There will be happiness from kinsmen and from one's son, enthusiasm, increase in wealth and name and fame, giving grains, etc., in charity
- Agony, anxiety, danger from diseases, antagonism with wife and kinsmen, wrath of the king (government), quarrels, loss of wealth, danger from Brahmins (wrath of Brahmins).
- There will be physical distress.

Mercury-Saturn

Effect of the Antar Dasha of Saturn in the Maha Dasha of Mercury

- There may be an increase in valour and arts and crafts may be profitable.
- Love of friends, wealth, sympathy, religion and pious deeds may be enhanced.
- Laziness may increase and there may be an inclination towards other women and secretive and sinful deeds.
- Happiness may be derived from simple people. There may be agricultural losses and pain due to gastric ailments.
- Effects like well-being in the family, acquisition of a kingdom (attainment of a high position in government), enthusiasm, increase in cattle wealth, gain of a position, visits to sacred shrines, etc.

- Danger from enemies, distress to wife and children, loss of thinking power, loss of kinsmen, loss in ventures, mental agony, journeys to foreign lands, and bad dreams.

DASHA INTERPRETATIONS

KETU MAHA DASHA

General Interpretations

General effects which are felt during the Maha Dasha of the Ketu are as follows:

- During the Maha Dasha of Ketu, there is a lack of happiness.
- Physical hardships may increase and ailments are possible.
- There may be an interest in sinful deeds arising out of conflicts, lack of prudence and mental restlessness.
- There may be hardships caused by those in positions of authority, and fear of theft, poison, water, fire, weapons and friends.
- Life is painful and unhappy and there may be lack of bliss from spouse and children.
- There may be obstacles in the acquisition of education and wealth, accident or fall from a vehicle, migration abroad and losses in agriculture are foreseen.

Specific Interpretations:

Interpretations based on the condition of the planet and other influences in the birth chart and divisional charts are as follows:

- During the Maha Dasha of Ketu, happiness will prevail and a lot of wealth will be attained.
- During the Maha Dasha of Ketu, there may be failure, loss of wealth, children and spouse, harm and trouble caused by the state.
- There may be loss of happiness, fear of vehicles, fire and public criticism.

- Children and the spouse may be fearful, there may be conflicts with family members and mother, and subsequent unhappiness.
- Food, land and house may be attained.

During the Maha Dasha of Ketu happiness and gain of wealth is moderate

EFFECTS OF SUB PERIODS *(ANTARDASHA)*

Ketu-Ketu

Effect of the Antar Dasha of Ketu in the Maha Dasha of Ketu

- Prudence and intelligence may be disturbed and public criticism is possible.
- There may be conflicts with wicked women, harm to son and wife or far of death.
- Wealth and happiness are destroyed and there may be pain due to fire and enemies.
- Happiness from wife and children, recognition from the king (government), but mental agony, gain of land, village.
- Heart disease, defamation, destruction of wealth and cattle, distress to wife and children, instability of mind, etc.
- There will be danger from disease, great distress and separation from kinsmen.

Ketu-Venus

Effect of the Antar Dasha of Venus in the Maha Dasha of Ketu

- Moderate amount of wealth may be attained.
- Wife and children may be ailing, there may be conflicts with them, bliss of wife may be disturbed and there is a possibility of separation.
- Friends and dear ones may be harmed and there may be disagreements with them. There may be fear of demotion.
- Ailments caused by heat and fever may cause pain.

- Beneficence from the king, good fortune, gain of clothes etc., recovery of lost kingdom (reinstatement in a high position in government), comforts of conveyances, etc., visits to sacred shrines, and gain of lands and villages by the beneficence of the king (government).
- There will be dawn of fortune.
- Sound health, well being in the family, and gains of good food and conveyances, etc.
- There will be quarrels without any cause, loss of wealth, and distress of cattle.
- There will be quarrels with kinsmen, headaches, eye troubles, heart disease defamation, loss of wealth and distress to cattle and wife.
- Physical distress and mental agony will be caused.

Ketu-Sun

Effect of the Antar Dasha of Sun in the Maha Dasha of Ketu

- There may be pain due to state displeasure because of enmity with some officials.
- There may be obstacles in work and business, migration and happiness may be disturbed.
- Father or some elderly person may suffer harm, there maybe opposition with dear ones and sudden problems may arise.
- Physical pain and ailments caused by cough and fever may strike.
- The effects like gains of wealth, beneficence of the king, performance of pious deeds, and fulfilment of all ambitions.
- Danger from the king (government), separation from parents, journeys to foreign lands, distress from thieves, snakes, and poison, punishment by government, antagonism with the friends, sorrows, danger from fever, etc.
- There will be physical fitness, gain of wealth or the birth of a son, success in performance of pious deeds, headship of a small village, etc.
- Obstacles in availability of food, fears, and loss of wealth and cattle.

- There will be distress at the commencement of the Antar Dasha with some mitigation at its end.

Ketu-Moon

Effect of the Antar Dasha of Moon in the Maha Dasha of Ketu

- In spite of great efforts the gains may be limited.
- Happiness and unhappiness may be attained, wealth may be acquired and both auspicious and inauspicious events may occur.
- Wife, children and servants may be overcome by laziness and lethargy, one's son may be harmed and the mind may be disturbed.
- Effects like recognition from the king (government), enthusiasm, well being, enjoyments acquisition of a house, land, etc.
- Abnormal gains of food, clothes, conveyances, cattle, etc., success in business construction of reservoirs, etc., and happiness to wife and children.
- The beneficial results will be realized fully if Moon is waxing.
- Unhappiness and mental agony, obstacles in ventures, separation from parents, losses in the business, destruction of cattle, etc.
- There will be the acquisition of a cow of cows, land, agricultural lands, meeting kinsmen and the achievement of success through them, increase in cows milk and curd.
- Cordial relations with the king (government) in he middle portion of the Antar Dasha
- Danger from the king (government) foreign journey or journeys to distant places in the end of Antar Dasha.
- Loss of wealth, anxiety, enmity with kinsmen and distress to brother.

Ketu-Mars

Effect of the Antar Dasha of Mars in the Maha Dasha of Ketu

- One may attain defame in work involving courage and there is a possibility of quarrels with neighbours.
- Work and business may suffer losses and the company of wicked persons may cause pain.
- There may be enmity towards wife, son, younger brother and family members.
- There may be physical pain due to ailments, poison and burning sensation.
- The king may cause pain and friends may be destroyed.
- Effects like acquisition of land, village, etc., increase in wealth and cattle, lying out of a new garden, gain of wealth by the beneficence of the king.
- There will be gain of land and enjoyment.
- There will be recognition from the king, great popularity and reputation and happiness from children and friends.
- There will be fear of death or disaster during a foreign journey, diabetes, unnecessary troubles and danger from thieves and the king and quarrels.
- High fever, danger from poison, distress to wife, mental agony.
- There will be enjoyment and gain of property.

Ketu-Rahu

Effect of the Antar Dasha of Rahu in the Maha Dasha of Ketu

- There is a possibility of physical ailments and accidents.
- Mental agony and disturbance of happiness may occur.
- Fear of king and thieves prevail, enmity with wicked people and obstacle in all work may occur.
- Increase of wealth and gain of wealth, grains, cattle, lands and village from a Yavan king (high dignitary of a foreign country.)
- There will be some trouble at the commencement of the Dasha but all will be well later.

- Frequent urination, weakness in the body, cold fever, danger from thieves, intermittent fever, opprobrium quarrels, diabetes, pain in stomach.

Ketu-Jupiter

Effect of the Antar Dasha of Jupiter in the Maha Dasha of Ketu

- Faith in God and elders prevail.
- The king will be favourable; there will be contacts with recognized people and financial condition remain good.
- Sympathy, philanthropy and a cool mentality cause happiness.
- Good health prevails, fame, land and bliss of son are attained
- Increase in wealth and grains, beneficence of the king, enthusiasm, gain of conveyances, etc., celebration like birth of a son at home, performance of pious deeds, Yagyas, conquest of the enemy and enjoyments.
- Danger from thieves, snakes, and wounds, destruction of wealth, separation from wife and children, physical distress, etc.
- Some good effects may be felt at the commencement of the Antar Dasha, there will be only adverse results later.
- There will be gains of many varieties of garments, ornaments by the beneficence of the king, foreign journeys, taking care of kinsmen, availability of decent food.

Ketu-Saturn

- Lack of ethical behaviour and mental restlessness prevails.
- The mind is agonized and fearful, there are conflicts with friends and one may have to leave one's native place.
- Loss of wealth and position and anxiety about money is possible.
- Effects like distress to oneself and one's kinsmen, agony, increase in cattle wealth.

- Loss of wealth as a result of imposition of fines by government, resignation from the existing post, journeys to foreign lands, and danger of thieves during travelling.
- There will be loss of wealth and lethargy.
- Success in all ventures, happiness from the employer, comforts during journeys, increase in happiness and property in ones own village, audience with the king (visits to high dignitaries).
- There will be physical distress, agony, and obstacles in ventures, lethargy, defamation, and death of parents.

Ketu-Mercury

Effect of the Antar Dasha of Mercury in the Maha Dasha of Ketu

- Prudence and intelligence prevails and education brings happiness
- Job and business brings moderate gains and the financial condition improves.
- There may be contacts and assistance from friends.
- At the end of the dasha there may be obstacles in work, wasteful expenditure and mental agony.
- Effects like acquisition of a kingdom (attainment of a high position in government), enjoyment, charities, gain of wealth and land, birth of a son, celebration of religious functions and functions like marriage suddenly, well-being in the family, gain of clothes, ornaments.
- There will be association with men of learning, dawn of fortune, and listening to religious discourses.
- Antagonism with government officials, residing in other people's houses, destruction of wealth, clothes conveyances, and cattle.
- There will be some beneficial effects at the commencement of the Dasha, still better results in the middle but inauspicious at the end.
- There will be good health, happiness from one's son, opulence and glory, availability of good food and clothes, and abnormal profits in business.

- Distress, unhappiness and troubles to wife and children, and danger from the king (government) may be expected at the commencement of the Antar Dasha.
- There will, however, be visits to sacred places in the middle of the Dasha

DASHA INTERPRETATIONS

VENUS MAHA DASHA

General Interpretations

General effects which are felt during the Maha Dasha of the Venus are as follows:

- During this period one may be endowed with jewels, ornaments and clothes.
- One may be blessed with spouse, children, wealth, prosperity, clothes and state honors.
- Interest in education, singing and dance may increase.
- One may be good natured and charitable.
- Skill in trading, profits in business and new ventures may commence.
- During the Dasha of Venus, one may acquire vehicles, have children and inherit the accumulated wealth of ancestors.
- During the Maha Dasha of a weak Venus, there may be domestic quarrels, weakness due to ailments related to gastric and cough problem
- There maybe mental restlessness, friendship and occasional opposition from lowly people.

Specific Interpretations:

Interpretations based on the conditions of the planet and other influences in the birth chart and divisional charts are as follows—

- Those in high position maybe favourable and may grant honors.

- One may be endowed with royal comforts, vehicles and animals.
- There will be plenty of servants.
- During this period there may be a loss of wealth, defame and constant unhappiness.
- There may be conflicts with women, migration and suspension due to lack of work.
- There may be many problems and fear due to thieves, those in high position, and fire.
- Agriculture, land and animals may be destroyed.
- In the beginning one may have to work hard to progress and wealth may be spent on pious deeds.
- At the end, wealth, honour and success in industry will be attained.
- One may be endowed with a good voice, good food, and happiness.
- One may be benevolent and those in high places may be favourable.
- One may be interested in poetry, arts and humour.
- Friendships with scholars, and an inclination to write a book may prevail.
- There may be progress in business, gain of wealth, enthusiasm and happiness.

One may be eager to travel abroad.

EFFECTS OF SUB PERIODS *(ANTARDASHA)*

Venus-Venus

Effect of the Antar Dasha of Venus in the Maha Dasha of Venus

- Fame and gain maybe attained at work and business.
- There will be interest in arts, crafts and music, friendship with women and the bliss of their company.
- Wealth may be attained, worldly comforts may be acquired and fame may be enhanced.

- Gain of wealth, cattle, etc., through Brahmins, celebration in connection with the birth of a son, well being, recognition from the king (government), acquisition of a kingdom (attainment of a high position in government.)
- Construction of a new house, availability of sweet preparations, happiness of wife and children, companionship with the friend, giving grains, etc. in charity, beneficence of the king (government), gain of clothes, conveyances and ornaments, success in business, increase in the number of cattle, gain of garments by performing journeys in the western direction, etc.
- There will be acquisition of a kingdom (high position in government), enthusiasm, beneficence of the king (government).
- Well being in the family, increase in the number of wives, children, and wealth, etc.
- Danger from thieves etc., antagonistic relations with government officials, destruction of friends and kinsmen, distress of wife and children

Venus-Sun

Effect of the Antar Dasha of Sun in the Maha Dasha of Venus

- Fear from the king & obstacles in government work are possible.
- There may be physical hardships and ailments related to the head, eyes, chest and stomach.
- There may be conflicts with friends and loss of wealth, agricultural yields and animals.
- Enemies may increase and poverty may prevail.
- Fear of pain because of infertile wife or wicked person or due to imprisonment is possible.
- There will be a period of agony, wrath of the king (government), quarrels with the coparceners, etc.
- Effects like acquisition of a kingdom (attainment of a high position in government), and wealth, happiness from wife and children, happiness from employer, meeting with friends, happiness from parents, marriage, name and fame, betterment of fortune, birth of a son, etc.

- Distress, agony, distress to members of the family, harsh language, distress to father, loss of kinsmen, wrath of the king (government), danger at home, many diseases, destruction of agricultural production.
- The period will not be very favourable for health in general

Venus-Moon

Effect of the Antar Dasha of Moon in the Maha Dasha of Venus

- Loss of health, pain in the head and nails, acidity, venereal diseases etc. may cause pain.
- There may be quarrels.
- There may be victory in conflicts, sufficient gain in business and gain of wealth from women.
- Interest in the worships of gods and pious deeds like fire worship and oblation may be performed.
- Enemies may cause pain, happiness may be lacking and tigers and other animals may give cause fear.
- Gain of wealth, conveyances, and clothes by the beneficence of the king, happiness in the family, great opulence and glory, devotion to deities and Brahmins.
- In the above circumstances, there will also be association with musicians and men of learning, and receiving of decoration, gain of cows, buffaloes and other cattle, abnormal profits in business, dining with brothers, etc.
- Loss of wealth, fears, physical distress, agony, wrath of the king (government), journeys to foreign lands or pilgrimage, distress to wife and children and separation from kinsmen.
- There will be sovereignty over a province or village by the beneficence of the king (government), clothes, etc., construction of a reservoir, increase in wealth, etc.
- There will be physical fitness at the commencement of the Antar Dasha and Physical problems towards the end of the dasha.

Venus-Mars

Effect of the Antar Dasha of Mars in the Maha Dasha of Venus

- Enthusiasm increases and interest in courageous deeds may arise.
- Land may be attained, wealth may be acquired and desires may be fulfilled.
- The wife may suffer harm.
- Blood infection may cause physical pain, acidity etc. may cause agony.
- Effects like acquisition of kingdom (attainment of a high position in government), property, clothes, ornaments, land, and desired objects.
- There will be fever from cold, disease (like fever) to parents, loss of position, quarrels, antagonism with the king (government) and government officials, extravagant expenditure, etc.
- Physical distress, losses in profession, loss of village, land, etc.

Venus-Rahu

Effect of the Antar Dasha of Rahu in the Maha Dasha of Venus

- Sudden fear, loss of wealth and insult are possible.
- There may be enmity with friends; loss due to friends & distress may be caused by wicked people.
- Fear of fire and ailments of the urinary organs is possible.
- Some black product may be acquired and it will prove to be very beneficial.
- Effects like great enjoyment, gain of wealth, visits of friends, successful journeys, gain of cattle and land.
- Enjoyments, destruction of enemy, enthusiasm, and beneficence of the king.
- Good effects will be experienced up to 5 months from the commencement of the Antar Dasha, but at the end of the Dasha there will be danger from fevers and indigestion.

- In the above circumstances except for obstacles in ventures and journeys, and worries, there will be all enjoyment like those of a king. Journeys to foreign lands will bring success and the person will return safely to his homeland. There will also be blessings from Brahmins and auspicious results consequent to visits to holy places.
- There will be inauspicious effects on oneself and one's parents and antagonism with people.
- Physical distress.

Venus-Jupiter

Effect of the Antar Dasha of Jupiter in the Maha Dasha of Venus

- A lot of work will be accomplished and authority may be acquired.
- Gain of education, inclination to perform yagyas and enhancement of fame and name is possible.
- Wealth, prosperity, clothes & ornaments are gained.
- Bliss of wife and children prevails but they may suffer from painful disease.
- Effects like recovery of the lost kingdom (reinstatement in a high position in government), acquisition of desired grains, clothes, and property, etc.
- Reverence from one's friend and the king (government), and gain of wealth, recognition from the king, good reputation, gain of conveyances.
- Association with an employer and with men of learning, industriousness in the study of Shastras, birth of a son, satisfaction, visits of close friends, happiness to parents and son, etc.
- There will be danger from the king (government), and from thieves, distress to oneself and to kinsmen, quarrels, mental agony, loss of position, going away to foreign lands, and danger of many kinds of diseases.
- There will be physical distress.

Venus-Saturn

Effect of the Antar Dasha of Saturn in the Maha Dasha of Venus

- One may become the head of a town or village and attain a high position.
- Land, wealth and house will be attained. Friends will progress.
- Inclination in immoral deeds may prevail. One may fall in love with an elder woman.
- Laziness and excessive expenditure is possible.
- Enemies are destroyed and children suffer pain.
- Effects like great enjoyments, visits of friends and kinsmen, recognition from the king (government), birth of a daughter, visit to holy places and sacred shrines conferment of authority of the king (government).
- There will be lethargy and more expenditure than income, if Saturn is in his Debilitation Rashi.
- Many kinds of distresses and troubles at the commencement of the Antar Dasha, like stress to parents, wife and children, going away to foreign lands, losses in profession, destruction of cattle, etc.
- There will be physical distress

Venus-Mercury

Effect of the Antar Dasha of Mercury in the Maha Dasha of Venus

- There may be friendship with the king and honour may be received from him.
- Gain of wealth is possible from business of trees, fruits and animals.
- Valour is enhanced and interest in performing bold deeds exist.
- Bliss of wife, children, friends, prosperity and wealth prevails.
- The mind is firm and the body is healthy.
- Effects like dawn of fortune, birth of a son, gain of wealth through judgement of court, listening to stories from the Puranas, association with persons competent in poetry, etc.,

visit of close friends, happiness from employer, availability of sweetish preparation, etc.

- There will be agony, loss of cattle, residence in other peoples house, and losses in business.
- There will be some good effects at the commencement, moderate in the middle portion and distress from fever etc. at the end of the Antar Dasha.
- There will be physical distress

Venus-Ketu

Effect of the Antar Dasha of Ketu in the Maha Dasha of Venus

- There may be defaming in government work and loss of wealth.
- The mind may be restless and unstable and physical hardships are foreseen.
- There may be conflicts with friends and brothers or ones brother may come to harm.
- Enemies may cause pain and there may be a shortage of money.
- Auspicious effects like availability of sweetish preparation, abnormal gains in profession and increase in cattle wealth.
- There will be definite victory in war at the end of the Antar Dasha.
- Moderate results will be experienced in the middle portion of the Antar Dasha, and sometimes there will also be the feeling of distress.
- There will be danger from snakes, thieves and wounds, loss of power of thinking headache, agony, quarrels without any cause or reason, diabetes, excessive expenditure, antagonism with wife and children, going away to foreign land, loss in venture.
- There will be physical distress.

CHAPTER 7

ASTROLOGICAL HINTS MICROSCOPY OF ASTROLOGY

YOUR JAMAN (BIRTH) NAKSHATRA

Your birth Nakshatra (Janma Nakshatra) determines your thinking patter, nature as well as basic destiny. It also determines the instincts as well as the subconscious aspects of the personality.

Ashwini
Bharani
Krittika
Rohini
Mrigasirisa
Ardra
Punarvasu
Pushya
Ashlesha
Magha
Purva Phaguni
Uttara Phaguni
Hasta
Chitra
Swati
Vishakha
Anuradha
Jyeshta
Moola
Purva Ashadha
Uttara Ashadha

Abhijit
Sravana
Dhanishta
Satha Bishta
Poorva Bhadrapada
Uttara Bhadrapada
Revati

ASHWINI NAKSHATRA

Male Natives

1. Physical features: Male born in Ashwini Nakshatra will have a beautiful countenance. His eyes will be bright and large. Forehead broad and nose a little bigger.

2. Character and general events: The native may appear to be very calm and quite, but capable of getting his work done un-noticed and is more predominant in the case of native born during the period from April 14th to April 28th, when the sun will be transiting his exaltation place in Ashwini and from October 14th to October 28th, when the sun will be transiting his debilitation place in Swaati. There is a saying that even Yama, the God of Death, cannot change his adamant attitude. Those born in the Ashwini of other months will have stubbornness in a lesser degree.

He will remain faithful to those who love him and will not hesitate to sacrifice anything for such persons. Ashwini born is the best friend in need provided others understand him? He keeps his patience even at the time of greatest perils. But it will be a hurricane task to console the native when he goes berserk. He is the best advisor to the persons in agony. But he deeply resents and fears criticism; see suggestions from others, as a frightening attempt at manipulation.

He takes his own time to do any work. Even so, his actions may be slow but well thought. He will not jump upon any matter without examining prose and corns of each item of work. He cannot be easily influenced. Once he carries out an action or work, whether it is good or bad, right or wrong, he will stick to what he has done, come what may. He is a firm believer of God. But there is no room for religious or other sentiments. He is orthodox but in new style i.e., he believes in modernization of orthodox method and belief.

Even though he is quite intelligent, at times he makes mountain of even small matters. This leads him in a state of lack of mental peace and will always be in desperate mood. He is always interested in keeping the entire surroundings neat and clean.

3. Education and sources of earnings / profession: He is jack of all arts. He is generally fond of music and interested in literary pursuits. Period up to his 30th years of age will be full of struggle. He has to face obstacles even for small matters. From the 30th year of age, there will be steady and continuous progress, which will continue up to 55 years of age.

One of the predominant features noticed is that he is very stingy, but his expenditure will be more than his income due mainly to his pomp and show. He is inclined to meet his desires and needs at any cost.

4. Family life: He loves his family in entire sincerity. However, he is subjected to hatred by his own family members due to his adamant behaviour. Affection that was expected and the care that was required cannot be derived from the father of the native. In other words, their father will neglect the natives as also his co-borns. Whatever help he may derive is only from the side of his maternal uncle. Maximum possible help will come from those who are outside the family circle.

Normally marriage takes place between 26 to 30 years of age. There will be more sons than daughters.

Female Natives

Females born in this Nakshatra will have more or less the same general results as mentioned in the case of male natives. In addition, she will have the following results:

1. Physical features: Eyes will be bright and small resembling to that of a fish. She has a magnetic look.
2. Character and general events: She has the technique of bringing anybody near to her with her sweet speech. She maintains utmost patience. She indulges in too much sexual operation. She is pure hearted. Even while living in the modern society she maintains the age-old tradition of respecting elders.
3. Education, sources of earning / profession: If employed she may either be not interested in the work after 50 years of age and may quit the job or seek voluntary retirement. It is not a negative point. She may do so, as her financial or other conditions would have improved by her 50th years of age, and she no longer requires any work for her livelihood. She will thereafter devote herself to the welfare of the family and to some extent do social work, provided other planetary positions are not adverse. Administrative type of job (including possibility of Indian Administrative Service for an Indian) is earmarked for her.
4. Family life: Normally marriage takes place between the period of 23 years to 26 years of age. It has been noticed that in case marriage takes place at a young age i.e., before the age of 23 years, such marriage ends either at divorce, separation from the husband for long time or even death of the husband.

There will be more female children than male children. She is quick to respond to the needs and desires of her children to pursue the interest of the children. Whenever time permits, these females do cleaning of the house and household articles and they force others to do the same.

5. Health: Her health will generally be good. Main cause of her ailments is unnecessary mental worry and anxiety. In some cases, when such worry or anxiety goes beyond control, it has been noticed that brain disorder of mild type takes place at a later stage. She should always be careful while cooking or while handling fire. In the modern society, motor vehicle accidents have also been noticed.

BHARANI NAKSHATRA

Male Natives

1. Physical features: He is of medium size, with less hair, large forehead, and bright eyes, with beautiful teeth. His complexion will be ruddy and fairly long neck and face. It has been found that if birth takes place during mid-day, the native is very tall. His head will be broad at the temples and narrow at the chin. Bushy eyebrows.

2. Character and general events: Bharani born is not generally liked by all, in spite of the fact that he is pure hearted and does not like to harm anybody. When he wants to express his opinion in any matter he is just not bothered about the sentiments of others. He will not like to get anything for himself by buttering. Come what may, he is not ready to work against his consciousness whether he is according to others, right or wrong. Due to this attitude he has to face a lot of resistance and failures. He won't hesitate to spoil the relationship even with near and dear ones on small matters. But when he is convinced of his fault, when the opponent comes forward with folded hands, he will completely forget their enmity and start reciprocating sincerely.

Tactful behaviour is alien to him. He is far away from the state of obedience. Arrogance quite often leads him to miseries. Subordination is equal to death for him. When he was to bow to others, he becomes pensive. Advice and encouragement have no room in his mind.

He will generally be having a good all-round knowledge. He has the capacity to go deep into any matter. Even though Bharani born will shine well in public life, he tends to face criticism and loss of wealth.

He likes to command others and will always be eager to establish supremacy. He cannot march forward without hurdles and will have to face stiff competition, and in the run he quite often faces failures. For others, he may appear to be arrogant, but the truth is that he is pure hearted. His life is full of ups and downs.

It is advisable that Bharani born should not involve in unnecessary arguments or competition. He will fight for certain principles, which will ultimately lead him into trouble. He is fond of spreading rumours and wasting time by humours. As already mentioned above his life is full of ups and downs, there will not be any good or bad periods for long time. In short, ha has to face a life of mixture of good and bad always. He is quite capable of looking after others but he needs some one to look after him. Ultimately his beneficiary and friends turn against him. He cannot establish permanent relationship with anyone.

3. Education, sources of earnings / profession: There is never a permanent good or bad time. After his 33 years of age there will be a positive change in his surroundings, in his life, and in his livelihood. He is fit for any type of work, particularly in administrative job, business, sports, music, art advertisement, automobile or restaurants. He can also be a good surgeon or a judge. He can be successful in the business of tobacco items or cultivation of tobacco. He will attain success in all undertakings provided he establishes or starts any activity by proceeding to the Eastern direction first and also if possible the place of activity or business may also be in the eastern side or eastern direction from his house.

4. Family life: Marriage comes around 27 years of age. They are fortunate in conjugal bliss. His companion will be expert in household administration and well behaved. He will cause the death of his father if birth is in the 1st or 2nd quarter of Bharani Nakshatra. His wife must save money for a rainy day, as he makes some impulsive purchases, whether there is money

left for other purposes or not. He loves his family. He dislikes being away from his family members even for a day.

5. Health: While he does not take care of his health, there won't be any serious health problems. Main possible diseases are dental problem, diabetes and severe body pain, affections of brain, high fever, apoplexy, ringworms and malaria. Normally he is a very poor eater. He believes in the principle of 'eating to live and living to eat'. He is afraid of water and as is the thought, he should be careful while travelling through water, taking bath in rivers, oceans and ponds. Injury in the forehead and just around the eyes. Since he is a chain smoker he has to be careful about his lung.

Female Natives

1. Physical features: She will have a very beautiful figure. White teeth but not in proper arrangement.

2. Character and general events: She will possess a clean, admirable and modest character. She respects her parents and elderly persons, but she does not relish suggestions from others and acts according to her own sweet will. She is bold and impulsive and over optimistic.

3. Education, sources of earning/ profession: She earns her own livelihood. She will be successful as a receptionist, guide or sales woman. She will not wait for opportunities to come but will go out and create opportunity to fulfil her desires. She may earn through sports activities.

4. Family Life: Marriage comes around her 23rd years of age. She will have an upper hand in all matters and she will behave like a commander. While she will enjoy full confidence, love and satisfaction from her husband, her in-laws often trouble her. She always speaks high of her own family. She will obey only such a man whom she can admire. In case she marries a simple man, who is lowly placed in life, she will over power her husband in all walks of life. As Bharani born females are a little aggressive, married partner should have patience and deal with them tactfully for avoiding daily friction in life.

5. Health: Her health will be good. She will have frequent menstrual problems, uterus disorders, and anaemia and in some cases tuberculosis has also been noticed.

ROHINI NAKSHATRA

Male Natives

1. Physical Features: He is normally of slim physique. However, based on other planetary positions and aspects, short structured and fatty persons have also been seen. His eyes are very attractive with a special magnetic touch. Appearance is very beautiful and attractive, big shoulder and well developed muscles.

2. Character and general events: He is short tempered. Once he gets angry, it will not subside so easily, and nobody can change his decision. He becomes extremely obstinate if some one attempts to over-ride his opinions or thwart his plans. He remains oblivious to any advice or ideas counter to his own.

He has special knack to find faults of others. Whereas, he cannot work with a fixed aim. He is ruled by his heart rather than his brain. While he is ready to sacrifice everything for his loved ones, he will not hesitate to cause extreme trouble to the hated. He feels impressed upon his own work.

Acceptance of the truth and discard of the false is his plus point. His life is full of ups and downs, as he does not try to pre-plan his objectives. He can attain great success in his life provided a little restraint is kept in the freedom of his mind. There is no tomorrow for him. He spends everything for today's comfort.

3. Education, sources of earning / profession: As far as possible he tries to be more sincere and honest in all the work he undertakes. But he lacks patience and forgiveness. He tries to be jack off all arts and in the process he fails to pass through the path of requisite rhythm and system.

His freedom of mind will quite often lead him to the downfall. It is also seen that some Rohini born persons have risen from the lowest rung of life due to the finest placements of other planets.

He may earn from milk products, sugarcane or as a Chemical Engineer. He is best adapted for mechanical or laborious work.

Periods between the age of 18 years and 36 years will be the most trial some periods. He will have to face a lot of problems economically, socially and on health grounds. It is often noticed that such people enjoy their life's best between the age of 38 years and 50 years and 65 years and 75 years of age. One of the primary factors to be born in mind is that he should never take anybody into confidence. He has to be extra careful in his business partners and employees. There is an inherent drawback in him that he blindly believes others. For a happy existence, it is suggested that he should screen the persons thoroughly before confidence is bestowed on such persons.

4. Family life: While he cannot enjoy full benefit from his father, he will be more attached to his mother and maternal uncle or maternal things. He will not hesitate to throw away any social or religious laws when warranted for. Hence his married life will be marred with disturbances.
5. Health: He is prone to diseases connected with blood, blood cancer, jaundice, urinary disorders, blood sugar, tuberculosis, respiratory problems, paralysis and throat trouble.

Female Natives

1. Physical Features: She is beautiful. Her eyes are very attractive. She is of medium height and fair complexion.
2. Character and general events: She is well behaved and well dressed. She shows a lot of pomp and show but at the same time she has a very weak heart. Like the males, females born in Rohini, are also short tempered and invite troubles. She is practical, secretive and violent when instigated.
3. Education, sources of earnings / profession: She possesses inherent aptitude for any work entrusted to her or done by

her. She earns from oils, milk, hotels, and paddy fields and as a dressmaker. Middle level education is indicated for her.

4. Family life: Her family life will be good. She will have the comfort of her husband and children in full. She must curb the tendency of stubbornness for a hormonal married life. She must avoid doubting her own husband as otherwise marriage may end in divorce.

5. Health: Her health will generally be good. She will have pain in the legs and feet, pain in the breast, sometimes breast cancer, irregular menses and sore throat, pimples and swelling above the neck.

MRIGA SIRISA NAKSHATRA

Male Natives

1. Physical feature: He will have a beautiful and stout body, tall, moderate complexion, thin legs and long arms.

2. Character and general events: There is a peculiar tendency seen in him. He has a doubting nature. He is always suspicious of everything. He is very sincere in his dealings with others and he expects the same reciprocal sincerity nature others find it pleasant to deal with him. But a word of precaution is necessary here that he has to be very careful while dealing with his friends and relatives as also in any partnership business as he may be cheated. Blind trust put on others will quite often lead him into later frustration and repentance.

He has a knack to deal with even those who ditch him. He has a natural initiative, awareness, brilliancy of mind, eagerness and active agility, but as a result of his affectionate regard for others, he is buffeted by both circumstances and people.

He is very simpleton. He prefers a life of simplicity and principled. He always expresses impartial and sincere opinion. He can be impatient to the point of intolerance when confronted with prejudice, judgment or action by others. While he expresses to others opinion, it is never brought into his life. He acts according to his own sweet will.

Outwardly expresses to the public that it is very courageous and will not hesitate to do anything which requires extreme courage, whereas he is an inborn coward.

He will not have peace of mind and get irritated even on small matters. His life up to 32 years of age will be full of trials and errors and would appear to be like a lost boat in the centre of the ocean i.e., the question of where to go, how to go and why to go will permanently rampage his mind without any conclusion. His 32nd age onwards, life will start settling down to the maximum satisfaction provided other planetary positions are good.

3. Education, sources of earning / profession: He will have good education. He is a very good financial adviser. He advises others to curb the spending but he cannot control the expenditure and at last finds himself in the extreme economic conflict. He achieves success in life, including business if engaged after the age of 32 years. Till that time he has to face several ups and downs. He often begins projects rather than finishing the tediously routine tasks of the one in hand. It is mainly due to percipience rather than weakness and above all his ability to understand the possibility of success or no success of a project in hand, discard it immediately and replaces it immediately and replaces it with another, which is more viable. In other words, he cannot undertake any permanent or continuing nature of work.

Period between 33 years and 50 years will be a period of full of strength and activities followed by utmost satisfaction. During this period he can achieve the benefits unexpectedly. But whatever he will be earning during this period will be wasted later on due to his own fault.

4. Family life: No benefit will be derived from the co-borns. Co-born will not only cause troubles and problems to the native, but also maintain extreme enmity so as to harm the native? His sincere love and affection will not have any effect in his relatives. In other words, the native is mistaken

absolutely for no fault of his own. That is why we are bound to believe the existence of God and the relationship of stars over the human beings.

His spouse may not keep good health. Moreover, his married life is not cordial, mainly due to difference of opinion on silly matters, and the adamant nature of the native. In some cases, it is seen that the reason for the disharmony between the couple is mainly due to the better occupation in life by one of them, and the consequent inferiority complex.

5. Health: He has to face ill health during his childhood. Frequent constipation ultimately leading to stomach disorder, cuts and injuries, pains in the shoulders near collarbones.

Female Natives

Female natives born in this Nakshatra will also enjoy more or less the same results as mentioned above in the case of male natives. In addition they will enjoy the following results:

1. Physical features: She is tall, sharp look, leaning body. Her countenance and body very beautiful.
2. Character and general events: She is very intelligent. She takes keen interest in the social work. Mentally always alert, quick-witted, selfish. Since she has a poisonous tongue, she has to be careful when entering to arguments or getting angry as in case she curses others, such curse has the power to harm others. She is educated, fond of fine arts. She will have children and devotes to her husband. Acquires considerable wealth. Enjoys good food. She will be lucky to have ornaments and fine clothing. She is greedy for wealth.
3. Education, sources of earnings / profession: Attains good knowledge in the mechanical or electrical engineering, telephones, electronics etc. It may become surprising that being a female native, how she is more interested in the jobs that are normally done by males.

4. Family life: Even after marriage, she keeps busy in various activities. She keeps her husband under her control. There may be one or two love affairs early in her life, which has not culminated into marriage. However, after marriage she is very much attached to her husband, as if nothing has taken place in the past.

5. Health: Intermittent health problems will take place. She is prone to goitre, pimples, venereal diseases, menstrual troubles and shoulder pains.

ARDRA NAKSHATRA

Male natives:

1. Physical features: It has been noticed that various natives of Ardra have different shape of structure, right from the slim and short structure to fat and lengthy structure.

2. Character and general events: He undertakes any work entrusted to him in a responsible manner. In the public meetings he creates an atmosphere of humour and keeps every body attracted to him. He has intuitive perception. He is good psychologist.

His dealings with his friends and relatives will be of very much cordial type. In some cases it is also noticed that the native is thankless to the persons who have given him help. He does not have a constant type of behaviour.

3. Education, sources of earning/profession: He has the capacity to acquire and keep knowledge of almost all the subjects. However, in spite of these good qualities he cannot attain much fame or reward out of such knowledge. Since he is over sincere in the work and as also to the persons even the slightest problem, which may be confronted, will land him into maximum mental agony. However, even during the time of extreme hardships both financial and mental, he can keep his head cool; behave in a most respectable an attractive manner. Because of this quality he is very much involved in others heart.

He will not stick to only one line of work, whereas he would like to undertake so many works at a time. Even when he comes to know that the line of action or though which he has taken is the correct approach but according to others it is not like that he will not hesitate to subdue and respect others. In case he undertakes research work on any particular line he can shine well. In the business field also he can attain much success.

It has been noticed that most of the selfless social workers are born in this Nakshatra. He has the capacity to undertake any number of jobs at a time and complete perfection in all the fields can also be obtained. In case he undertakes a travel for a specific job, he will oversee other connected work, which can be carried out simultaneously.

Normally, the native earns his livelihood away from his home and family. In other words he is settled in foreign places. Period between 32years and 42 years of age will be the golden period for him. He may be employed in transport, shipping, communication departments or industries. He may also earn as a bookseller or finance broker.

4.   Family life: His marriage will be delayed. In case marriage takes place early he will be compelled to live separately from the family either due to difference of opinion between the couple or due to other circumstances beyond his control. He will have to face several inherent problems of the life. But he will not reflect his problems outwardly.

When the marriage takes place at a late stage his married life will be good. His spouse will exercise full control over him.

5.   Health: He may have some diseases, which may term to be sometimes incurable. For example, paralysis, heart trouble and dental problems. He is also prone to Asthma, eosinophilia, and dry cough, ear trouble.

Female natives

1. Physical features: She has handsome body with charming eyes, prominent nose.
2. Character and general events: She is well behaved and peace minded. She is extravagant. Has good intelligence, helpful to others but clever in finding fault in others. In some female horoscope, possibility of having two mothers or two fathers has been noticed.
3. Education, sources of earnings/profession: She can attain a good amount of distinction in the educational or scientific field. Mostly Ardra born specializes in Electronic items or drugs and pharmaceutical. She also earns out of various consultation works.
4. Family life: Like male folk, she also marries at a late stage. But she cannot enjoy full requisite love and affection either from her husband or husband's family. Her married life will be full of thorns. Even children cannot give her the required happiness. In some cases it has been noticed that either death of the husband of divorce takes place.
5. Health: She is prone to menstrual troubles, asthma, spoiled blood, lack of blood or uterus trouble, ear trouble, mumps, bilious and phlegmatic.

PUNARVASU NAKSHATRA

Male Natives

1. Physical features: Handsome, long thighs and long face. Some identification mark on the face or on the backside of the head.
2. Character and general events: The native has complete faith in God. He is religiously inclined. Initially he will have good behaviour but later on according to the circumstances he changes his behaviour. Therefore, others have to be careful while approaching him. It is very difficult to know his inner thought. He is contended with little but at the same time he is hot tempered. He sticks to ancient tradition and belief.

He will not stand a party to any illegal activities and will try to resist others from doing so. He does not like to cause trouble to others; on the other hand he tries to help the needy. He will lead a simple life.

3. Education, sources of earning/profession: He can shine and get success in almost all the subjects except in partnership business. He can attain much name and fame as a teacher or as an actor. Writer, physician etc. Period up to 32 years of age will not be so good. Hence he should not involve himself in any major business till 32 years of age. He may not be in a position to accumulate wealth but he can attain public honour. The main reason why the native is not in a position to accumulate wealth is lack of business trick and straightforwardness. One peculiar expression can be seen in his face i.e. an innocent and frustrated looking.

4. Family life: He is the most obedient child of his parents. He respects his father and mother as also his teacher. His marriage life may not be good. He may either divorce his wife or another marriage, even while the first wife is alive. In case he does not go for the second marriage the health of the spouse will give a lot of problems and mental agony. However, his spouse will have all the qualities of a good housewife. Frequent friction between other family members will take place. All these simultaneous problems will lead to mental wreckage.

5. Health: While there may not be any serious health problem, even the slightest problem will be a cause of concern for him. He drinks lot of water. He has strong digestion.

Female Natives:

1. Physical features: Her eyes are red, curly hair, sweet speech and high nose.

2. Character and general events: While she will generally have a calm nature, she has argumentative tongue, which will lead her into frequent friction with her relatives and her neighbours. However, she is charitable and shows respect. She will have many servants. On the whole she will be leading a comfortable life.

3. Education, sources of earning/profession: She is fond of music, gets mastery over dances.
4. Family life: Her husband will be most handsome man.
5. Health: She cannot enjoy good health. This is mainly due to her non-care nature about her health. Jaundice, tuberculosis, goitre and pneumonia, stomach upset and ear trouble.

PUSHYA NAKSHATRA

Male Natives

1. Physical Features: It is very difficult to define or describe the body structure or the look of Pushya born native, as there is no specific structure exclusively enjoyed by Pushya born. In other words, varying sizes are noticed. One rare sign, as a mark of identification noticed in these persons, is that there will be a distinguished mark, may be a scar or a black mole on their face.
2. Character and general events: He is very weak at heart. He finds it difficult to reach at conclusion on any matter. He will have good knack of behaviour but that behaviour is only for the sake of selfish interest. This clearly indicates that his outward expression is hypocritical and against his consciousness i.e. the inner expression is negative and the outward expression is positive. Respecting others is unknown to him whereas expectation of respect is within him. He responds quickly to admiration and become quickly deflated by criticism, giving himself to love and affection with sincerity and appreciation, yet he is ever mindful of slights and he hesitate to form strong attachments.

As already explained above, the inherent freedom available in all walks of life will lead to him to the bad company. Hence he has to be very careful with his friends. He is fond of good dresses.

3. Education, sources of earning/profession: He will jump upon any work without judging or thinking whether he is capable

of doing such work or not, and ultimately push him into utter failure in any work he undertakes. While I say that he is not a good anticipator, he is very good in certain work and sweet words are just a natural expression for him. It would be better if he assess his capacity and ability for the specific field where he can shine well and then start doing the job. If that is done, nobody on earth can stop him in achieving the requisite result. One of the plus points for him is that he is not easily vulnerable to defeat and he pushes his way up through several obstacles.

Even if he does not have any basic education, he will show extra-ordinary intelligence and knowledge on any matter of discussion. Another plus point for him is that he will resist tooth and nail any idea or programme or work which is not within the spirit of law. He is of the opinion that all wrong doers must be punished whether they are his friends or relatives or enemies. He will carry out any work entrusted to him with utmost sincerely and certainty. While he wants to complete the work, which he commences or assigned to him in perfect, condition, the outcome in most of the cases i.e. negative because of his too much independent nature. His abilities are many faceted but his success is as probable in the theatre or the arts of in commerce.

In most cases it is seen that Pushy born will have to face the grip of poverty up to the age of 15-16 years of age and thereafter he will enjoy a mixture of good and bad, where plus will be less and minus will be more up to the age of 32 years. From the age of 33 years, there will be remarkable all round improvements i.e. economically, socially and in health.

In most cases it has been seen that Pushya born will stay away from his native place and family for his bread earning. He normally undertakes the work where maximum travelling is involved.

4. Family life: There will be lot of problems in the family circle and he will have to depend on others for even day-to-day requirements. Due to this dependency during childhood he becomes quite independent when he grows up.

Circumstances will be so warranted that he will be forced to stay away most of the time from his wife and children even though he very much wants to be attached with them. He expects his wife to be thoroughly self sufficient, with creditable talents and to be correct and conservative in manner and dress. If the marriage of the native is performed without proper comparison or tallying of the horoscope, he may lose all rational perspective and begin to doubt his wife rather than admitting his own lack of discernment. He is very much attached to his parents.

5. Health: He will not keep good health during his childhood i.e. up to the age of 15years. Gallstones, gastric ulcer, jaundice, cough, eczema and cancer are the possible diseases.

Female Natives:

1. Physical Features: She has a short stature, moderate complexion, well-proportioned face and body. Generally handsome.

2. Character and general events: She will not enjoy peaceful existence. She has a very amicable character and is peace-minded, very submissive to the elders but oppressed by all. She is sincere, affectionate but moody. She is religious and god fearing. Respects her elders. She is conservative. Does systematically and methodical action.

3. Education, sources of earning/profession: She may have income from land and buildings. She may be employed in a job where maximum trust is required e.g. Private Secretaries, Secret departments of a country. She may also have income from Agriculture.

4. Family Life: Even though she is 'Pativrata' (attached to won husband only) she is quite often mistaken by her husband for her moral character. This situation can be avoided if she keeps a little control and restriction over her husband by shedding away her shyness and her outward expression is made clear to her husband and others. Reasons for most of the turmoil in her life is mainly attributable to what she thinks inside and what she expresses outside. She wants to say a lot of things but she

is prevented by her inherent quality of shyness, which often misleads others, and a negative opinion is formed about the native. She will have good duty bound children.

5. Health: She will have respiratory problem. She is prone to tuberculosis, ulcers, breast cancer, and jaundice, eczema, bruises in the breast or gastric ulcer.

ASHLESHA NAKSHATRA

There is a saying that persons born in Ashlesha Nakshatra possess serpent's sight that even the look of these persons on others will have the effect of penetration of certain unknown force. In order to escape from such sight, it is the ancient traditional practice that the neighbours grow bamboos on the border or fences of their houses. Probably the bamboos have magnetic power to catch both sight and sound.

Male Natives

1. Physical Features: Ashlesha born normally possess rude appearance. He may appear to be having stout body and rude features but inside built up is void.

2. Character and general events: He will not be grateful to anybody even to those who have given him life. Outwardly he tends to show that he is very sincere and would like to share the tragedy of others but he is not like that. He is very talkative. One of the added advantages is that he can attract people with hypocritical words and he is fit to man various organizations. Since there is an inherent quality of leadership and eagerness to reach the top he can shine very well in the political field. In spite of all those mentioned above, which may appear to be an adverse indication of the character, he is the most intelligent person who can give suitable leadership to a country.

It is also seen that some Ashlesha born who are cowards, poor-hearted and soft-spoken. They are not arrogant by themselves but they are arrogant to the world, because of the peculiar expression they show to the world.

He does not believe others blindly. Even then it is seen that he mostly associates himself with black marketers, thieves and murderers. He does not keep any distinction between rich and poor, good and bad people. He does not like to have any resistance to his independence from any circle and has a good liking towards the persons who are ready to accept his leadership and obey his orders whether in the negative or in the positive approach. To such persons he is ready to sacrifice anything. He never likes to cheat others nor he likes to engulf others property. But it is seen that others quite often mistake him.

One of the drawbacks with the Ashlesha born is that his brain always supports the persons who are not in need and reject the request of the persons who are in need. Suppose he renders a helping hand to a needy person he will not hesitate to publicize such act.

Whatever may be the plus and minus points in the Ashlesha born, it is generally noticed that he is luckiest, popular but hot-tempered person. If anybody closely watches him it will be seen that he loses his temper where it is not required and where it is required he keeps silent. On the one side when we say that the Ashlesha born is luckiest, he cannot enjoy the fruit of that lucky existence.

Mostly the relations and friends betray the unknown extends him and helping hand.

2. Education, source of income/profession: He may have his education in Arts or Commerce line. In the professional field, the native gets speedy promotions and sudden reversals.
3. A heavy loss of money at the age of 35-36th years of age and unexpected and unearned income when he is 40 years of age.
4. Family life: He will have to shoulder much of the family responsibilities; most probably it may be due to the native being the eldest in the family. His wife cannot understand him. She does not want to share her wealth with other relatives (sister-in-law or cousin brother etc.)
5. Health: He will have flatulence, jaundice, and pains in legs and knees, stomach problem. He will be addicted to drugs.

Female Native

Females born in Ashlesha will also enjoy almost all the results mentioned for the male natives.

1. Physical features: Most of the females born in this Nakshatra are not good looking. However, if Mars is associated in this Nakshatra, she will have beautiful figure.
2. Character and general events: She will be self-restrained and will possess non-caring attitude. The inherent quality of shyness in the females is present in a greater degree in the case of Ashlesha born females. Her moral is of a very high order. She will enjoy good respect and recognition from her relations. She has the capacity to conquer her enemies mainly through vocabulary twisting.
3. Education, sources of earning/profession: She will be very efficient in her official work. She maybe, if educated, employed in an administrative capacity. Illiterate females may be engaged in selling fishes or work in the agricultural field.
4. Family Life: She is very efficient in the household administration. She should be careful while dealing wit in-laws, as there is a possibility of making some plot against her so as to create friction with her husband.
5. Health: Joint pains, hysteria, dropsy, jaundice and indigestion. She will have frequent nervous breakdown.

MAGHA NAKSHATRA

Male Natives

1. Physical features: He has a prominent neck and a hairy body. There is a mole in the hands and also beneath the shoulder. Medium size height. Innocent looking countenance.
2. Character and general events: He is very enterprising. He will respect elders. He will be God fearing. He enjoys his life. He is expert in various sciences and soft spoken. He likes to lead a noiseless life. The native will be receiving honour and recognition from the learned persons. He has good knowledge about various arts.

He will devote his valuable time for the expansion of his culture and actively involves in various cultural activities.

His dealing with others will be with a well thought planning and he doesn't want to hurt the feelings of others. In case any of his action is responsible for hurting the feeling of others, he is immediately a try to rectify such action. He also does not like any person who makes hindrance or causes troubles to others. That is why there may be several hidden enemies in the native's life. He is hot-tempered. He cannot tolerate any action or activity, which is not within the purview of truth. But this mental feeling leads him into a state of failures. Selfishness is a remote question for him. He does several things for the community or society not with the intention of getting anything in return but for mental satisfaction. This is the reason why the native is able to catch the eyes of the public.

3. Education, sources of earning/profession: He will have many servants and great wealth. In the professional field he cannot attain much success in the material field as he is not business minded and mainly due to his straightforwardness. However, he will be a fitting example of sincerity and hard work. This inherent quality of sincerity and hard work do sometimes pay him some lift but not to the extent when we see the balance. He is bound to change his field of earning business. Once he takes a decision, he will stick to that decision. His dealings with his superiors and subordinates are very cordial and most technical. Hence he is able to be a link between his boss and subordinates.

4. Family life: Most of the Magha born male natives will enjoy a happy and harmonious married life. He has to shoulder several responsibilities, to be more specific, burden of his co-borns.

5. Health: He may suffer from night blindness, cancer if Saturn and Mars jointly aspects Moon in this Nakshatra or conjoin in this Nakshatra, asthma or epilepsy.

Female Natives

1. Physical features: A most beautiful and attractive feature. If Saturn aspects Moon in this Nakshatra, she will have long bunch of hair.
2. Character and general events: While she is fond of quarrelling and anger is at her nose, she is charitable, god fearing. She will enjoy royal comforts. She can attain mastery over both household and official activities. She is religiously much inclined. Whenever somebody is in trouble she will help them without any selfish motive.
3. Education, sources of earning/profession: If Jupiter is also placed in this Nakshatra, she will be employed in a very high position or she will be like a queen i.e. her marriage will be with a wealthy person.
4. Family life: One of the drawbacks for the female native born in this Nakshatra is that she invites friction in the family, make conflict between her husband and in-laws, resulting in mental torture for everybody in the family. This mental tendency must be curbed for a happy family life. She will have good children; preferably the first will be a son and next two daughters.
5. Health: Her eyes may be affected. Blood disorders, uterine trouble and hysteria. She may also have jaundice

PURVA PHAGUNI NAKSHATRA

Male natives

1. Physical features: He has attractive personality. A stout body with mixed colour. Frequent sweating. A snubbed nose.
2. Character and general events: He likes full freedom. It is seen that the native becomes famous in one or the other field. However, his mind will be full of disturbances on one or the other matter. He has inherent intuitive powers to know the problems of others. Hence, even before the help is requested for, the native extends his helping hand to the needy. He has sweet speech. He is fond of travelling.

3. Education, sources of earning/profession: He cannot be a slave to anybody. Because of this quality often noticed that he would not take up a job, which involves subordination in its true meaning. There is a drawback in the native, that he cannot be a 'yes master' even to his boss in the case of employed persons. Hence he is not in a position to derive much benefit from his superiors.

He wants to be sincere in all the work he undertakes. Neither he can be a party to any illegal activities not has he the power of tolerance to see such activities. This condition of his mind drags him into several complications in life and he is ready to face such problems. He does not like to get any benefit at the cost of others pocket. There will be several hidden enemies to him. Hence, such enemies stand as a main obstacle in the progress. However, the native is able to crash such enemies and attain much success in all the work he undertakes. He is a power monger. He gives preference to the position and authority rather than money. He observes right path to the progress and may devote his valuable time for such a cause. Even though the native is able and intelligent he cannot reach the place where he thinks to be. It does not mean that the native will not rise in the life.

In the employment field, he will frequently change his job, particularly at the age of 22,27, 30, 32, 37 and 44 years. He will attain the requisite position only after his 45th years of age. While he does not want other's money he will be frequently in trouble in the financial matters from others. In other words, borrowers will not return the money to him.

In spite of all the adverse positions mentioned above he, after his 45th years of age, will reach a good position where power and authority vests in him. In the business field he can shine well.

4. Family life: His married life will be happy. He will have good wife and children and also derive much happiness from them. In some cases it has been noticed that the native does not marry the girl of his choice. He will lead a life away from his native place and other family members.

5. Health: His health will generally be good. However, he is prone to dental disease, abdomen problem and diabetics. Even so, no permanent nature of disease is noticed in the native.

Female natives

1. Physical features: Medium height with round face and a long nose. Double chin. Overall an attractive personality.
2. Character and general events: She is polite, agreeable temper, virtuous and has the knowledge of arts. She does charitable deeds. She will be happy. She does righteous deeds. In spite of all the good characteristics mentioned above, she has one peculiar quality of self-imposed showy image and believes that there is none above her. This tendency must be curbed for success in life.
3. Education, sources of earning/profession: Her learning is towards scientific subjects. Attains a good degree of education. She may be a lecturer. She will have reasonable wealth.
4. Family life: She has a loving husband and good children. She is also a duty bound wife. She is ready to sacrifice everything for the sake of family and she always remembers the persons who have rendered some helping hand at the time of need. However, she can be called an obstinate daredevil. According to her, she is the most intelligent member in her family and others are fools. This attitude takes her to the path of frequent friction between the family members. She cannot have a cordial relation with her neighbours. It is mainly due to her arrogance in regard to money and position of her husband.
5. Health: Suffers from frequent menstrual trouble, asthma, jaundice or breathing trouble.

UTTARA PHAGUNI NAKSHATRA

Male Natives

1. Physical features: Normally a tall and fat figure. Large countenance and long nose. A black mole in the right side of his neck.

2. Character and general events: The native enjoys a happy existence. He is lucky in several respects. He has a neat behaviour. He shows extreme sincerity in all the work he undertakes. Religiously also he is much inclined. He enjoys good reputation for his social work.

While he is clean hearted, he is hot tempered also. He does not have the requisite patience or tolerance.

Once he heats up, it will be very difficult to calm him. But later on he repents over such expressions when it is too late. However, he will not admit his fault at any cost. Even if he is convinced that he has done a wrong thing he will not admit the fact. However, he has good reasoning and is tactful.

3. Education, sources of earnings / profession: He has an independent nature. However, he undertakes all the responsibilities and does the same in a perfect manner. He does not like to deceive others or to be deceived by others. He can shine well in the profession or work where public contact is required. This success is attributable to the inherent quality of behavioural techniques. However, he earns a good amount as commission out of the public dealings. He is not sincere in his own affairs, whereas he is sincere in other's work. Once he takes a decision nobody can change the decision. Since he is a born hard-working person he can reach a good position through his hard work. He is suited to the profession as a teacher, writer or research fellow in the scientific field. In some cases it has been noticed that he earns extra money out of tuitions.

Period upto 32 years of age will be a period of complete darkness. Thereafter slight upward trend commence upto 38 years of age. From his 38th age onwards, his progress is much faster and achieves much of his desires. A smooth sailing in his life goes on upto his 62 years of age. He will be lucky to earn fame and wealth during his fifties. He has only self-acquired assets. He is good in mathematics or engineering, astronomy and astrology. He can also be successful in advertising business.

4. Family life: His married life will be more or less good. He is quite contended with his family life. His wife will be most efficient.

5. Health: His health will be generally good. However, he is prone to body ache, dental problems, gastric trouble, liver and intestine problems.

Female Natives

Females born in his Nakshatra will also enjoy more or less the same results as mentioned in the case of male natives born in this Nakshatra, in addition to the following results:

1. Physical features: Medium height, soft body, medium complexion, nose a little bigger. A peculiar identification mark in the form of a black mole on the face has been noticed in this native.

2. Character and general events: She will have very calm and simple nature. She does not keep enmity for long. She is principled, always joyful.

3. Education, sources of earnings / profession: She has inherent mathematical aptitude or scientific background. Hence she is fitted for the profession of teacher or lecturer or in administrative field. She may also be associated with sanitary department or hospitals. She may also earn money as a model or as an actress.

4. Family life: She can enjoy happiness from her husband and children. She is very clever in managing domestic work. Her husband will be moderately wealthy. She must curb the tendency of pomp and show, as she is likely to become the object of jealous neighbours, who may create unexpected problems in her family life in alliance with her in-laws.

5. Health: Generally she does enjoy good health. However, possible diseases for this native are Asthma of mild nature, menstrual trouble, and severe headache.

HASTA NAKSHATRA

Male Natives

1. Physical features: The native is tall and stout. Mixed colour with short hands comparing to the body structure. There will be a scar mark on the upper right hand or beneath the shoulder.
2. Character and general events: The native will have a calm nature. There is a peculiarity while he is smiling i.e. his sweet smile has the magnetic power to attract others. This inherent quality produces a vibration on others and it becomes difficult to leave the native once such acquaintance takes place. He can easily get respect and honour from the public. He is always in readiness to help the needy for nothing in return. He does not like to deceive others even if it costs him his life. In spite of this good quality, the reward he gets in return is nothing but criticism and opposition. He does not believe in a posh living.

Unlike other Nakshatra born persons, the life of Hasta native is full of frequent ups and down. At one moment he rises to the top and another moment he falls to the bottom whether in profession al field or in the mental world. In other words, luck and unlucky comes to them without intimation. Hence we cannot categorise him as a permanent poor or wealthy. When he enters in a particular field and starts gaining the object, reversal is already in store for him. While he tries to get out of such reversal with his own effort, helps comes to him from the unexpected quarters and he achieves medium success in the undertaking. It may appear that there is some hidden curse on the native as otherwise, the sincerity and hard work, which he shows in every work, should have given him a wonderful boost.

While the native does not want to cause any trouble to others, once he is hurt, he will always be in search of revenge, but at the same time takes consolation in the feet of god by thinking that let god give him the punishment and he slowly withdraws from the scene of conflict.

3. Education, sources of earning/profession: In the work field, he keeps strict discipline. Normally employment in a subordinate level is not fit for him. Only very few cases where the Hasta native is working in a low level job has been found. Most of the cases either they are engaged in business or in a high position in the industries.

Hasta native even with a preliminary academic background will possess excellent all-round knowledge. He will show to the world that he is not being anybody on any matter. He is a good adviser as he has the capacity to intervene and settle various disputed matters. Lot of responsibilities will have to be undertaken by him before he can climb one step of ladder of success.

Period up to his 30th years of age will bring in unexpected circumstantial changes both in the family front as well as in the academic and professional or business field. Period between 30 to 42 years of his age will be his golden period, when the native can settle down in his life. If the native lives beyond 64 years of age, there will be remarkable accumulation of wealth and all-round success in the business field.

4. Family life: He is able to enjoy an idle married life, even though occasional friction as is expected in a family will definitely be there. His wife will be a homely lady with all good qualities expected from a housewife. One of the hidden factors noticed in the wife of a hasta native is that she may indulge in homosexual activities in her youth period.
5. Health: He is prone to have severe cough and cold, frequent emanation of water from the nose and clotting of such fluid, asthma or cynos.

Female Natives

Female natives born in Hasta Nakshatra also will enjoy more or less the same results as mentioned for a male native born in Hasta native. In addition, they will also enjoy the following results:

1. Physical features: Her eyes and ears will be extremely beautiful and entirely different from those born in other Nakshatras. A typical shoulder. Very attractive with soft body.
2. Character and general events: She will have the inherent shyness of a female sex. While she will respect the elders, she may not like to live like a slave. She will not hesitate to express her views openly. She is not bothered about the outcome of such expression. Hence she is subjected to enmity from her relatives. If she curbs the tendency of open expression of her views she can attain good amount of success in the family front and enjoy her life in full.
3. Education, sources of earning/profession: In most of the cases, hasta female is not employed mainly due to good financial stability of her parents as well as her husband. In some cases it has been noticed that hasta female, if born in a poor family is employed in the agricultural field and in the construction activities.
4. Family life: She can enjoy a happy married life. Her husband will be wealthy and loving. She can enjoy good benefit from her children. First will be a son and followed by two daughters.
5. Health: Her health will generally be good. However, she may have high blood pressure and twisting of veins, asthma in her old age.

CHITRA NAKSHATRA

Male Natives

1. Physical features: He has a lean body. He can be recognized or identified even from a crowd of hundreds of people through his magnificent dealings and expressions.
2. Character and general events: He is very intelligent and peace loving. He will not hesitate to go to any extreme for the sake of selfish benefits. There is a hidden inherent Godly gift for this Nakshatra born i.e., the ideas or opinions or advice expressed by him would initially appear to be a sheer nonsense but later on the same idea or opinion or advice will only prevail upon. There is also an inherent gift of intuition. Hence he is the type of person who is very much fit for the Astrological profession where intuition is very much needed.

In some cases, it is also noticed that the native quite often see a lot of dreams, which are actually becoming true. This would indirectly indicate that a divine power is automatically installed in the brain of Citra born.

He is not the type of person who is not bothered about the sentiments of others nor is he selfish to others. But in spite of this adamant attitude his dealings with the poorer section of the society will be very cordial and full of kindness. Quite often he is mistaken by others that he is very rude and stingy. He has a tendency of giving reply on any matter without forethought and he wakes up at the eleventh hour and try to rectify his utterances when it is too late.

He has to confront his enemies at every step but he is capable of escaping any conspiracy. He has soft corner for the downtrodden people and he devotes his time and energy for the uplift of this section of the society. But one of the hidden factors is that initially his approach to the down trodden will be without any selfish motive, which later on culminates into selfish motive.

3. Education, sources of earnings / profession: Obstacles in the life is not a hurdle for the advancement for him. He can overtake all these hurdles with his courage and hard work. He will not be leading a comfortable life up to the age of 32 years. Period between 33 years and 54 years of age will be his golden period.

One of the redeeming features of Citra born is that he gets help and reward from unexpected quarters without putting much effort. From several horoscopes examined by me, it is seen that the age of 22, 27, 30, 36, 39, 43 and 48 years of age will be very bad in all respect. The native may earn as a sculptor or mechanic or as a factory employee or the native will be in the political arena or the native may be an engineer or a textile technologist.

4. Family life: While on the one hand he sincerely loves his co-borns, and parents, on the other hand he suspects the activities of the co-borns and parents. Citra born cannot, in

most of the cases enjoy the benefit, love and affection from his father. It is also noticed that the father of the native leads a separated life. In any case, he has a life away from his father. One of the points noticed is that his father in spite of separation from the native have some distinct identity of his own i.e., will be famous or known in a particular field. He is more attached to his mother and enjoys benefits from the maternal side.

There is a saying that the Citra born cannot stay in the house where he is born. Either the native will leave the house and settle down somewhere else or the house he is born it will be sold or destroyed. In other words, he will be settling down in an unknown and distant place away from his native house.

Normally he cannot enjoy a happy married life. When we say a happy married life, while the marriage will be stable the relationship between the couples will not be cordial leading to frequent friction on small matters. He has to shoulder lot of responsibilities and face lot of criticisms throughout his life.

5. Health: Inflammation of kidney and bladder, brain fever, diseases connected with worms. Abdominal tumours or appendicitis also have been noticed.

Female Natives

Females born in this Nakshatra will also equally enjoy the same results mentioned above for the male natives, except that the females are more subjected to the hands of unlucky fate.

1. Physical features: She has a beautiful envious body. She will be tall with equally matched fleshy body. While she has natural long hair, she in the modern world will have a cut hair.
2. Character and general events: Her eagerness for excess of freedom and unrespectable behaviour makes problems still complicated. She is proud for no merits. A veracious and

sinful, laziness. She will have very few friends. Commits sinful deeds.

3. Education, sources of earnings / profession: She will have her education in science subjects. She may be a nurse or a model or a film actress. If planets are not well or moderately placed, she may be employed in agricultural field.

4. Family life: Unless the horoscope of a female native is compared properly there is likelihood of death of the partner, divorce or complete absence of pleasure from the husband. In some cases, childlessness is also noticed. She is advised to observe the remedial measures mentioned at the end of this mentioned at the end of this chapter for a happy existence.

SWATI NAKSHATRA

Male Natives

1. Physical features: One of the peculiar features of Swati born is that his under part of the feet will appear to be curved and the ankle risen. His feature is very attractive to the women folk. His body will be fleshy type.

2. Character and general events: He is a peace loving person, but adamant and independent. He does not like neither to swallow others property nor ready to part with his own property. He does not like criticism of his work. Once he loses temper, it will be very difficult to calm down. Hence for a better tomorrow it would be better if he uses his proper balance of mind.

He is willing to extend any helping hand to others provided his own freedom is not questioned. He keeps limit of respect to be given to others irrespective of the position or level of persons that is to say he is not hypocritical in giving respect. He is the best friend in need and worst enemy of the hated. He does not hesitate to take revenge on the persons who is against him. His childhood days will be full of problems. He initially tries to give protection and helping hand to the most dear and near ones but he changes his mind later on due to the unwanted criticism received from such persons.

3. Education, sources of earning/profession: His intelligence and capacity to do the work are excellent. He has to suffer, financially and mentally, even if born in a wealth family, till his 25th years of age. However, he cannot expect much progress and advancement in profession or business up to the age of 30 years. Thereafter he can have a golden period up to his 60 years of age.

The native will earn through the profession as Gold Smith, travellers or drug seller, an actor or dramatist or a textile worker; may join defence (navy); one may be an astrologer or a translator; the native may be a mechanical engineer.

4. Family life: His married life will not be so much congenial. For the outsiders it would seem that they are the most adjustable couple but in reality they are not.
5. Health: Normally the native has a very good health. However, as every human being has to have certain diseases, he is also prone to diseases connected with the abdomen, heart, piles and arthritis.

Female Natives

Females will enjoy a little different result than those mentioned above.

1. Physical features: She can be distinctively identified from the way of her walk because she is very slow in walking.
2. Character and general events: She is sympathetic and loving, virtuous and enjoys a very high social position. Fond of religious rites. She is truthful. Have many friends. She will win over enemies. While most of the women folk prefer to wander, this native is not inclined to do so.
3. Education, sources of earning/profession: In case she takes up some employment she will attain much fame even beyond anticipation. As the fate would have it, while she does not like to travel, she is forced due to circumstances to accept a job where more travelling is involved.

4. Family life: She will have to act against her consciousness in regard to moral due to some peculiar circumstances and atmosphere prevalent in the family. However, she will enjoy complete satisfaction from her children.

5. Health: Outwardly her health will not look to be very good. But internal constitution is weak. She may suffer from bronchitis, asthma, breast pain, broken feet ankles and uterus trouble.

VISHAKHA NAKSHATRA

Male Natives:

1. Physical Features: His face will be round, bright and physical appearance extremely attractive. We have noticed two types of physical appearance i.e. one with fatty and long structure and the other with very lean and short structure.

2. Character and general events: He will have full of vigor and vitality as also intelligence of the highest order. He is firm believer of god and leads a life of truthful existence. He does not believe in the orthodox principles not the age old tradition. He is fond of adopting modern ideas.

Mostly he lives away from his family. He is ready to give weight to others in excess of what is actually required depending on the weight of the persons to whom he is dealing in. Slavery is suicidal for him. While he is very much religiously active, he does not follow any superstitious religious fanaticism. He treats all religions, castes and creed as one. He is a follower of Gandhian philosophy of 'Ahimsa Paramodharma' (Religion is Non-violence) and 'Truth is God'. In certain cases I have seen that such type of persons accept Sanyasa (saintism) when they touch 35 years of age. When we sanyasa it does not mean that complete detraction from the 'Grihastashram' (duty towards the family). He will simultaneously look after the family and follow sanyasa.

3. Education, sources of earning/profession: He is a very good orator and has the capacity to attract crowd. He will win

several prizes in elocution competition. Hence he is the fittest person to be in the political circle. There is a peculiar spending tendency in him. While on the one side he is very stingy on the spending on the other side he is extravagant in the spending where it is not required.

He is fit for doing an independent business; job involving high responsibility, banking and religious professions, mathematician or a teacher or a printer.

4. Family life: He cannot enjoy love and affection of mother. One of the primary reasons for such lack of care may either due to mother's death or unavoidable circumstances and atmosphere which warrant his mother to be away from the native. There may be several beneficial points of his father with which he can always be proud of. Even then, not much help will be derived from his father also. In other words, we have to come to a conclusion that the native leads more or less a life of an orphan. There may be a lot of difference of opinion between his father and him on several points where an amicable settlement on any matter may not be possible. It is due to these reasons he is right from the childhood a hardworking and self made person.

He loves his wife and children very much. Even so, he has two bad qualities. One is that he is addicted to alcohol and another is that he indulges in too much sex with other ladies. In spite of these weaknesses he will not make this weaknesses as hindrance either in the family or social life.

5. Health: Since has inherent vigour and vitality given by the god, his health will normally be very good. However, he is prone to paralytic attack. I have in more than 70 percent of Vishakha born people noticed this paralytic attack after the age of 55 years. In the remaining 30 percent cases, I have every doubt that the native could not provide me the correct birth time as otherwise the same symptom of paralytic attack would have in one form or the other present in them. It is also seen that they are prone to asthmatic attack.

Female Natives:

Females born in this Nakshtra will enjoy more or less the same results mentioned for the male natives and in addition they will enjoy the following results:

1. Physical features: Her features extremely beautiful. This inherent godly gift of attractive physical features normally attract the men folk and she has to face lot of problems on this account.

2. Character and general events: She has a very sweet tongue. She is expert in the household activities and if employed in the official activities also. Arrogance is very rarely noticed in these females. She does not believe in pomp and show and she is very simple. She does not like to increase her beauty by make up. She is subject to jealousy of other female friends and relatives. She is a firm believer of religious principles and quite often observes fast and perform poojas and visit holy places frequently.

3. Education, sources of earning/profession: She is interested in poetry. If there are other good planetary combinations, particularly when Moon and Venus are together, she may become a famous writer. She will have academic excellence in arts or literature.

4. Family life: She treats her husband as her god. Her religious attitude will confer love and affection from her in-laws. As she looks after the welfare of all family members and even distant relations, she will have power and authority conferred on her. She will have more attachment to her father-in-law. She may frequently be visiting sacred places.

5. Health: She will generally have good health. However, she is prone to kidney trouble, goitre and weakness due to homosexuality.

ANURADHA NAKSHATRA

Male Natives

1. Physical features: The native will have a beautiful face with bright eyes. In some cases where combination of planets is not good, the native has cruel looks.

2. Character and general events: He is liable to face several obstacles in his life. Even then he has special aptitude to handle the most difficult situation in a systematic way. However, if we look at his face, a peculiar frustrated face can be noticed. The main reason for such a gloomy appearance is the problems, which he has to confront on several occasions. to be more specific, there will not be peace of mind in his life. Even a smallest problem will start pinching his mind repeatedly runs after one and the same problem.

He always thinks of taking revenge whenever opportunity comes. In spite of these drawbacks he is the most hardworking and ever ready to complete the task before him. Come what may, March forward is the motto of this native. Here I may add that after several reversals he ultimately achieves the desired result.

He is a firm believer of god. He cannot keep a permanent stable relationship with anybody. His life is full of helplessness but independent. Even in several reversals he will not leave optimism.

3. Education, sources of earning/profession: He can be successful in the business field. If he is employed he has a special calibre of how to pocket his superiors. He starts earning his bread at quite young age say on or about 17 or 18 years of age. Life between the periods of 17 years to 48 years of age. Life between the periods of 17 years to 48 years of age will be full of problems. When we say full of problems, it does not mean that there will not be any good period in between the above-mentioned period. Occasional, benefits and favourable results will be definitely noticed. The life after the age of 48

years will be extremely good. It is in this period he can settle down n his life to the desired way and become free from most of the miseries of the life. If Moon is in the company of Mars, he may be a person dealing with drugs and chemicals or a doctor.

4. Family life: No benefit will be derived from the co-borns under any circumstances. He cannot enjoy or derive any benefit from his father. In some cases, frequent friction with his father has also been noticed. Same way there is no luck of receiving love and affection from the mother also. Normally, he settles down away from the place of his birth. Even though several adverse results have been commented above, one of the favourable points is that his married life will be completely satisfactory. His spouse will have all the qualities of a good housewife. As is the god's gift, he always looks back to his life while dealing with his own children and at any cost he likes to provide all necessities of life as far as possible and the love and affection. Hence his children reach a height position, much more than that of the native.

5. Health: His health will generally be good. He will be prone to asthmatic attack, dental problems, cough and cold, constipation and sore throat. Due to non-care nature of his own health he does not take medicines properly.

Female Natives

1. Physical features: Her face is innocent looking. Even an ugly looking woman with beautiful waist is attracted to man. Whereas, in the Anuradha native, in addition to her attractive face and beautiful body her beautiful waist is further added to her attraction to males.

2. Character and general events: There is no room for arrogance in her life. She is pure hearted. She does not believe a life of fashion whereas she likes to lead a simple life. A selfless, agreeable and attractive disposition. She can shine well in social and political field. She will respect her elders. Her friends will cordon her as if she is the head of friend's circle.

3. Education, sources of earning/profession: She will be more interested in music and fine arts. She may obtain an academic degree or high degree of knowledge in music or dance. Professional dancers are also found to have been born in this Nakshatra.
4. Family life: She is very much devoted to her husband and observes religious norms. She can be called as a model mother as far as upbringings of her own children are concerned. Her devotion to her in-laws pours further glory in her personal life.
5. Health: She may suffer from irregular menses. Severe pain will be felt at the time of bleeding, as the flow of spoiled blood will be quite intermittent. In some cases it has been told that, after appearance of monthly menses, there will be break for some hours or for one or two days before commencing actual flow. She may also suffer from headache, nasal catarrh.

JYESHTA NAKSHATRA

Male Natives

1. Physical features: He has a very good physical stamina and attractive countenance. It may be noticed that most of the persons born in this Nakshatra have defective teeth, either the teeth will have gap between them or bulged out. If these two defects are not there, then the colour of teeth will be different.
2. Character and general events: He is very clean in his mind and is very sober. But these good qualities will not be noticed by others, as he does not believe in show. He cannot face even a small problem. He is the type of person to whom no secret should be told or given. He cannot keep anything hidden in his mind even if it pertains to his own life. Unless he keeps it open to others he feels that something is missing in his life and good sleep is disturbed. Several persons born in this nakshatra have been coming to me and complaining that they do get good sleep. When the reason for such a state of affairs was enquired into, they have all admitted that a peculiar vibration takes place in their mind and unless the reason for

that vibration is leaked out they cannot rest. So they always wait for the next morning and try to tell these things to the persons who meet them first.

He is hot tempered and obstinate. Due to this temperament he often faces a lot of problems and forms a wall to his progress in life. He never accepts the advice given by others+, whereas he acts upon his own consciousness.

For the sake of principle he takes on the spot decisions on several matters without seeing the opportunity and circumstances, which ultimately leads him to a precarious state. Due to the condition of the hot temperament he will not hesitate to cause problems and troubles even to those who rendered him all possible help when required and even ill treat those persons. He cannot expect any help from the relations. Outwardly, he appears to be very proud but when we go closer to him it will be evident that it is just the opposite.

He must keep away all drugs and alcohol as he is prone to go out of control quickly which will spoil his hard earned reputation, put an hindrance to his profession as also in the family life.

3. Education, sources of earning/profession: He will leave his home at a very young age and seek refuge in a distant place. He has to earn his bread strictly due to his own effort. Because of the sincerity shown in the work field he normally come up quickly in any position he holds. Constant change of jobs or professions are noticed.

Period up to 50 years of age will be full of trial and any stability in his life starts thereafter only. Period from 18 years of age to 26 years of age will be period of maximum troublesome. During this period he will have to undergo financial problems, mental agony as also in some case mental disarrangement. Period from 27th years of age will be a beginning of progress towards stability, even though the pace will be very slow up to his 50 years of age.

4. Family life: He cannot expect any benefit from his mother and co-borns, whereas they become his enemies. He is generally disliked by his near and dear ones. This is mainly due to the fact that Jyeshta born likes to keep a separate identity and existence.

His spouse will always have an upper hand and resist tooth and nail the activity of intoxication. While his married life will be completely harmonious and enjoy to the maximum occasional health problems of his wife or separation due to some unavoidable circumstances will greatly affect the mind of the native.

5. Health: Frequent temperature, dysentery, cough and cold, asthmatic attach and stomach problems are the possible diseases. It is noticed that these people are affected with one or the other health problems frequently. He may also have severe pain in arms and shoulders.

Female Natives

Females born in this Nakshatra will also enjoy more or less the same results mentioned for the male natives of Jyeshta Nakshatra. In addition, they will enjoy the following results:

1. Physical appearance: Well-proportioned and muscular body with long arms. Height above average. Broad face, short and curly hair.
2. Character and general events: She has strong emotions, passionate jealousies and deeper loves. She is intelligent, thoughtful, perceptive. She is more eager to know what other's talk of her. Although her natural inherent feminine character will not allow her to appear domineering, she is good organiser.
3. Education, sources of income/profession: She is active in sports. Medium academic education. She is often contended herself in the home, seeking to enrich her own life through her husband's success. Hence most of the Jyeshta born females are not involved in any earning job.

4. Family life: She lacks marital harmony and loss of children is also noticed. In some cases it has been that such native is subject to harassment by in-laws and several concoctions stories are framed against her. She has to be very careful while dealing with her neighbours and relatives, as they are persons who put poison in her life. A worriless period is very rarely available for her. Since she makes her own rule to be abided by her children, she will be neglected by her children as a vengeance to what she has done to them during childhood.

5. Health: Her health will not be so good. It is seen that some of the females born in this Nakshatra suffer from disorder of the uterus. She is also prone to prostrate gland enlargement or pain in arms and shoulders.

MOOLA NAKSHATRA

Male Natives

1. Physical features: He has good physical appearance. He will have beautiful limbs and bright eyes. He will be the most attractive person in his family.

2. Character and general events: He has a very sweet nature and is a peace loving person. He has a set principle in his life. There is a general fear about the persons born in Moola Nakshatra. It isn't like that always. He can stand against any adverse tidal wave. He has the capacity to penetrate that wave and reach the destination.

He is not bothered about tomorrow nor he is very serious about his own matters. He keeps all the happenings in the hands of god and become prey to optimism.

3. Education, sources of earning/profession: He does not keep control of the balance of receipt and payment resulting in debt. He is the type of person who renders advice to others but not capable of keeping the same principles for his own use. This peculiar characteristic generally fits them for the profession of financial advice or religious advice.

Since he is skilled in several fields there will be frequent changes of profession or trade but stability in this direction seems to be a very rare phenomenon. Because of this inherent quality of frequent changes he is always in need of money. Moola born has a peculiar characteristic of mixing with his friends. It is quite natural that when expenditure is more than income and the native is not ready to earn anything by illegal mode the balance will always be in the negative. Hence it is advisable that he must keep away such friends and while he believes that all that is taking place on the earth is due to the blessings of HE, he should also try to be a little selfish and find a way to improve the inflow of income.

Out of all the28 Nakshatras, I have come to a conclusion that these are the people who devote their entire energy with utmost sincerity to their employers as also to any persons who have kept faith or trust in Moola born. A deep study of the life of these persons has revealed some facts about their separate entity than other Nakshatra born i.e. some sort of internal force or some external force is briefing the natives in all the work they undertake.

He earns his livelihood in a foreign place. It is advisable that he must, as far as possible, try to get an opportunity either in the professional field or in the business field in a foreign land or country as he cannot have good luck in the native place; whereas he can have much better success in a foreign land.

As already mentioned above, he is capable of shining in all walks of life, particularly i the field of fine arts, as a writer and in the social work.

4. Family life: Excepting a few cases, it is seen that Moola born cannot have any benefit from his parents whereas he is all self-made. His married life will be more or less satisfactory. He gets a spouse with all the requisite qualities expected from a good wife.
5. Health: Probable problems he will be affected with are tuberculosis, inosemia, and paralytic attack or stomach problem. Whatever may be the nature of disease it will not be

visible in his appearance or face as even when he is critically ill, his expression and the attraction of the face will not change? Normally it is seen that the native is not in the habit of taking care of his own health. With the result, some severe health problems can be noticed in his 27th, 31st, 44th, 48th, 56th and 60th age.

Once he is addicted to any drug it will be very difficult to control such addiction. Hence it must try to keep away from any material of intoxication.

Female Native:

1. Physical features: Medium complexion—neither black nor white or swarthy in hot countries. Reddish colour in cold countries. Her principal teeth will not be close with great distance, wealthy sign.

2. Character and general events: Mostly these natives are pure hearted. However, obstinacy cannot be ruled out. Even on small matters she will be very much adamant. Since she lacks knack of dealing she quite often lands into problems.

3. Education, sources of earning/profession: Mostly, Moola born females do not acquire much education. These females don't show any interest in studies. Most of these females spent more than two terms in the same standard or class. Ultimately they leave further education. The only exception is that if Jupiter is placed in opposition i.e. aspects or placed in Magha Nakshatra, the native may be a doctor or employed in an envious position i.e. such females will have excellent academic record and reach to the top.

4. Family life: Females born in this Nakshatra, unlike the males, cannot enjoy full conjugal bliss. She will have a separated life, mainly due to the death of her husband or divorce. This result cannot be blindly applied as other planetary positions of favorable nature will, blindly applied, as other planetary positions of favorable nature will, to a certain extent, nullify the bad effects. There may be delay in the marriage and also some hurdles. If the position of Mars is unfavorable she will

have to face a lot of problems either from her husband or from children.

5. Health: She is prone to rheumatism, lumbago, hip or backache combined with pain in arms and shoulders.

PURVA ASHADHA NAKSHATRA

Male Natives

1. Physical features: He will have lean and tall body. His teeth will be very beautiful, ears long, eyes bright, waist narrow and arms long. In other words, he has good attractive physical features.

2. Character and general events: He has exemplary intelligence. There is a tendency of jumping to a conclusion on the matters he deals with. Nobody can defeat him in argument. He has extra-ordinary convincing power. He will not under any circumstance subdues to others, whether he is right or wrong. On the one side you can have a lot of advices from him but you cannot render any advice to him.

While he expresses that he is very courageous he cannot reach that state unless he is forced either by circumstances or by persons to show the requisite courage. In decision-making he is very poor. He finds it difficult to take decision even on small matters. Once he is aroused by instigation or argument he takes decision without thinking the merits and demerits of such action and he sticks to that decision till the end. Even if he is completely wrong in his steps, nobody can change his decision. Such is the obstinate character of the native.

He likes to do a lot of things for others for nothing in return but he will be subjected to a lot of criticism. He derives maximum benefits from the unknown persons. He cannot keep any permanent relationship with anybody. If he can work with a particular aim with full sincerity he can reach to the top of life. He hates external show. He is God fearing, honest, humble and far from hypocrisy. He can never think of doing anything, which will disturb the progress of others.

He will be highly religious and always interested in feeling revered class and will devote much of his time in puja or others religious act. He is good collector of antiques. He may also take interest in writing poems.

3. Education, sources of earning / profession: Even though he can shine in almost all the fields, he is particularly fit for doctor's profession or fine arts. He is advises not to venture for any business unless he has dependable employees or managers. He will be attracted to the studies of occult philosophy and sciences and he can shine well. Period up to 32 years of age will be period of trial and error. Thereafter he slowly starts climbing ladder of success. Period between 32 years and 50 years of age will be very good.

4. Family life: He cannot enjoy any benefits from his parents. However, he will be lucky to have benefits from his co-borns, particularly from his brothers. He will be spending most of his life in foreign land.

His married life will be more or less happy. His marriage may be delayed. In some cases it has been noticed that the marriage takes place in a most competitive way. He is more inclined towards his wife and in-laws. Even then there will be frequent disharmony between the couples. At last he finds peace in the company of his wife. He will be lucky to have the most talented and respectful children, who will bring name and fame to his family. There may be at the most two children.

5. Health: While his outward appearance is extremely good, his internal constitution may not be good i.e., his health may not be good. It is quite often noticed that this native is prone to a particular incurable disease. Still he will not care for his health. He is prone to severe whooping cough, breathing trouble, bronchitis, tuberculosis, heart attack and malaria or inosemia is also found in such native. Even in the state of critical illness he will not hesitate to jump into the work, which he feels, should be completed. He may face problems with his thighs. He must take care about his lungs, as he is liable to suffer from rheumatic pains.

Female Natives

1. Physical features: She is extremely beautiful. Her almond eyes play the role of a magnet. Long nose and graceful look, fair complexion, brown coloured hair.
2. Character and general events: She is intelligent. She has energy, enthusiasm, vigor and vitality. Hence she is greedy and aspiring for everything. However she is not obstinate. She can attain more success when adverse conditions prevail. She will weigh the merits and demerits of each case and come to a final decision after deep consideration. She will speak out what she feels is right whether others will digest it or not. She will be fond of dogs and other pet animals. She makes promises but will not be fulfilled. Tendency of hatred towards her parents and brothers has been noticed. She will be leader among her relations. A determined, truthful character.
3. Education, sources of earnings / profession: Generally females born in this Nakshatra are educated. She may be a teacher, bank employee or attached to religious institutions. If mercury is also placed with Moon, she may earn as a publisher or writer.
4. Family life: She is very good in household activities. When the age goes by, she develops more and more attachment to her husband; with the result her life becomes more and more happier. Benefit from the children will be to a limited extent only.
5. Health: Her health will generally be good. In addition to the diseases mentioned in the case of male natives above, she will have acute disorder of the womb and uterus. Problems connected with thighs.

UTTARA ASHADHA NAKSHATRA

Male Natives

1. Physical features: A well proportioned body. Broad head. tall figure. Long nose, bright eyes. Charming and graceful appearance with fair complexion.

2. Character and general events: He will be refined, soft spoken, pure hearted and an innocent looking countenance. In case he happens to occupy a very high position in the society, he will not like to express pomp and show and will dress like a simpleton. He gives respect to all and particularly women folk. He is god fearing. It is not easy for others to find out the underlying merits and demerits. It is only after several acquaintances and dealing one can come to a conclusion about the behavioral aspect of this native. In most of the cases, it has been noticed that there will be black mole around his waist or on the face. A slight reddish colour is noticed in his eyes.

He will be very plain in his dealings and will show utmost sincerity in all the work he undertakes. He will not deceive others and would not like to cause any trouble to others. So much so, due to his inherent good behavior quality he often lands into uncalled for problems. While he is plain hearted, he will not subdue to any pressure and will not bestow full confidence on anybody. But once he takes into confidence a person nobody can change him. To certain extent, he is slave to flattery and expects that others must look after his welfare. He will not take any hasty decision, whereas full consultation. With trusted persons will be obtained before coming to a conclusion. While he is very much involved in all the activities he undertakes, usually he is a lazy fellow.

Even in the state of conflict he cannot utter harsh words directly to any person and in spite of difference of opinion he will not like to express his unhappiness to others. Any discussion he makes with others will be without expressing any ill will. He is bound to shoulder much responsibilities at a young age. Due to this he is fully trained to shoulder any responsibility with perfection. Once he is convinced that any action carried out by him or words uttered by him happens to be wrong he will not hesitate to repent and express sorry.

His every action requires recognition by others. Otherwise, he is dragged into the state of unhappiness. He is subjected to maximum happiness at one stage and the maximum unhappiness at the next.

3. Education, sources of earning/profession: He has to be very careful in any controversial dealings. Before any collaboration is made, he has to completely screen the persons with whom he is entering into such collaboration. Otherwise, failure is certain. Period after the age of 38 years will mark all round success and prosperity.
4. Family life: Normally his childhood will be somewhat better. But later on he may have to face a lot of unexpected reversals and problems in the family front. It has noticed that between the age of 28 and31 years some important change takes place in the family circle.

His married life will be more or less very good. He normally gets a responsible and loving wife. At the same time the health of the spouse will be a cause of concern for him. His wife will be having problems of acidity or uterus disorder. In spite of the comparative advantages mentioned above, he lacks happiness from the children whereas his children will be main cause of concern.

5. Health: He is prone to stomach problems, paralysis of limbs, pulmonary diseases. Poor eyesight or some defects in the eyes.

Female Natives

Females born in this Nakshatra will also enjoy more or less the same results mentioned above in the case of male natives. In addition the following results will be enjoyed:

1. Physical features: Her forehead will be much wider, nose larger, eyes attractive, teeth beautiful, body stout but not so beautiful hair.
2. Character and general events: One of the worst qualities of these females is that they are the 'obstinate daredevil'. Her utterances are not well thought, whereas she jumps into conflict with others. This category of females very well fit to the proverb "There are two horns for the rabbits I have got". In spite of this disadvantage she would like to lead a very simple life.

3. Education, sources of earning/profession: Generally, females born in this Nakshatra are educated. She may be a teacher, bank employee or attached to religious institution. If Mercury is also placed with Moon, she may earn as a publisher or a writer.

4. Family life: She cannot enjoy her married life in it's fullest sense whereas quite often her mind will be disturbed due to either husband's separation or some other problems connected with him. She is very much religiously inclined and observes all the religious formalities.

She derives complete happiness and contentment by marrying a Revati or Uttara-Bhadra Pada boy.

5. Health: She will have wind problems, hernia or uterus problems etc.

ABHIJIT NAKSHATRA

Male Natives

1. Physical features: Medium height well proportioned body. Magnanimous personality. Shining countenance and graceful expression. Penetrating looks.

2. Character and general events: The native will be respected by the learned and respected class. His behaviour is extremely courteous. He will be famous in one or the other field. God fearing and religious. Soft spoken. Inherent optimism and ambition. Tendency for occult study.

3. Education, sources of income/profession: He will be most learned highly placed and most famous man in his family. He will be engaged in a profession where much power and authority vests.

4. Family life: More than one wife is indicated. Marriage comes to him around 23rd year. Large number of children. Does not follow family planning norms. Severe financial problem upto his 27th year. Thereafter there will not be any occasion when he will be short of money. There may be loss of children, one

or two, when they will be in their twenties. Living children will reach a comfortable position. However, he will prefer to live with the eldest one.

5. Health: Health will be poor during childhood. Parents of the native will have to spend several anxious moments due to the poor health condition of the native. However, His health will improve after his 20th year. He may suffer from piles, jaundice. There is a danger or risk to life when he is in his 19th or 20th year. If he can cut through that period, there will not be any serious health problem.

Female Native

1. Physical features: Slim body with long face, long and double chin, large feet. She will be quite fat upto her 16th year.

2. Character and general events: Subject to crossing her 18th year, a sudden unexpected positive event will take place. She is then a matured lady, who has thoroughly learned value of life after a severe jolt. She is everywhere. Her capacity to handle several works at a time is excellent. Excellent executive talent. She is the employee, She is the master and she is the owner i.e. she does not believe in distinction between employer and employee, she will mingle with her employees or subordinates. She will earn considerable wealth on her own effort.

3. Education, sources of income/profession: Since she is optimistic and ambitious, she will make her own career. Business seems to be preference of the native rather than career.

4. Family life: Since she hates the men folk due mainly to an unforgettable sexual assault on her at a very young age, on or about her 12 to 14 years of age, she may not be inclined to marry initially. However, marriage may take place between her 27 to 30th year. Her marital life will be good and will have good children.

5. Health: Health will be very bad during childhood. May suffer from whooping cough, rheumatism, arthritics or skin diseases. Her 15th year will be most troublesome period. Parents are advised not to venture to scold the native. On the other hand,

keep a watch over the native secretly and try to make her understand about her drawbacks, with love and affection. If she can prolong beyond the age of 18 years, there is nothing to worry, she is at the top thereafter.

SRAVANA NAKSHATRA

Male Natives

1. Physical features: He has a very good attractive physical feature. Normally his height will be small. There will be a peculiar sign on his face, may be in the form of a mole or some other marks which appears to be a kind of disfigurement. In some cases it has been noticed that black mole beneath shoulder.

2. Character and general events: He is very sweet in the speech and also maintain neatness in every work he undertakes. There is a set principle for him in his life. He expects his surroundings to be very clean and he dislikes the persons who do not have the tendency of maintaining neatness. Once he notices a person in untidy condition he will not hesitate to open his mouth. He takes pity on the condition of others and try to help others as far as possible. He likes to have a very neat and delicious food. It is because of this he is found to be a very good host.

He is God fearing and has full Guru bhakti (respect to the teacher). He is a believer of 'Satyameva Jayate' (Truth only will win). He cannot expect much benefit or return from those persons whom he has helped whereas it has been noticed that he is subject to deceit from others. Even if a thief is caught by him, he will try to find out the truth of the circumstances which led that person to become a thief and if he is convinced he will let that fellow go. His inherent quality if peaceful appearance and the knack of dealings will penetrate to the minds of the public, hence he is fittest politician for the modern times. His one smile is enough for others to be attracted and once he is attracted they cannot forget the native.

Whatever may be the ups and downs in his life, neither he will reach to the top nor he will be at the bottom. In other words, a mediocre life will be enjoyed by him.

Even illiterate born in this Nakshatra will show complete maturity and will be eager to gather knowledge whenever they get opportunity.

He is a very good adviser. Others will look upon him for solving individual as well as collective problems. He is a versatile genius. He has the ability and capacity to undertake different jobs at a time. If he is installed in a seat where some power and authority vests, he will shine well. He is always in search of authoritative job.

Since he has to shoulder many responsibilities and spend for fulfilling his responsibilities he will always be in need of money. He will not like to take any revenge even to his bitterest enemies. On the other hand he will think that let the God give them the due punishment to them.

3. Education, sources of earnings / profession: Normally period upto 30 years of age will undergo several changes. Period between 30 years to 45 years of age will mark stability in all walks of life. In case he goes beyond 65 years due to beneficial planetary positions he can expect remarkable progress both economical and social.

The native is suitable for taking up mechanical or technical work or engineering. He may also be connected with petroleum or oil products.

4. Family life: His married life will be filled with extra ordinary happiness. He will have most obedient wife with all good qualities that is expected of a wife. Even then occasional sex relationship with other ladies are not ruled out.
5. Health: He may suffer from ear problem, skin disease, eczema, rheumatism, tuberculosis and indigestion.

Female Natives

1. Physical features: She is tall and lean. Her head is comparatively big with broad face. She has large teeth. There will be distance between the front teeth. Prominent nose.

2. Character and general events: She believes in charity. She is highly religious; hence she will visit several holy places. She is internally very cunning. However, sympathy towards the weak and generosity towards the needy are the notable features. She likes lot of show. She has the knack to adapt to the required circumstances but not in the matters concerning her husband. She is a 'chatter-box' without having any control over her tongue.

3. Education, sources of earning / profession: She is a very good dancer and takes interest in various fine arts. Illiterate women will normally be engaged in agricultural field, digging wells etc. Other females with medium type of education are normally employed as typists, clerks or receptionist etc.

4. Family life: Her family will always take pride in her name. However, since she wants perfection in all matters, she has to confront frequent friction with her husband. She cannot expect others to have the same perfection; hence for a happy home she should avoid such enforcement. As already mentioned above, while she can adapt to any circumstances, this behavior is applicable only with outsiders and not with her husband, whom she always looks upon to be a perfect gentleman.

5. Health: She may be infected with some kind of skin disease. She is also prone to eczema, filarial, pus formation, and tuberculosis. Leprosy of low intensity is also not ruled out. She may also have ear problem.

DHANISHTA NAKSHATRA

Male Features

1. Physical features: Normally, the native has a lean body with lengthy figure. In exceptional cases there are some natives with stout figure.

2. Character and general events: He will be expert in all the works he undertakes. He has extremely intelligent mind and all-round knowledge. He does not like to cause any trouble to others "Manasa, Vacha or Karmana" (by mind, by word or by work). However, it has been seen that he has religious spirit. He always likes to live with his own calibre and effort. He dislikes expressing his disagreement with others till the last moment. Most of us are probably aware of the elephant's revenge. That is, if any person or any animal causes trouble to the elephant, the elephant waits for an opportunity to bounce upon them. In the same way Dhanishta born also waits for an opportunity to bounce upon others with whom he has to settle a score.

3. Education, sources of earning/profession: A number of horoscopes examined by me have revealed that most of the scientists and historians are born in this Nakshatra. Since there is an inherent talent of keeping secret, the native is quite suitable for secret service, private secretaries to the senior executives. Whatever may be his academic background his intelligence is beyond questionable? In argument also he is much ahead of others. Hence lawyers' profession is the best for him. Normally, period from 24th years of age onwards will show progress in the earning field. Since he will be engaged in the profession or trade where he has to trust others, he should be very careful before putting trust on others.

4. Family life: In the family circle also he will be the uppermost administrator. His relatives will cause a lot of embarrassment and problems. He is more inclined to his brothers and sisters. He will have ample inherited property subject to the placement of planets in beneficial position. He cannot have

much benefit from his in-laws. But this drawback will be nullified due to the presence of good qualities in his wife. His wife will be an incarnation of "Laxmi" (goddess of wealth). To be more specific, any improvement in the financial field of the native will be only after the marriage.

5. Health: His health may not be so good. Even then he will not think of his own health. It is only when the disease reach at the peak he starts finding remedy. Slightest improvement out of the severest disease will drag him to the work field. He is prone to whooping cough, anaemia etc. However, he will not be on a prolonged state of illness.

Female Natives

Females born in this Nakshatra will also enjoy more or less the same results mentioned above.

1. Physical features: Handsome and ever sweet seventeen i.e. she will look very young even while she crosses her forty.

An inviting appearance with thick lips. In some cases, ugly appearance due to teeth protruding outside the lips have been noticed.

2. Character and general events: She has great aspirations in life and is a spendthrift. A modest and liberal disposition. She has sympathy towards the weak. As in the case of Sravana born, she is an enforcement master. She should curb this tendency for a congenial atmosphere in the home front.

3. Education, sources of earning/profession: Mixed nature of talents have been noticed in the field of education. Some are interested in literature and some in sciences. Hence usually, teachers or lecturers or research fellows.

4. Family life: She will be an expert in the household administration.

5. Health: Her health will not be good. She is prone to anaemia, uterus disorders of acute intensity and spoiled blood

SATHA BISHTA NAKSHATRA

Male Natives

1. Physical features: He will have a soft body, excellent memory power, wide forehead, attractive eyes, bright countenance, prominent nose and bulged abdomen. He would appear to belong to a aristocratic family at the first sight itself.

2. Character and general events: He is of the type "Satyameva Jayate". He will not hesitate to sacrifice his own life for upholding the truth. As he is born with certain principles, he has to quite often confront with others, as he cannot deviate from his principles of life. Selfless service is his motto. He insists on following the religious traditions. He is also of the adamant type. Once he takes a decision it is not easy for others to change his decision. While he is very intelligent and efficient in most of the walks of life, he is very soft in his heart. He is the mixture of good and bad.

When he is provoked, he will rise like a bulldog, but that anger is soon subsided. As he does not believe in pomp and show, he has a feeling of shyness to exhibit his talents. However, his talents will be unearthed due to his interesting and attractive conversation, which will be highly instructive and educative.

3. Education, sources of income/profession: Period upto 34 years of age will be a trial some period in his profession field. Period after 34 years will be the period of constant progress. He is highly suited for the practice of astrology, psychology and healing arts. His literary capacity and greatness will come to limelight even when he is very young. He is capable of acquiring very fine and high education. This Nakshatra has produced eminent doctors and research fellows in medicines.

4. Family life: Generally he has to face a lot of problems from his dear and near ones. Even then, he always extents his helping hand to his near and dears even without asking for such help. It has been noticed that native has to undergo maximum

mental agony due to his brothers. He cannot also enjoy much benefit from his father, whereas full love and affection is derived from his mother.

It has also been found that he is not capable of leading a happy married life. In some cases, when there is severe affliction of Saturn and Jupiter, it has been found that the native remains a chronic bachelor throughout his life. While on the one hand he does not enjoy happy married life, his wife will have all the good qualities that are expected of a companion.

5. Health: Outwardly he may appear to have very good health but it is not like that. He cannot tolerate even the slightest affliction to the body. He is prone to urinary diseases, breathing trouble and diabetics. As he is too much inclined in the sexual pleasures, he may have sexually transmitted diseases. Even though he may keep illicit relationship with other females it will be kept a secret from all. He may have problems with his jaws. He is also liable to suffer from colic troubles and must take precautions to protect himself from the diseases incidental to exposure to cold weather.

Female Natives

1. Physical features: Tall and lean, fairly handsome, elegant disposition. Fleshy lips and broad cheeks with prominent temples and buttocks.
2. Character and general events: She will be very calmed natured. But at certain times she is also hot-tempered. She is very much inclined in the religious activities as she is god fearing. Due to her hot-temperament, she is mostly confronted with family quarrel and this will result in frequent lack of mental peace.

She has very good memory. She is highly sympathetic and generous. While she does not expect anything in return for her humanitarian action, she is quite often misunderstood not only by the general public but also by her own family members.

3. Education, sources of income/profession: Interested in the scientific study. Percentage wise assessment shows that most of the female doctors are born in this Nakshatra.
4. Family life: While she loves and adore her husband, her life will be full of problems. Sometimes long separation from her husband or widowhood has also been noticed.
5. Health: Her health will be a cause of concern for her. Urinary and uterus disorders have been noticed. She may also suffer from colic troubles and chest pain.

POORVA-BHADRAPADA NAKSHATRA

Male Natives

1. Physical features: One of the peculiar body phenomena is that he has a lifted ankle of the foot. He is of medium size. Broad cheeks with fleshy lips.
2. Character and general events: He is generally a peace loving person but occasional blasting has also been noticed. He is a very simpleton type. Since he is very much principled, he has to suffer a lot mentally as he takes into his heart even a small confrontation or problem. He likes good food and is a voracious eater. He is not very particular about dresses.

He normally expresses impartial opinion. He does not believe in the blind principles of religion. He is ever ready to lend a helping hand to the needy. Even so, hatred and resistance will be his reward in return. He can easily enjoy the respects and confidence of others even if he is financially weak. He is God fearing and performs religious rites in accordance with the scriptures. While the native will be moderately rich, he likes to have respect and honour from the public rather than accumulating money. He is impartial in expressing his views.

3. Education, sources of earnings / profession: As he is a born intelligent and has the knack of trade he can shine in any type of job he undertakes. If he is employed in a government organization he can look forward for unexpected gains or promotions from the government. He is capable of quite

independent life both socially and financially. Period between 24 and 33 years of age will mark remarkable all-round progress in his life. Even though occasional mental tension is not ruled out during this period. Period between 40 years and 54 years of age will be his golden period when he can establish fully. He keeps much restriction on the spending activities.

He can shine in the field of business, banking, government job, or as a teacher, actor or writer, research worker and astrologer or astronomer. If in government service, most of the Poorva-Bhadrapada born is engaged in the revenue collection department or in any capacity where cash transactions take place.

4. Family life: He cannot enjoy fully the love and affection from his mother. As per the learned in astrology, the native will cause death or separation of his mother early. But in my personal experience, the native cannot derive full love and attention of his mother, as she will be working. Naturally, being a working mother, she is away most of the time and the native is automatically separated. Hence our ancients who have written this dictum are also correct to the extent of separation, but not to the extent of death. For causing death other planetary affliction is also necessary and birth in this Nakshatra alone is not sufficient.

One of the redeeming features is that there will be a lot of things with which he can be proud of his father. Subject to other favorable planetary positions, father of the native has been found to have fame and possess a very good moral character. Such popularity may be mainly in the field of fine arts, oration or in the writing field. In spite of these good qualities of his father, the native quite often disagree with the opinion and confrontation takes place.

5. Health: He is prone to paralytic attack, acidity and diabetes. He may have problems with the ribs, flanks and soles of the feet.

Female Natives

Females born in this nakshatra will also enjoy more or less the same results as mentioned above in addition to the results mentioned below:

1. Physical features: She is neither lean nor fatty, and neither tall nor short. In some cases very slim figure have also been noticed. However, she is very beautiful in appearance.
2. Character and general events: Honesty and sincerity are the main characteristics of this native. She is of the type who believes that let her head is cut down; she will not deviate from the right path and principles. She is a born leader. She is capable of extracting work from others. Hence she will be successful when she gets power and authority. Example of extreme optimism.

While she has the humanitarian doctrine, she will not extend her helping hand unless she is convinced fully that such kindness, sympathy and generosity are actually required. There is a peculiar politeness in her behavior.

3. Education, sources of earnings / profession: Her education will be in the scientific or technical field. Hence the native is earmarked for the profession of teacher, statistician, astrologer or research worker.
4. Family life: She will have more attachment towards her husband and will be blessed with children. She has good ability in the house hold administration. She will enjoy lots of benefits from her children. She will have many children if she marries a Rohini boy.
5. Health: She is prone to low blood pressure, dropsy or swollen ankles, apoplexy and palpitation. Perspiring feet and enlarged liver.

UTTARA-BHADRAPADA NAKSHATRA

Male Natives

1. Physical features: Most attractive and innocent looking person. There is an inherent magnetically force in his look. If he looks at a person with a mild smile, rest assure, that person will be his slave.

2. Character and general events: He keeps equal relationship with high and low people i.e. irrespective of the status of the person. He has a spot-less heart. He does not like to give troubles to others. The only drawback noticed in this native in the behavioral field is that temper is always on the tip of his nose. However, such short-temper is not of a permanent nature. He will not hesitate to sacrifice even his life to those who love him. At the same time once he is hurt he will become a lion. He has wisdom, knowledge, and personality.

He is expert in delivering attractive speeches. He is capable of vanquishing his enemies and attains fairly high position. He is sexually inclined always and desirous of being in the company of other sex.

3. Education, sources of earning/profession: He can attain mastery over several subjects at the same time. Even if he is not academically much educated, his expression and knowledge put forward to the world will equal to that of highly educated persons. He is much interested in fine arts and has ability to write prolonged articles or books.

In the work field, he can shine well due to his extraordinary capacity and capability. Laziness is a remote question for him. Once he opts to undertake a job he cannot turn back till that job is completed. Even in the case of utter failure he is not desperate. If he is employed he will reach to the top. In most of the cases it has been noticed that even if this Nakshatra born persons are employed initially in the lower or middle level positions, they later on reach to a good position and they always receive reward and praise from others.

It has been noticed that his stability in life or even the slightest upward movement begins after his marriage. He starts his livelihood at a very young age say 18 or 19 years of age. He will have important changes in the professional field at his 19th, 21st, 28th, 30th, 35th and 42nd years.

4. Family life: While he keeps praising his father on the one side due to the prominent personality and religious rigidity of his father, he cannot virtually derive any benefit from his father. He leads a neglected childhood. He is normally subjected to a life away from his hometown.

His married life will be full of happiness. He will be blessed to have a most suitable wife. His children also will be an asset, most obedient, understanding and respecting children. He will be blessed with grandchildren also. He is an ornament in his family.

5. Health: His health will be very good. He is non-care about his own health. Hence he will search for a doctor only when he is seriously ill. He is prone to paralytic attack, stomach problems, piles, and hernia.

Female Natives

Females born in this Nakshatra will also enjoy more or less the same results, as that is applicable for male natives mentioned above. In addition, the following results will also be enjoyed:

1. Physical features: She is of medium height with stout body. Large and protruding eyes.
2. Character and general events: She is a real "Lakshmi" (goddess of wealth) in the family. She is the embodiment of a real family woman. Her behavior is extremely cordial, respectful and praise worthy. Adaptability as the circumstances warrants. Suitability as the occasion warrants and lastly impartiality as the country needs is her main characteristics. When all these three essentials required for the present day are combined in one, what more I can describe or attribute to her character.

3. Education, sources of earning/profession: Employed females can attain good positions due to their own effort. She is best suited to the profession of a lawyer or arbitrator. She is also a good nurse or a doctor.

4. Family life: These females will be a gem in any family they are born or married. In other words, their footsteps are sufficient to bring in Laxmi (goddess of wealth).

5. Health: She is prone to rheumatic pains, acute indigestion, constipation, and hernia and in some cases tuberculosis of low intensity.

IN REVATI NAKSHATRA

Male Features

1. Physical features: Revati born will have very good physique, moderately tall and symmetrical bodies with fair complexion.

2. Character and general events: He is very clean in his heart, sincere in his dealings and soft-spoken. He has knack of dealing with others as per the occasion warrants. He does not give much heed to others unnecessarily. Since he has a completely independent life he easily gets hurt when resistance arises. He cannot keep anything secret for too long time. He will not blindly believe even his loved ones. But once he takes somebody into confidence, it is not easy to keep away them out of his attachment.

He is very hot tempered. Come what may, act according to his inner calling is his principle. He tries to observe the principle, which he feels, is correct and resist tooth and nail till the end for achieving or following that principle. He draws premature conclusion on any matter. He is God fearing, superstitious, religious and rigid in the observance of orthodox culture and principles.

He is stubborn and ambitious. Even a slightest failure of his ideas or plan will give him maximum torture. Out of all the Nakshatra born persons, Revati born persons are the most God fearing and religiously much inclined. Hence they also enjoy the maximum blessings of the Almighty.

3. Education, sources of earnings / profession: He will be interested in the scientific solutions, historical research and ancient cultures. He will be known publicly for the merits in any one of the three fields mentioned above. Ancient cultures include astrology and astronomy also.

He can be a good physician, astrologer or poet. If he is employed in a government organization he can be the most successful person. Revati born are mostly settled in foreign countries. When I say foreign countries it includes quite a reasonable distance from one's own birthplace. He will come up in his life with his own efforts. His intelligence and abilities are the inherent qualities at birth. He cannot stick to any particular field of job for long time.

He cannot expect to gain much compared to the ratio between work and reward till his 50th age. Period between 23 years and 26 years will be a good period whereas period between 26 to 42 years of age will mark a lot of problems financially, mentally and socially. It is only after his 50th year he can think of worriless and stable life.

4. Family life: He cannot have any help from his relatives and even from father. In other words, he is unlucky to enjoy the benefits from his near and dear ones. However, his married life will be moderately good. His spouse will be quite an adjusting type.
5. Health: He is prone to fever, dysentery or dental diseases, intestinal ulcers and ear problems.

Female Natives

1. Physical features: She will be extremely beautiful. She can be recognized easily even out of thousand persons due to her magnificent attractive personality.
2. Character and general events: She is somewhat stubborn. Likes to exercise authority over others. Like male natives, she is also God fearing, religious and rigid in the observance of orthodox culture and principles. Highly superstitious.
3. Education, sources of earnings / profession: She will have her education in the field of arts, literature or mathematics.

She may be in the general line as far as professional field is concerned i.e., she may be a telephone operator, typist, teacher or a representative of companies. When good aspect of benefice planet is received, she may be an ambassador or a person representing her country for cultural or political matters.

4. Family life: She will enjoy a most harmonious married life.

5. Health: She may have some deformities of the feet, intestinal ulcers or abdominal disorders. In some cases, deafness has also been noticed.

CHAPTER 8

ASTROLOGICAL HINTS MICROSCOPY OF ASTROLOGY

NUMEROLOGY

Know About Your Self through Numerology

KNOW YOUR FUTURE THROUGH NUMBERS

IF YOU ARE BORN ON THE FOLLOWING DATE OF ANY MONTH. YOUR FORECAST READS AS:

1	2	3	4	5
6	7	8	9	10
11	12	13	14	15
16	17	18	19	20
21	22	23	24	25
26	27	28	29	30
31				

YOUR RULING NO.1 (ONE)

IF YOU BORN ON THE 1. (FIRST) 10th (TENTH), 19th (NINETEENTH) OR 28th (TWENTY-EIGHTH) OF ANY MONTH THAN KINDLY READ THE FOLLOWING:

THE NUMBER ONES

In general ones are leaders independent active, speedy, adventures, original and easily bored. One take a heroic stance in life and thrive on obstacles which they prefer to see as challenge They are depressed when they are not achieving their ideals (which are very strong and positive rarely unrealistic. Ones love what is new in the fashion scene. They pride them selves on being up to that and ahead in their thinking. They identify with groundbreakers pioneers achievers. They are dominant peoples with a great deal of fairs they are ambitious decisive and often have an ironic scene of humour.

IF YOU BORN ON THE1. FIRST

You strive to stand in the first from the crowd. A natural leader you have a strong will and need to goal to work towards. You may run yours own business. You do not take no for an answer but have to push yourself to follow through (you tend to procrastinate). You like to plan rather than implement and are talented in diagnosis and troubleshooting. You are the one of the most idealistic people but consider yourself pragmatic rather than emotional. You may not be demonstrative emotionally but you love very deeply and are sometime romantic. You value loyalty very highly. You want things to be done correctly.

IF YOU BORN ON THE 10th

You have great deal of vitality and recover yourself from any setback. You are creative and have much interest and are always forward thinking. You may have little help from others because you structure situation so that you are I n dispensable you would do well in design.

IF YOU BORN ON THE 19th

Take note this is one of the four Karmic numbers and signifies that you have chosen some special direction or have a special goal in life you will always being trying to fulfil It; your nature is complex due to the combination of the one and the nine. Extremely discerning and perceptive you may put up an aloof or formal front use your intellect as a shield until you get to know someone. Verbal sparring and a keen sense of humour usually a dry wit characterize your social interaction your emotional attachment are deep but you strive to maintain self control at all times your negative attribute is often cynicism, rigidly, or xenophobia.

IF YOU BORN ON THE 28th

You love your independence and freedom and yet are much more loving and affectionate than other ones. You love to be the centre of attraction with people that you admire and respect. You always have quality friends. Your mate will have to be a strong person in his/her own right. And you will never settle for less then your ideal.

Like all ones you are an executive capable of sacrificing for your ambition, you would be successful in any profession, especially teaching, law engineering, architecture, and design. You have dramatic flair in you all do and will chosen a mate who shares this trait.

IF YOU BORN ON THE 2. (SECOND) OR 11th (ELEVENTH), OR 20th (TWENTIETH) OR 29th (TWENTY-NINTH) OF ANY MONTH THAN KINDLY READ THE FOLLOWING:

THE NUMBER TWOS

In general Twos are very sensitive emotional people. They do not have the one raging ambition but are content to work more in the back ground often as support for more dominant people. Two's analyse a situation and are conscious of the dynamics of emotional interrelationships at work and at home. They tend toward perfectionism (even-net picking) and should be allowed to work at their own pace. They will do anything to bring harmony into situation and often they will stay with an unpleasant situation longer then they should.

Two's tend to be plagued by worries that stem from a fear of the unknown.

IF YOU BORN ON THE 2. SECOND

Your social life and the mate are very important to your sense of well-being. You may find more accomplishment through having good friends then you do from your employment. You are easily affected from environment and should only work with people with whom you are compatible. In a conflict, you tend to be a peacemaker.

You may not let on what your real feelings are in the conflict. You may work long ours to please someone. You crave affection and usually remember other people's birthdays. You reply conversation looking for things you might say or wondering if someone has an ulterior motive. You are high strung and should not overtax your talents for music and arts. You love beautiful things but often don't want to push yourself to get them. You are patient and excel at detail work. Do not compare yourself and your accomplishment with those who may have more assertive or competitive numbers.

IF YOU BORN ON THE 11th

your birth date is the master of inspiration. All Twos are sensitive and this is especially true for you. This is the number of the teacher or of someone who function as exemplar. If you are female you may be unusually pretty. If male you may have refined characteristics or be interested in aesthetic pursuits. You may find yourself in the limelight. Successful areas are Television, poetry, metaphysics, art, psychology and spiritual work. You have a tendency to fall in love with peoples and ideas. You may always be on the verge of success yearning to do something almost impossible. Eleven can fall into menial work while nurturing a strong sense that they are meant for better things. Try to find some talent that you can express.

IF YOU BORN ON THE 20th

You are extremely conscientious person, friendly, compassionate, and eager to help. You may do well in small business but will probably not want to take on a large project without help from others. You will be attracted by spiritual matters and do quite a bit of searching through out your life.

You would make a sensitive therapist, artist, photographer, or writer on subject of interest of women. You work slowly because of attention to detail. You need to order to help you from feeling anxious.

IF YOU BORN ON THE 29th

Your spiritual interest is generally heightened. Your number adds up too eleven, which is the master number of inspiration in the mystical spiritual world. Like the11, you need to stay grounded by activities that offer discipline and immediate reward (such as working in the garden, cooking, sewing, building). You will have to watch your moods and know what to do before they get out of hand. You may be an inspiration to others and may attract the lime light through teaching or your art. You can also find success in occupations such as accounting and waiting tables, while pursuing your artistic interest. If a women, you may be very pretty, or as a man you have rather gentlemanly features.

IFYOU BORN ON THE 3. (THIRD) OR 12th (TWELFTH), OR 21st (TWENTY FIRST) OR 30th (THIRTIETH) OF ANY MONTH THAN KINDLY READ THE FOLLOWING:

THE NUMBER THREES

Happy outgoing, forever, optimistic, vivacious, talkative, scattered all these describe the threes. Lovers of social life and recreation, Threes do not enjoy hard physical employment. They may excel at sales and will always have several projects going on at once. Work must feel creative for them to be happy. They are not overly concern about money or the future. They are spontaneous and impulsive. They must learn to be focused and not overly self indulge. When positive they bring joy and light to all situations. All Threes easily overcome physical illness.

IF YOU WERE BORN ON THE 3rd

You are charming quick to see the humour in any situation but can be somewhat unreliable. You may spread yourself thin over several projects because you like to keep busy. You are energetic, but easily distracted.

Your social life is of a great concern to you. Having many friends you need to budget a sizeable amount of gifts because you are also generous. You love spontaneous get-together and may be the one in the office to suggest the going out of drinks or taking up a collection for a birthday party. You naturally embellish stories and events. You are known for youthfulness, certain intensity in style and while friends may laugh about your scattered ness, you are love by them. You adore an audience. Creative hobbies are a necessity for you.

IF YOU WERE BORN ON THE 12th

You have one of the most magnetic birth dates. You have an exceptional ability to express yourself, be convincing, and persuade others.

Your mind goes right to the heart at any issue. You are idealistic, yet logical and can be brilliant. You are easily bored and often tired of people ones you have picked their brains. You have a great need to charm and need to flirt. Your eye for colour and design, especially in photography, is outstanding. You love the media-movies, magazines, and television and keep up to date on who is who. You are something of a celebrity of yourself.

IF YOU WERE BORN ON THE 21st

You may be a bit quieter and less impulsive then other Threes, very sensitive and more likely to think things through before speaking. You have a great imagination and may be prone to dreaming, perhaps writing poetry. You may be natural singer or songwriter. You may be content to have fewer, but closer friends then other Threes. You are high strung and should avoid analysing things too much. You may find you have a tendency of infatuations (due to seeing people in a rosier light through your imagination and sense of drama). You may be gullible. You love pleasure and aesthetic pursuits. You definitely avoid manual labour if at all possible.

IF YOU WERE BORN ON THE 30th

You have exceptional high energy. Your enthusiasm is infectious; you can motivate and persuade others. You are outspoken and have a flair for having just the right word or fact to win an argument. You may have strong psychic ability. You would be an excellent teacher, actor, or musician. You would make a wonderful minister.

You are serious and intense about what interest you, but will find it difficult to fulfil old promises. Like other Threes, you are flirtatious. Guard against a tendency to drink too much or overspend on cloths and socializing.

IF YOU BORN ON THE 4. (FOURTH) OR 13th (THIRTEEN), OR 22nd (TWENTY SECOND) OR 31st (THIRTY FIRST) OF ANY MONTH THAN KINDLY READ THE FOLLOWING:

THE NUMBER FOURS

In general those with a birth date of four are called the "salt of the earth". Loyal, productive, earnest, Fours love home, family, and country. They prefer secure environments and stability. They take a cautious approach and enjoy working with their hands. They are builders and managers. While Fours are traditionalist they are also enthusiastic supporters of measure that result in reform, improvement and efficiency.

IF YOU WERE BORN ON THE 4th

You succeed through business, management, production, and anything connected to building and the earth. You learn things the hard way and have confidence that you can learn anything if shown the principles. You may have trouble seeing the "big picture". You can be very cautious and careful in approach to work and life in general.

You must make an effort to keep up to date. With fundamentals no frill thinking you have strong ideas about the right way to do things. You may work on several manual jobs in your life before working your way up to a position where your experience is respected.

IF YOU WERE BORN ON THE 13th

You do well in business involved with manufacturing commerce real estate and building (especially remodelling). You are more capable of verbal expression then those born on the 4th and posses creative ability that absorb you. You would like to be more socially successful, find a great deal of satisfaction in your work. You have an exceptional ability to reform and improve any situation or condition. You may have strong emotional nature that erupts suddenly because you have tendency to ignore your feelings.

IF YOU WERE BORN ON THE 22nd

This minister number requires you to work for the universal good rather then for personal ambition. This means that spiritual study should be a large part of your education. You are competent at almost anything you undertake. You will find that your varied experiences will some day be appropriate in a very challenging project. Your work must meet your ideals; you may pursue a hobby because you feel it will eventually pay off. You are not interested in status or luxury, but in making a significant contribution and living your life in a meaningful manner. You may have many Aquarian friends. You will recognize a special quality in others Twenty-two you meet, who will also display originality, competence and reformative abilities. You can be single minded and serious and need to feel in control. You must realize your power is channelled from above. You are sensitive, analytic, and judgmental.

IF YOU WERE BORN ON THE 31st

You derive great satisfaction from working with your hands and may be a sculptor or painter. You may have very high ambition for yourself. You are very traditional love your friends and remember their birthdays. You may be a great cook. You love to travel and socialize, but work for extremely long hours if motivated. You do not enjoy living alone and will take on solicitous attitude towards your mate.

You love talk about yourself and your plans and expected others to be interested.

IF YOU BORN ON THE 5 (FIFTH) OR 14th (FOURTEENTH), OR 23rd (TWENTY THIRD) OF ANY MONTH THAN KINDLY READ THE FOLLOWING:

THE NUMBER FIVES

In general, Fives are active, adaptable, curious people who insist on your independence. They prefer flexible hours and will always add a new dimension to what ever they do. Fives are very good sales people gregarious and persuasive. Fives love a good deal and want to be successful. They are spontaneous and know how to take advantage of an opportunity. They move quickly and do not brood over losses.

They are charming not always too serious and love being the devil's advocate. Fives open new territory, promote big business deals, and do not except the word "can't".

IF YOU WERE BORN ON THE 5th

You enjoy travelling. You may want to marry late so that you cal explore first. Adventures, you need work that is challenging, risky, and different. You would be an excellent promoter being something of a ham yourself. You are known as a good storyteller and jokester and will learn much through love affairs. You tend to use things up quickly and seek new stimulation. You are always on the alert, curious, and questioning and love to rock the boat. You will have a variety of jobs and will leave home early to seek your fortune, which, you are convinced in just around the corner. You see yourself as something of a hobo prince or lucky lady.

IF YOU WERE BORN ON THE 14th

You may have most interesting life, studded with setbacks that cannot keep you down. You must be careful to know your boundaries. You will meet people throughout your life with which you feel a "karmic" connection. You are vigorous, competitive and can be discipline when there is some short-term goal to be gained. You like to experiment and crave stimulation. You should be in business for yourself; anything to do wit travel, promotion, the public, performing and entertainment appeals to you. You want to live, not just exist.

You may have a very opinionated nature based on what you have "experienced in the past". You have a highly visible sexual nature. You may be eccentric.

IF YOU WERE BORN ON THE 23rd

You are extremely independence and self-sufficient. You may have an eccentricity for which you are known. You may be interested in art and music or new age ideals. You have an interesting way of viewing life and turns events to your advantage. Verbal expression, witty, and, at times, defiant you can be petty and critical under stress. Generally however you excel in persuasion and know what other peoples will buy. You may appear youthful a log time.

IF YOU BORN ON THE 6 (SIXTH) OR 15th (FOURTEENTH), OR 24th (TWENTY FOURTH) OF ANY MONTH THAN KINDLY READ THE FOLLOWING:

THE NUMBER SIXES

In general, those with a Six birth dates are the responsible type who prefer traditional lifestyle and domestic comfort. They are parents, teachers, practical artist, and healers. They accomplish through their hands and hearts. Sixes are often plagued by worries, and will wither if not doing something useful. Great community workers and upholders of moral justice, they understand compromise, and always search for an answer that serves the broadest interest. They are stubborn in their opinion as to what is "right".

IF YOU WERE BORN ON THE 6th

You have a very loving, but territorial nature. You are natural teacher and your ideas on how to parent are strong. Your home is of the uttermost importance to you; you take responsibilities very seriously. You love luxuries and crave romantic attention. You may have necessary worries about "going broke", something which seldom happens to Sixes since you are able to find financial backing for your business ideas. Your social position and contacts are important to you. You know the value of reciprocity. Family and friends always come first. Buy a good backpack and/or well-outfitted camper.

IF YOU WERE BORN ON THE 15th

Your home is very important to you. You have great financial protection (all Sixes do), and people come to you for advice. You are more open-minded, spirited, independent, and well travelled then other Sixes. If female, you need a carrier outside the home (although you consider your home an accomplishment in itself). You would make great fashion or interior designer, emergency nurse, or teacher. You need a wide social circle of educated people as friends. Your family is your first priority, but friends soon become "family" to you. You can be quite creative. Singing is a possible talent; at the very least, you will be noted for a pleasing voice.

IF YOU WERE BORN ON THE 24th

You want to build a family empire. You will be very unhappy alone or without domestic responsibilities. You love to accumulate wealth for yourself and others and will do well in traditional occupation such as teaching, accounting, banking, and real estate. Your ideas were set earlier in life and will tend not to change. Your admire creative and spontaneous people and may be inclined to marry one (since you feel very secure with your own abilities). You consider yourself liberal and open; other may not. You may be very emotional or prone to jealousy. You are careful, cautious and productive. Most of your plans come to fruition.

IF YOU BORN ON THE 7 (SEVENTH) OR 16th (SIXTEENTH), OR 25th (TWENTY FIFTH) OF ANY MONTH THAN KINDLY READ THE FOLLOWING:

THE NUMBER SEVENS

In general, those with a seven-birth date are unusual people with special talents. Intellectual and absorbed, they are often considered loner and lover of solitude. They generally love nature, animals, and serene environments. Material success means less to them then being able to live life by their own rules. By nature they are deep peoples, intuitive and observant with spiritual and technical abilities. Seven are usually cautious and move very slowly when making decisions. Alcoholism is sometime a problem for sevens. They do not take advice well.

IF YOU WERE BORN ON THE 7th

You will succeed if you will learn to concentrate on one thing at a time. Your intuition will lead you to the right opportunities and then you have to get specialized training in the field you have chosen. You may have fine technical abilities. Your work may involve a great deal of research or you may be a farmer or a rancher, immersed in the land. Always follow your hunches rather then someone else advises. You should realize that you have strong opinion that you may not want to compromise, and relationships may suffer from your intractability. You will find your opportunities coming to you though patient waiting; if you try to be aggressive, you may experience frustration at the pace of events. Never gamble.

Your attitude of caution in regard to money is correct. You may play an esoteric instrument or have unusual hobbies and friends. You have an affinity for the country and animals, and meditation and solitude are absolute necessities for you. You may be prone to be quite and have few special friends rather then many.

IF YOU WERE BORN ON THE 16th

Yours is one of the most unusual birthday numbers. It brings startling events, which become turning point in your life. Your friends will be highly unusual. You may chosen an eccentric lifestyle and always have a feeling that you are somehow different. The 16 are a karmic number. This may mean that you have connections with people based on past life experiences and you will feel a special quality when you meet them-or by the way you meet them. Life is never dull with the 16. Many things are learned the hard way. You do not take undue risks. Your attitude may complicate your working or marital situations. Because of the nature slowness of the Sevens, you may procrastinate. You are analytic and may pursue technical or historical fields. You may uncover facts of great significance or invent something entirely new. You insist that friends be of high quality. You may love antiques and stamp collections.

IF YOU WERE BORN ON THE 25th

You are very intuitive and impressionable and must guard against emotional instability through the intensity of your emotion. You may be hard for others to understand.

You can be extremely talented in artistic or musical fields and have great rapport to animals. You may even choose to be a veterinarian. Three may be difficult times (especially around ages 27 and 28) when you will find some type of therapy valuable in assisting your personal growth. There may be a bisexual nature. Do not cut yourself off from family and friends when you are feeling melancholy. Find a stable diet and exercise routine.

IF YOU BORN ON THE 8. (EIGHTH) OR 17th (SEVENTEENTH), OR 26th (TWENTY SIXTH) OF ANY MONTH THAN KINDLY READ THE FOLLOWING:

THE NUMBER EIGHTS

In general, Eight are hard working, practical people. They are never without a desire to better their position and posses a knack for knowing how to do it. They have a natural self-confidence and do not stay in subordinate position for long. They are natural leaders and managers and, while their associates may admire them, are also somewhat feared. They are not usually considered "one of the gang". As women eight must acknowledge an ability to direct and achieve. Eight knows the power value and mechanic of money by second nature. They may be strict, but are always fair and loyal to those who serve them. They may appear somewhat formal. They are dependable, objective, and dominant.

IF YOU WERE BORN ON THE 8th

You are very ambitious person, highly motivated to do well. You will stop at nothing to move forward to your chosen work. You need a career of business that will challenge you. You will not stay in a subordinate role, but will rise to the level of supervisor, manager, foreman, head of department, or professional very quickly usually through your own hard work unaided by "lucky breaks". Women who were born on the 8th need to work outside the home. Eight will find the success in any large structured organization, such as factories, law firm, criminal justice system, military, financial institution, hospital or government. In business, you should be your own boss. You have a way with money and will do very well in life. When success evades you, you have a tendency to become cynical or bitter. You are serious and mature, discipline and competent.

You may have trouble sharing your emotional side with the opposite sex; as a woman you may seem very independent and dominant to men. Eight need a partner who is willing to differ them. You buy only name brands.

IF YOU WERE BORN ON THE 17th

You are dynamic go-getter. You have the daring and courage to undertake large projects and the executive ability to delegate to the right people. You have one of the best business and financial outlook possible. Your business may be at the cutting edge of its industry.

You have vision and determination-unbeatable qualities. If you are male, opposite sex will be highly attracted to your power. If female, you will instill admiration in others, although you may need to emphasize your feminine qualities to attract men.

The number should attain the highest achievement; integrity is the key. Your judgment is nearly infallible and you are outstanding trouble-shooter. Do not get bogged down with details delegate! You admire scholars and historians and will excel in technical, factual writing. You are never vague.

IF YOU WERE BORN ON THE 26th

You are much less intense then the 17. You have a strong emotional capacity and love nature. Harmony is very important to you. You will be oriented towards marriage as much as work. You love to dress well, have a fine house, and well brought up children (for which you take credit). You are the more generous Eight. You may brood about the past, hanging on to old arguments and beliefs. You may have big ideas, but want to include others to help you, as you may not be as self-confident as the other Eight. You are more introspective and psychologically analytic. You might consider a catering business, diplomacy, or administrative work in the social science.

IF YOU BORN ON THE 9. (NINTH) OR 18th (EIGHTEENTH), OR 27th (TWENTY SEVEN) OF ANY MONTH THAN KINDLY READ THE FOLLOWING:

THE NUMBER NINES

In general, nine are broad minded, idealistic, generous loving people with multiple talents.

They are interested in universal good and often go into fields where there is broad scope. Music, Art, drama, healing arts, the ministry, metaphysics, social reform any area is open to them. They have a strong need to express the self, but not necessarily in the more ego-cantered way of the One or Eight. Nines can be diffused and vague. They are very vulnerable to outside influences and often experience difficulty in deciding what they are going to be or in making decision in general.

Young Nines may choose an eccentric life style to rebel against tradition. They may or may not continue on that path depending on who they meet and the experiences that influence them. Nines need too learn not to take everything personally. They will take up causes and wonder why others are not so involved as they are. They will do well in groups that strive to reform and educate. All nines have dramatic style whether in their dress, speech, manner, or philosophy. They can be distant and cool.

IF YOU WERE BORN ON THE 9th

You can succeed in any artistic, healing, teaching, philanthropic, or musical line of work. You are idealistic and emotional. Life is serious for you and you feel such a need to be of service to the world that you have trouble making up your mind about which carrier you follow. You are very capable but have some trouble concentrating on everyday details. You become absorbed in whatever interests you and you have many interests. You may have a metaphysical outlook towards world problems. You will find yourself involved with much group work through out your middle years. You may travel extensively and your life will always be full of surprises. You may be drawn to transformational work through therapy.

IF YOU WERE BORN ON THE18th

You can accomplish very great things when you put your mind to it. You have the drive and ambition of the one and the executive capacity of the Eight. You will have to push yourself a bit to get through the obstacles that will force you to acquire more knowledge and understanding. As a child you may have displayed a nature kind of maturity. You will not like to take advice from others.

Your own critical power are good and could be used professionally (especially in drama, art. And music). You definitely need to work the good for others.

IF YOU WERE BORN ON THE 27th

You are quieter then other Nines, but a keen observer of life. You may have musical or artistic ability and will yearn for distant places; you enjoy the poetry of the East, perhaps wish to be a member of an eastern religious community.

You would make an excellent journalist, wild life photographer, calligrapher, or antique dealer. The Nines has many talents and interests, which cam takes a while to find. You are generous and forgiving of friends. To be happy and fulfilled, you need to have an ideal to follow. You are always learning about letting go.

CHAPTER 9

ASTROLOGICAL HINTS MICROSCOPY OF ASTROLOGY

VASTU-STUDY

It is an ancient science, based on astrology and developed by the sages to ensure good fortune for the homebuilder and dwelling units. It aims at providing guidelines for proper construction. Its a study of planetary influences on dwelling units and the people who live in it.

In order to lead a prosperous and happy life and to receive all round happiness, along with increase in health, wealth and all round peace one should give importance to VASTU STUDY in making of the dwelling units. It is for this reason one gains or looses, if the dwelling units are made according to the principles of Vastu Study.

The effect of Vastu Study can be expressed in the following ways.

There are three actions to create harmony namely Wind, water and fire.

If these forces are kept in their accurate places, then there will be no disturbance. But if water is placed in place of fire and wind is placed in place of water or if in any other combination are made, the forces will start acting accordingly and create disharmony and unhappiness.

Vastu Study says that the all the planets influence everything on earth in some form or other; hence every home is under the influence of the said governing planets.

Some planets have good influence on certain rooms. Each of these planets guards a separate direction.

East	Sun
South East	Venus
South	Mars
South West	Dragon's Head
West	Saturn
North West	Moon
North	Mercury
North East	Jupiter
North East	Dragon's Tail

"HOME MY SWEET HOME"
"EAST OR WEST". "MY HOME IS THE BEST".

MY HOME NEEDS TO BE MADE ACCORDING TO THE BASIC PRINCIPLES OF VASTU STUDY, WHICH ARE AS UNDER:

NW	NORTH	NE	
STUDY ROOM	STRONG ROOM AND SAFE	WORSHIP ROOM	
DINNING ROOM	MISCELLANEOUS	BATH ROOM	EAST
JEWELERY & EQUIPMENTS	BED ROOM	KITCHEN	
SW	SOUTH	SE	

CHAPTER 10

ASTROLOGICAL HINTS MICROSCOPY OF ASTROLOGY

GEMS

PROPERTIES AND ITS IMPORTANCE

Gems are being widely used as a popular Astrological Remedy. They act as a remedial measure to counter the adverse planetary effects. Gems have their own power of attraction an individual by their brilliance and beauty. The ancient science of India called them as Ratnas (Jewels) and used them to help an individual native. Though they are many Gemstones Lunar Astrology Specialties use nine stones to counteract the adverse effect of planets. Gemstones should be carefully selected after determining planetary positions in one's chart, one's Ascendant Planetary Cycle and the moon sign. Careful selection of a Gem can bring about Prosperity, Mental Peace and Success.

This is the basic introduction about the effects of Gems. The Most important thing is to ascertain which is the Gem that will bring about maximum benefit to an individual. It is most important to identify which gemstone will suit an individual's chart. Gemstones such as Blue Sapphire, Cat's eye, Coral are so strong that if not chosen carefully they actually act in a negative manner and bring about the downfall of a person.

There are various methods for choosing the right Gemstone. The question that arises is should a Gemstone be selected of the planet placed favourably in an individual's chart or the other way round. For that consultation with a Reputed Astrologer shall definitely solve the native's problem.

NAME OF THE GEM AND ITS SIGNAFIANCE

Planet	GEM NAME	Indian name	Activity
Sun	RUBY	Manick	Excellent for rulers, leaders, people involved in government and political works.
Moon F:\other sites details and office 2010\Htm1\remedies-2-MOON.htm	PEARL	Moti	Good for mental peace, Anger and Moods.
Mars	RED CORAL	Moonga	For strength, Valour, Energy and Vitality
Mercury	Emerald	Panna	For mental activities. Good for accountants, Business Managers, Orators and those involved in research work.
Jupiter	Yellow Sapphire	Pukhraj (Yellow)	For spiritual thoughts, Spiritual advancements, and good luck, knowledge, academic success.
Venus	Diamond	Hira	For domestic bliss, attracting good things of life curing genital diseases.
Saturn	Blue Sapphire	Neelam	For countering the ill effects of Saturn.
Dragon's Head (RAHU) F:\other sites details and office 2010\Htm1\remedies-5-RAHU.htm	Hessonite	Gamed	Good for mental balance, stability.
Dragon's Tail. (KETU)	Cat's eye	Lehsunia	To counter the ill effects of Ketu.

GEMS AND STONE ITS PROPERTIES
AND IMPORTANCES

Represent Planet	Stone	Colour	Metal	Worn on Finger	Auspicious Day
Sun	Ruby	Reddish Brown	Gold	Ring	Sunday
Moon	Pearl	White	Silver	Little	Monday
Mars	Coral	Blood Red	Gold/ COPPER	Ring	Tuesday
Mercury	Emerald	Green	Gold	Little	Wednesday
Jupiter	Yellow Sapphire	Yellow	Gold	First	Thursday
Venus	Diamond	Transparent	Platinum	Little	Friday
Saturn	Blue Sapphire	Blue	FIVE METAL	Middle	Saturday

CHAPTER 11

ASTROLOGICAL HINTS MICROSCOPY OF ASTROLOGY

YANTRAS

PURE YANTRAS

Our Holy sages had the DIVINE STRENGTH with which they could foretell the effects of planets, which the individual would be subjected to due to his/her past deeds. They also had the divine power to reduce the evil effects of planets through various MEANS. One of the effective means was through Yantras.

KUBER YANTRA

For increasing wealth & prosperity.

SHREE YANTRA

For attaining power and authority.

BAGLA MUKHI YANTRA:

For achieving success in Competitive Examinations and Victory in Legal Battles, Court Cases. Also shields from Cuts, Operations and Accidents.

SHREE GANESH YANTRA

Ganesh puja is an essential ritual to be performed for any new venture, fulfilment of desire, achievement and attainment of wealth & objectives.

BESSI YANTRA

This helps the native to pay his debts.

GAURISHANKAR YANTRA

For success in attainment of comforts & Worldly Pleasures

KARYA SIDHI YANTRA

For success in all the Endeavours.

BUSINESS ENHANCEMENT YANTRA

Widely used and tested with success at factories, offices etc.

MAHALAKSHI YANTRA

For Fulfillment of desires & to bring Good Luck, Fortune and Prosperity.

MAHA MRITYUNJAY YANTRA

For Health, Wealth, Peace and Prosperity. This is powerful enough to ward off evil effects and give relief from dreaded diseases.

SARASWATI YANTRA

With the Blessings of Goddess Saraswati, it showers wisdom, sharpens intellect and ensures success in examinations.

KALSARPA YOGA YANTRA

For reducing the ill effects of Kalsarpa Yoga, if it is found in horoscope.

MARRIAGE SUSTAINING YANTRA

Maintains Bondage & Harmony in marital relations and reduces tension in marriage.

Other YANTRAS ARE

a) SHREE DURGA YANTRA b) SHREE HANUMAN YANTRA c) SHREE GAYATRI YANTRA d) SHREE NAVGRAH YANTRA e) SHREE SANTAN GOPAL YANTRA

CHAPTER 12

ASTROLOGICAL HINTS MICROSCOPY OF ASTROLOGY

MANTRAS

Our Accentors have given due importance to Mantras for the purification of planets. Their importance in Astrology is supreme. It is of utmost importance in Astrology to recite the Mantras with all Devotion and Pure Heart to obtain their blessings and get relief from Pain, Anguish and Agonies which blesses us with fruitful results unexpectedly in life most of the time.

The best time to recite them is during their main and sub periods. We have translated these mantras from Sanskrit to Roman English for Proper Recitation. May the planets bless all with their power and strength.

Sun "Om hraam hreem hraum sah suryaya namah"
Moon "Om shraam shreem shraum sah chandramasay namah"
Mars "Om kraam kreem kraum sah bhaumaya namah"
Mercury "Om braam breem braum sah budhaya namah"
Jupiter "Om graam greem graum sah brihasptaye namah"
Venus "Om draam dreem draum sah shukraya namah"
Saturn "Om praam preem praum sah shanayishraya namah"
Rahu "Om bhraam bhreem bhraum sah rahave namah"
Ketu "Om straam streem straum sah ketave namah"

CHAPTER 13

ASTROLOGICAL HINTS MICROSCOPY OF ASTROLOGY

REMEDIES OF PLANETS

PLANET

SUN

Effects and Remedies

The Sun is the father of our solar system, around which all planets resolve. The power of light in the sky, the temperature of the earth, the power of presentation and progress are represented by the sun. His presence means the "day" and absence means the "night". The soul in human body and the power of rendering bodily services to others have also been referred to the Sun—a royal planet of power, authority and finances.

The effects and remedies of Sun in different houses are as below:

Sun in 1st House

Benefic:

(1) The native will be fond of constructing religious buildings and digging of wells for public purposes.

He will have permanent source of livelihood—more from the government. Money earned from honest sources will keep multiplying. He will believe only his eyes, not in ears.

Malefic:

The native's father may die in early childhood. Having sex in the daytime will make the wife constantly ill and have infection of tuberculosis if Venus is placed in the 7th house. Malefic sun in the 1st house and Mars in the 5th house will cause the death of sons, one after the other. Similarly, the malefic Sun in the 1st house and Saturn in the 8th house will cause the death of wives, one after the other. If there is no planet in the 7th house the marriage before 24th year will prove lucky for the native, otherwise the 24th year of the native would prove highly disastrous for him

Remedial Measures:

(1) Marry before 24th year of life.
(2) Don't have sex with wife during the daytime.
(3) Install a hand pump for water in your ancestral house.
(4) Construct small dark room in the left side at the end of your house.
(5) Either of the spouses must stop eating "GUR" i.e. jiggery.

Sun in 2nd house

Benefic:

(1) The native will be self-dependent, skilled in handiwork and would prove highly helpful to parents, maternal uncles, sisters, daughters and in-laws.
(2) The Sun in the 2nd will become more auspicious if the Moon is placed in the 6th house.
(3) Ketu in the 8th house will make the native very truthful.
(4) Rahu in the 9th house makes the native a renowned artist or painter.
(5) Ketu in the 9th house makes him a great technician.
(6) Mars in the 9th house makes him fashionable.
(7) The generous nature of the native would put an end to growing enemies.

Malefic:

(1) The Sun will affect very adversely the things and relatives associated with the planets inimical to the Sun i.e., wife, wealth, widows, cows, taste, mother etc. Disputes regarding wealth property and wife will spoil the native.

(2) Never accept donations if the Moon is placed in the 8th house and the Sun in the 2nd house is not auspicious; otherwise the native will be destroyed altogether.

(3) The Sun in the 2nd house, Mars in the 1st and Moon in the 12th house make the native's condition critical and pathetic in every manner.

(4) Mars in the 8th house makes the native extremely greedy if the Sun in the 2nd house is inauspicious.

Remedial Measures:

(1) Donate coconut, mustard oil and almonds to religious places of worship.

(2) Manage to avoid disputes involving wealth, property and ladies.

(3) Avoid accepting donations, specially rice, silver and milk.

Sun in 3rd House

Benefic:

(1) The native will be rich, self-dependant and having younger brothers.

(2) He will be blessed with divine grace and will earn profits intellectual by pursuits.

(3) He will be interested in astrology and mathematics.

Malefic:

(1) If the Sun is not auspicious in the 3rd house and the Moon is also not auspicious in the horoscope, there will be daylight robbery or theft in the native's house.

(2) If the 9th house is afflicted, the forefathers would have been poor. If the 1st house is afflicted, the neighbours of the native will be destroyed.

Remedial Measures:

(1) Obtain blessings of the mother by keeping her happy.
(2) Serve others with rice or milk.
(3) Practice good conduct and avoid evil deeds.

Sun in 4th House

Benefic:

(1) The native will be wise, kind and a good administrator. He will have constant source of income. He will leave a legacy of great riches for his off springs after death.
(2) If the Moon is with the Sun in the 4th house, the native will earn great profit through certain new researches.
(3) The Mercury in the 10th or 4th house will make such a native a renowned trader.
(4) If Jupiter is also with the Sun in the 4th house, the native will make good profits through gold and silver trade.

Malefic:

(1) The native becomes greedy, inclined to commit theft and likes to harm others. This tendency ultimately produces very bad results.
(2) If the Saturn is placed in the 7th house he becomes victimised by night blindness.
(3) If the Sun is inauspicious in the 7th house and mars is placed in the 10th house, the native's eye will become seriously defective, but his fortunes will not dwindle.
(4) The native will become impotent if the Sun in the 4th is inauspicious and the Moon is placed in the 1st or 2nd house, the Venus is in the 5th and Saturn is in the 7th house.

Remedial Measures:

(1) Distribute alms and food to the needy people.
(2) Do not take up business associated with iron and wood.
(3) Business associated with gold, silver, cloth will give very good results.

Sun in 5th house

Benefic:

(1) The progress and prosperity of family and children will be assured. If the Mars is placed in the 1st or 8th house and Rahu, Ketu, Saturn are placed in 9th and 12th houses, the native will lead king's life.
(2) If in 5th house placed with any planet inimical to sun, the native will be bestowed hour by the government everywhere.
(3) If Jupiter is placed in 9th or 12th house, the enemies will be destroyed, but this position will not be good for children of the native.

Malefic:

(1) If the Sun in the 5th is inauspicious and Jupiter is in 10th, the wife of the native will die and wives in subsequent marriages will also die
(2) If the sun in the 5th house is inauspicious and Saturn is placed in 3rd, sons of the native will die.

Remedial Measure:

(1) Do not delay in having a child.
(2) Build your kitchen in the eastern portion of your house.
(3) Drop a lit the quantity of mustard oil on the ground continuously for 43 days.

Sun in 6th House

Benefic:

(1) Native will be lucky, prone to anger, will have beautiful spouse and will benefit from that government.

(2) If Sun is in the 6th house and Moon, Mars and Jupiter in the 2nd house, following tradition will be beneficial.

(3) If sun is in 6th house and Ketu in 1st or 7th house then the native will have a son and after the 48th year great fortune will follow.

Malefic:

(1) The native's son and maternal family will face bad times. Will also affect native health adversely.

(2) If there is a no planet in the 2nd house, the native will get a government job in the 22nd year of his life.

(3) If Mars is placed in the 10th house the native's sons will die one after the other.

(4) Mercury in the 12th house causes high blood pressure.

Remedial Measures:

(1) Ancestral customs and ritu also should be strictly followed; otherwise the family progress and happiness will be destroyed.

(2) Underground furnaces should not be constructed with in the premises of the house.

(3) After taking dinner blow off the fire of the kitchen stove by sprinkling milk over it.

(4) Always keep Gangajal in the premises of your house.

(5) Offer wheat or Gur to monkeys.

Sun in 7th House

Benefic:

(1) If Jupiter, Mars or Moon are placed in the 2nd house, the native will occupy a ministerial position in the government.
(2) If the Mercury is exalted or Mercury in the 5th or 7th house is expected by Mars, the native will have unending sources of income.

Malefic:

(1) If the Sun is inauspicious in the 7th house and Jupiter, Venus or any malefic planet is placed in the 11th house and Mercury is malefic in any other house, the native will encounter the death of several members of his family together. Obstacles from the government diseases like tuberculosis and asthma will victimise the native.

Incidents of fire, embalmment and other family troubles will madden the native who may go to the extent of becoming a recluse or committing suicide.

(2) Malefic Sun in the 7th and Mars or Saturn in the 2nd or 12th house and Moon in the 1st house cause leprosy or leucoderma.

Remedial Measures:

(1) Lessen the amount of salt intake.
(2) Start any work after taking a little sweet with water.
(3) Offer a little piece of your chapati to the fire of the kitchen before taking your meals.
(4) Serving and rearing up a black cow or a cow without horns, but make sure that the cow is not white.

Sun in 8th House

Benefic:

(1) Government favours will accrue from the 22nd year of life.
(2) Here the Sun makes the native truthful, saintly and king like. Nobody would be able to harm him.

Malefic:

(1) Mercury in the 2nd house will create economic crisis.
(2) Native will be short tempered, impatient & will have ill health.

Remedial Measures:

(1) Never keep a white cloth in the house.
(2) Never live in the house facing south.
(3) Always eat something sweet and drink water before starting any new work.
(4) Throw copper coins in a burning pyre (Chita) whenever possible.
(5) Throw Gur (jaggery) in running water.

Sun in 9th House

Benefic:

(1) Native will be lucky, good natured will have good family life and will always help others.
(2) If Mercury is in the 5th house, the native will have fortune after 34 years.

Malefic:

(1) Native will be evil and troubled by his brothers.
(2) Disfavour from government and loss of reputation.

Remedial Measures:

(1) Never accept articles of silver as gifts or donation. Donate silver articles frequently.
(2) Ancestral pots and utensils of brass must be used and not sold.
(3) Avoid extreme anger and extreme softness.

Sun in 10th House

Benefic:

(1) Benefits and favours from government, good health and financially stronger.
(2) The native will get a government job and comforts of vehicles and servants.
(3) The native will always be suspicious about others.

Malefic:

(1) If the Sun is in the 4th house, the native's father will die in his childhood.
(2) If the Sun is in the 10th house and moon is in the 5th house the native will have a very short life.
(3) If the 4th house is without any planet, the native will be deprived of government favours and benefits.

Remedial Measures:

(1) Never wear blue or black clothes.
(2) Throwing a copper coin in a river or canal for 43 years will be highly beneficial.
(3) Abstain from liquor and meat.

Sun in 11th House

Benefic:

(1) If the native is vegetarian he will have three sons and will himself be head of the house and will get benefits from government.

Malefic:

(1) The Moon is in the 5th house and the Sun is not expected by good planets, the will have a short life span.

Remedial Measures:

(1) Abstain from meat and wine.
(2) Keep almonds or radishes near the head of the bed and offer it in the temple next day for long life and children.

Sun in 12th House

Benefic:

(1) If Ketu in the 2nd house the native will earn wealth after 24 years and will have good family life.
(2) If Venus and Mercury are together then one will benefit from business and the native will always have steady source of income.

Malefic:

Native will suffer from depression, financial loss from machineries and will be punished by the government.

If the other evil planet is in the 1st house, the native will not be able to sleep peacefully at night.

Remedial Measures:

(1) Native should always have a courtyard in his house.
(2) One should be religious and truthful.
(3) Keep a Chakki in the house.
(4) Always forgive your enemies

GEM FOR PLANET SUN

SUN	RUBY	RED

REMEDIES OF PLANTS

PLANET

MOON

Effects and Remedies

As explained in the preceding issue, the Sun is regarded as the generator of power that gives spirit and life to all planets, the Moon is considered to be the conductor of power lent by Sun and rules over the lives of the beings on this earth. Sun represents individuality, whereas Moon shows one's personality.

Moon governs over impregnation, conception, birth of a child and the animal instinct. She represents mother, mother's family, grandmother, old women, horse, navigation, agricultural land, Lord Shiva, love, kindness, mental peace, heart, services rendered for other's welfare and the 4th house.

The Moon's effect comes up in the 16th, 51st and 86th year of the native and similarly its 1st cycle falls in the 24th year, the 2nd in the 49th year and the 3rd cycle falls in the 94th year of the native. The Jupiter, Sun and Mars are Moon's friends, whereas Saturn, Rahu and Ketu are inimical to her. For her protection, the Moon sacrifices her friendly planets—Sun, Mars or Jupiter. Moon is the Lord of 4th house, stands exalted in the 2nd house of Taurus and becomes debilitated in the 8th house of Scorpio. The Moon provides very good results if placed in houses 1, 2, 3, 4, 5, 7 and 9 whereas the 6th, 8th, 10th, 11th and 12th houses are bad for the Moon. The death of a domestic milch animal or a horse, drying up of a person's well or pond, the loss of the senses of touching and feeling are the signs of moon turning malefic.

The placement of the Ketu in the 4th house causes Matri Rina i.e. mother's debt.

In such a situation pieces of silver of equal weight and size be collected from every member of the family and the same should be thrown together into the running water of a river. Consequently all the ill effects would be warded off.

Moon in 1st House

In general, the 1st house belongs to Mars and Sun. When the moon is also placed therein, this house will come under the combined influences of the Mars, the Sun and the Moon i.e. all the 3 mutual friends will be treated as occupants of this house. The Sun and Mars will extend all friendly support to their natural friend Moon placed on the throne i.e. the ascendant house.

Such native will be softhearted and will inherit all the traits and qualities of his mother. He will be either the eldest brother or will certainly be treated so. As long as the native receives the blessings of his mother and keeps her happy, he will continue to rise and prosper in every way.

The things and the relatives as represented by Mercury, who is inimical to Moon, will prove harmful to the native, e.g., the sister-in-law and the green colour will affect adversely. Hence it is better to keep away from them.

Burning milk (for making Khoya) or selling milk for profit would reduce or minimize the power of the Moon placed in the 1st house, which means that the native's life and property would be destroyed if he engages himself in such activities. Such a native should serve others with water and milk freely for long life and all round prosperity. Such a native will get a life of about 90 years and will be bestowed with honors and fame by the Govt.

Remedies

1. Do not marry between the age of 24 and 27 years, i.e., marry either before 24 years of age or after 27 years of age.
2. Do not build a house out of your earnings between 24 and 27 years of age.
3. Keep away from the green color and sister-in-law. Do not keep a silver pot or kettle with a snout (Toti) in it in the house.
4. Offer water to the roots of a Banyan tree whenever you can afford.
5. Insert copper nails on the four corners of your bed.
6. Whenever crossing a river, always throw coins in it for the welfare of your children.
7. Always keep a silver Thali in your house.
8. Use Silver pots for drinking water or milk and avoid the use of glassware for the same.

Moon in 2nd House

The results of the 2nd house, when Moon is placed therein, will be influenced by Jupiter, Venus and the Moon, because this is the Puckka Ghar, the permanent house of Jupiter and Venus is the lord of the second Rashi Taurus. The Moon gives very good results in this house, as it becomes very strong here because of the friendly support of Jupiter against Venus.

Such a native may not have sisters, but will certainly be having brothers. In case he doesn't have, his wife will certainly have brothers. He will certainly receive his due share in parental properties. Whatever is the planetary position otherwise, but the Moon here will ensure male offspring to the native.

The native will receive good education, which will add to his fortune. The Business associated with the things of the Moon will prove highly advantageous. He may be a reputed teacher also.

The Ketu placed in the 12th house will cause eclipse of the Moon here, which will deprive the native either of good education or of male children.

Remedies

1. Temple within the native's house may deprive the native of male issue.
2. The things associated with the Moon, i.e., silver, rice, non-cemented floor of the house, the mother and old women and their blessings will prove very lucky for the native.
3. Offering green color clothes to small girls continuously for 43 days.
4. Place the things associated with the Moon into the foundation of your house, e.g., a square piece of silver.

Moon in 3rd House

The results of the 3rd house, when the Moon is placed therein, will be influenced by the Mars, Mercury and Moon. Here the Moon proves highly beneficial to ensure a long life and great wealth or riches for the native.

If there are no planets in the 9th and 11th houses, then Mars and Venus will give good results to the native because of the Moon being in the 3rd house.

With the advancement of the native's education and learning, the economic condition of his father will deteriorate, but without affecting his education adversely. If Ketu's placing in the horoscope is auspicious and not harming the Moon in the 3rd, the education of the native will bear good fruits and prove advantageous in every manner.

If the Moon is malefic, it will cause great loss of wealth and money at the age of the malefic planet placed in the 9th house.

Remedies

1. Offer in donation the things associated with the Moon, e.g., silver or rice, after the birth of a daughter and the things associated with the Sun e.g., wheat and jaggery when a son is born.
2. Do not make use of your daughter's money and wealth.
3. To avoid the evil effects of a malefic planet in the 8th house, serve the guests and others by offering them milk and water freely.
4. Worshipping Goddess Durga and obtaining the blessings of small girls by touching their feet after serving them food and sweets.

Moon in 4th House

The results of the 4th house are the general product of the total influences of Moon, the lord of the 4th Rashi Cancer and the permanent resident of the 4th house. Here the Moon becomes very strong and powerful in every manner.

The use of, and association with the things represented by the Moon will prove highly beneficial to the native. Offer milk in place of water to the guests. Obtain blessings of your mother or the elderly women by touching their feet. The 4th house is the river of income which will continue to increase expenditure. In other words, expenditure will augment income.

The native will be a reputed and honoured person with soft heart and all sorts of riches. He will inherit all the traits and qualities of his mother and will face the problems of life boldly like a lion. He will receive honour and favours from the government along with riches and will provide peace and shelter to others.

Good education will be ensured for the native. If Jupiter is placed in the 6th house and Moon in the 4th, parental profession will suit him. If a person has mortgaged certain valuables to the native, he will never come back to demand it.

If Moon be placed with 4 planets in the 4th house, the native will be economically very strong and wealthy. The male planets will help the native like sons and the female planets like daughters.

Remedies

1. Selling of milk for profit and burning of milk for making Khoya, etc., will have a very adverse effects on income, life span and mental peace.
2. Adultery and flirtation will be seriously detrimental to the native's reputation and prospects of wealth gains.
3. The more the expenses, the more the income.
4. Before beginning any auspicious or new work, place a pitcher or any container filled with milk in the house.
5. For warding off the evil generated by the Jupiter placed in the 10th house, the native should visit places of worship along with his grandfather and offer their oblations by placing their forehead at the feet of the deity.

Moon in 5th House

The results of the 5th house, when the Moon is placed therein, will be influenced by the Sun, the Ketu and the Moon. The native will adopt just and right means to earn wealth and will not yield to wrongdoing. He may not do well in business but certainly receive favours and honours from the government. Anyone supported by him will win.

The Moon in the 5th house will give 5 sons if the Ketu is well placed and benefic even if the Moon is joined by malefic planets. By his education and learning the native will undertake several measures for others welfare, but the others will not do good to him.

Further, the native will be destroyed if he becomes greedy and selfish. If he fails to keep his plans a secret, his own men will damage him seriously.

Remedies

1. Keep control over your tongue. Never use abusive language to ward off troubles.
2. Avoid becoming greedy and over selfish.
3. Deceit and dishonesty towards others will affect you adversely.
4. Acting upon the advice of another person before trying to harm anybody will ensure very good results and a life of about 100 years.
5. Public service will enhance income and reputation of the native.

Moon in 6th House

This house is affected by the Mercury and Ketu. The Moon in this house will be affected by the planets placed in the 2nd, 8th, 12th and 4th houses. The native will receive education with obstacles and will have to struggle a lot for reaping the benefits of his educational achievements.

If the Moon is placed in the 6th, 2nd, 4th, 8th and 12th houses it is auspicious. The native would enliven a dying person by putting a few drops of water in his mouth.

But if the Moon is malefic in the 6th house and Mercury is placed in the 2nd or 12th house, the native will have suicidal tendencies. Similarly, if the Moon is malefic and the Sun is placed in the 12th house, then the native or his wife or both will have severe eye defects and troubles.

Remedies

1. Serve milk to your father with your own hands.
2. Never take milk during night. But intake of milk during day time and use of even curd and cheese during night is permissible.

3. Do not offer milk as donation. It can be given only at religious places of worship.
4. Digging of wells for public will destroy the issues, but digging of wells in a hospital or within the premises of cremation ground will not be harmful.

Moon in 7th house

The 7th house belongs to Venus and Mercury. When the Moon is placed here, the results of this house will be affected by the Venus, Mercury and Moon. Venus and Mercury combined together give the effects of the Sun. The 1st house aspects the 7th house. Consequently the rays of the Sun from the 1st house would be enlightening the Moon if placed in the 7th, which means that the things and the relatives represented by the Moon will provide highly beneficial and good results.

Educational achievements will prove fruitful for earning money or wealth. He may or may not have properties but will certainly have cash money in hand always. He will have good potential for being a poet or astrologer, or else he will be characterless and will have great love for mysticism and spiritualism.

The 7th Moon also denotes conflict between the native's wife and mother, adverse effects in milk trade. Disobedience towards mother will cause overall tensions and troubles.

Remedies

1. Avoid marriage in the 24th year of your life.
2. Always your mother keep happy.
3. Never sell milk or water for profit.
4. Do not burn milk for making Khoya.
5. Ensure that in marriage your wife brings silver and rice with her from her parents, equal to her weight.

Moon in 8th House

This house belongs to Mars and Saturn. The Moon here affects the education of the native adversely, but if education goes well the native's mother's life will be shortened and very often such a native loses both—education and the mother. However, the evil effects of the Moon in the 7th house will be mitigated if Jupiter and Saturn be placed in the 2nd house.

The 7th Moon often deprives the native of his parental properties. If there is a well or pond adjacent to the parental property of the native, he will receive adverse results of the Moon all through his life.

Remedies

1. Avoid gambling and flirting.
2. Perform Shraddha ceremony for to your ancestors.
3. Do not build any house after covering a well with roof.
4. Obtain blessings of the old men and children by touching their feet.
5. Bring water from the well or water tap situated within the boundaries of a cremation ground and place it within your house. It will ward off all the evils generated by the Moon in the 7th house.
6. Offer gram and pulse in places of worship.

Moon in 9th House

The 9th house belongs to Jupiter, who is a great friend of the Moon. Hence the native will imbibe the traits and features of both these planets—good conduct, soft heartedness, religious bent of mind and love for virtuous acts and pilgrimage. He will live upto 75 years. A friendly planet in the 5th house will augment comforts and pleasures from the son and develops intense interest in religious deeds. A friendly planet in the 3rd house ensures great increase in money and wealth.

Remedies

1. Install the things associated with the Moon within the house, e.g., place a square piece of silver in the almirah.
2. Serve the labourers with milk.
3. Offer milk to snakes and rice to fish.

Moon in 10th House

The 10th house is in every manner ruled by Saturn. This house is expected by the 4th house, which is similarly ruled by Moon. Hence the Moon in the 10th house ensures a long life of about 90 years for the native. Moon and Saturn are inimical; therefore, medicines in liquid form will always prove harmful to him. The milk will act as poison if taken during night. If he is a medical practitioner, dry medicines administered by him to the patient will have a magical effect for cure. If a surgeon, he will earn great wealth and fame for surgery. If the 2nd and 4th houses are empty money and wealth will rain on him.

If Saturn is placed in the 1st house, the native's life will be destroyed by the opposite sex, especially a widow.

The things and business represented by Saturn will prove beneficial for the native.

Remedies

1. Visits to religious places of worship will enhance the fortune of the native.
2. Store the natural water of rain or the river in a container and keep it within your house for 15 years. It will wash off the poisons and evil effects generated by the Moon in the 10th house.
3. Avoid taking milk during night.
4. Milch animals can neither live long in your house nor will they prove beneficial or auspicious.
5. Abstain from wine, meat and adultery.

Moon in 11th house

This house is strongly influenced by Jupiter and Saturn. Every planet placed in this house will destroy its inimical planets and the things associated with them. In this way the Moon here will destroy its enemy Ketu's things, i.e., the sons of the native. Here the Moon will have to face the combined power of its enemies Saturn and Ketu, which will weaken the Moon. Now if Ketu is placed in the 4th house, the life of the native's mother will be endangered.

The business associated with Mercury will also prove harmful. Starting house construction or purchase of a house on Saturdays will strengthen the Saturn (the Moon's enemy) which will prove disastrous for the native. Kanyadan after the midnight and participating in any marriage ceremony on Fridays will damage the fortunes of the native.

Remedies

1. Offer milk in Bhairo Mandir and donate milk to others liberally.
2. Ensure that the grandmother does not see her grandson.
3. Heat up a piece of gold in fire and put it in a glass of milk before drinking it.
4. Throw 125 pieces of sweet (Peda) in a river.

Moon in 12th house

This house belongs to Moon's friend Jupiter. Here the Moon will have good effects on Mars and the things associated with Mars, but it will harm its enemies Mercury and Ketu and the things associated with them. Hence the business and things associated with the house in which Mars is placed will provide highly beneficial effects. Similarly, the business and things associated with the houses where Mercury and Ketu are placed will be strongly damaged. The Moon in the 12th houses causes a general fear in the native's mind about numerous unforeseen troubles and dangers and thus destroys his sleep and peace of mind. Ketu in the 4th house will become weak and affect the native's son and mother very adversely.

Remedies

1. Wearing Gold in ears, drinking milk after inserting hot piece of gold in it and visiting religious places of worship will ward off the evils of the Moon in 12th house and also that of the Ketu in the 4th house.
2. Never offer milk and food to religious saints/sadhus.
3. Do not open a school, college or any other educational institute and do not help children in obtaining free of cost education.

GEM FOR PLANET MOON

MOON	PEARL	WHITE

REMEDIES OF PLANETS

PLANET

MARS

Effects and Remedies

Mars is a dry, red and fiery planet. Masculine by nature it signifies energy, both constructive and destructive depending upon his position as Mars positive and Mars negative. If Sun and Mercury are placed together in one house, Mars would be positive but if Saturn and Sun are placed in one house Mars becomes negative.

Mars acts on the extremes—either soft like a wax or hard like a stone. The Sun, Moon and Jupiter are his friends, whereas Mercury and Ketu are his enemies. Rahu and Saturn are neutral to Mars. The first cycle of Mars runs between the ages 28 and 33, the 2nd between 63 and 68 years and the 3rd between 98 and 103 years. The 1st and 8th houses are the own houses of Mars and he gets exalted in the 10th house of his debilitation.

Mars acts as a malefic in the 4th and 8th houses, but he is benefic if placed in the 1, 2, 3, 5, 6, 7, 9, 10, 11 and 12th houses.

Mars is the signification of sex, brothers, land and property and rules over the animal instincts in man. A benefic Mars offers self-confidence, sharp wit, faculty of argumentation and adventurous spirit, strong determination and qualities of leadership in all human pursuits. On the contrary, a weak and afflicted Mars makes the native lose temper quickly, fool hardy, quarrelsome and brutal. Such a Mars makes the native a sexual pervert.

The general effects remedial measures of Mars can be delineated as follows:

Mars in IST House

Mars in the 1st house makes the native good natured, truthful and richer from the 28th year of age. He wins favours from the government and victory against the enemies without much effort. He earns large profits from the business associated with Saturn i.e., iron, wood, machinery etc. and the relatives represented by Saturn i.e., nephews, grandsons, uncles etc.

Spontaneous curses from the mouth of such a native will never go waste. Association of Saturn with Mars provides physical trouble to the native.

Remedies

1. Avoid the acceptance of things free of cost or in charity.
2. Avoid evil deeds and telling lies.
3. Association with saints and Faqirs will prove very harmful.
4. Things of ivory will give very adverse effects. Avoid them.

Mars in 2nd House

The native with Mars in the 2nd house is generally the eldest issue of his parents, or else he or she would always like to be treated so. But living and behaving like a younger brother would prove highly beneficial and ward off several evils automatically. Mars in this house provides great wealth and properties from the in-laws' family. Mars negative here makes the native a snake in disguise for others and causes his death in war or quarrels.

Mars with Mercury in the 2nd house weakens the will power and undermines the importance of the native.

Remedies

1. The business associated with Moon, e.g., trade in cloth, will provide great prosperity, and hence strengthen Moon.
2. Ensure that your in-laws make arrangements for providing drinking water facilities to the common people.
3. Keep deerskin in the house.

Mars in 3rd House

The 3rd house is affected by Mars and Mercury, who provide brothers and sisters to the native i.e., he will not be the only issue of his parents. Others will be highly benefited from the native, but he will not be able to receive benefit from others. Humbleness will bring rewards. In-laws will become richer and richer after the native's marriage. The native believes in the principle "eat, drink and be merry" and suffers from blood disorders.

Remedies

1. Be soft hearted and avoid arrogance. Be good to brothers for prosperity.
2. Keep articles of ivory with you.
3. Put on silver ring in the left hand.

Mars in 4th House

The 4th house is overall the property of Moon. The fire and heat of Mars in this house burns the cold water of Moon i.e., the properties of the Moon are adversely affected. The native loses peace of mind and suffers from jealousy to others. He always misbehaves with his younger brothers. The native's evil mission gets strong destructive powers. Such a native affects the life of his mother, wife, mother-in-law etc very adversely. His anger becomes the cause of his overall destruction in various aspects of life.

Remedies

1. Offer sweet milk to the roots of a banyan tree and put that wet soil on your navel.
2. To avoid havoc from fire, place empty bags of sugar on the roof of your house, shop or factory.
3. Always keep a square piece of silver with you.
4. Keep away from black, one-eyed or disabled person.

Mars in 5th House

The 5th house belongs to the Sun, who is a natural friend of Mars. Hence Mars ensures very good results in this house. The sons of the native become instruments of wealth and fame for him. His prosperity increases manifold after the birth of sons. The things and relatives represented by Venus and Moon will prove beneficial in every manner. Someone of his forefathers must have been a doctor or Vaidya.

The prosperity of the native will continue to grow more and more with the growth in age. But romance and emotional affairs with the opposite sex will prove highly disastrous for the native, which will destroy his mental peace and night sleep too.

Remedies

1. Maintain a good moral character.
2. Keep water in a pot below the head side of your bed at night and drop it in a flowerpot in the morning.
3. Offer Shraddha to your ancestors and plant a Neem tree in the house.

Mars in 6th House

This house belongs to Mercury and Ketu. Both are mutual enemies and inimical to Mars also. Hence Mars in this house will keep himself away from both. The native will be courageous, adventurous, lover of justice and powerful enough to set fire into water. He will be highly benefited by the trade and business associated with Mercury. His pen will wield more power than the sword.

If Sun, Saturn and Mars are placed together in one house, the brothers, mother, sisters and wife will be affected very adversely.

Remedies

1. Distribute salt in place of sweets on the birth of a male child.
2. His brothers should keep the native happy by offering him something or the other for their protection and prosperity.

But if he does not accept such things, the same should be thrown in water.

3. The male children of the native should not wear gold.
4. Adopt remedies of Saturn for family comfort. Worship

Ganeshji for parents' health and destruction of enemies.

Mars in 7th House

This house belongs to the influences of Venus and Mercury, who combined together provide the effect of Sun. If Mars is placed therein, the 7th house will be affected by Sun and Mars both, which ensures that the native's ambition will be fulfilled. Wealth, property and family will increase.

But if Mercury is also placed here along with Mars, very adverse results will follow regarding the things and relations represented by Mercury e.g., sister, sister-in-law, nurses, maid servant, parrot, goats etc. Hence it would be better to keep away from them.

Remedies

1. Place solid piece of silver in the house for prosperity.
2. Always offer sweets to daughter, sister, sister-in-law and widows.
3. Repeatedly build a small wall and destroy it.

Mars in 8th House

The 8th house belongs to Mars and Saturn, who jointly influence the properties of this house. No planet is considered good in this house. Mars here affects very adversely the younger brothers of the native. The native sticks to commitments made by him without caring for profit or loss.

Remedies

1. Obtain blessings of widows and wear a silver chain.
2. Offer sweet loaves of bread prepared on Tandoor to dogs.
3. Take your meals in the kitchen.
4. Build a small dark room at the end of your house and do not allow sunlight to enter it.
5. Offer rice, jaggery and gram pulse at religious places of worship.
6. Fill an earthen pot with 'Deshi Khand' and bury it near a cremation ground.

Mars in 9th House

This house belongs to Jupiter, a friend of Mars. Mars placed in this house will prove good in every manner to the native by virtue of the help and blessings of the elders. His brother's wife proves very fortunate for him. Generally he will have as many brothers as his father had. Living with brothers in a joint family will enhance all round happiness. The native will gain a highly prestigious administrative post upto the 28th year of his age. He may earn large profits in the trade of goods associated with warfare.

Remedies

1. Obedience to elder brother.
2. Render services to your Bhabhi i.e., brother's wife.
3. Do not become an atheist and follow your traditional customs and rituals.
4. Offer rice, milk and jaggery at religious places of worship.

Mars in 10th House

This is the best position of Mars in a horoscope, the place of his exaltation. If the native is born in a poor family, his family will become rich and affluent after his birth. If he is born in a rich family, his family will grow richer and richer after his birth. If the native is the eldest brother he will gain a more distinct recognition and reputation in society. He will be bold, courageous, healthy and competent enough to set traditions, norms and rules in society. However, if malefic planets Rahu, Ketu and Saturn or Venus and Moon are placed in the 2nd house, the aforesaid beneficial effects are reduced.

Further if a friendly planet is placed in the 3rd house, it will also affect the results of Mars in the 10th house adversely. If Saturn is placed in the 3rd house, the native will gain huge wealth and large properties in the later part of his life along with a kingly position. Mars in the 10th house but no planet in the 5th house provides all round prosperity and happiness.

Remedies

1. Do not sell ancestral property and gold of the house.
2. Keep a pet deer in your house.
3. While boiling milk, please ensure that it should not overflow and fall on the fire.
4. Offer help to one-eyed and childless persons.

Mars in 11th House

Mars gives good results in this house, because this house is influenced by Jupiter and Saturn. If Jupiter is in exalted position, Mars gives very good results. Native is courageous and just and usually a trader.

Remedies

1. One should never sell one's ancestral property.
2. Keeping Sindoor or honey in an earthen pot will give good results.

Mars in 12th House

This house is inhabited by Jupiter, so now both Mars and Jupiter will give good results. This is also considered as the "Pukka Ghar" of Rahu, so now Rahu will not trouble the native notwithstanding its position in native's horoscope.

Remedies

1. Take honey the first thing in the morning.
2. Eating sweets and offering sweets to another person will increase the wealth of the native.

GEM FOR PLANET MARS

MARS	CORAL	RED

REMEDIES

MARS

MANGLIK DOSH
AND
MARRIAGE

We often say that he or she is a "Manglik". . . . WHY?
What is Manglik Dosh?

He or she is said to be a "Manglik" if Mars occupies the 1st, 4th, 7th, 8th, or 12th house of the horoscope of the person.

"Manglik Dosh" is present at the time of birth and Mars is considered the most malefic planet as far as Marriage of the native is considered.

A "Manglik Dosh" has been regarded by astrologers since the times immemorial as the worst culprit.

There is exception in this; like in Cancer ascendant mars is a very beneficial planet so it doesn't make any harm etc. Some common Factors about "Manglik Dosh" are:

A person having the "Manglik Dosh" in his or her horoscope can only get married with a person having the same Dosh or in other words a Manglik should only marry a Manglik.

Remedies for Mars:

Sindoor to Lord Hanuman.
Throw in the running water pulse of
Masoor/ Honey.
Sleeping on deerskin.
Pure silver utensils to be used.

REMEDIES OF PLANETS

PLANET

RAHU (DRAGON'S HEAD)

Effects and Remedies

Unlike other planets of the solar system Rahu and Ketu are not observable, substantial heavenly bodies, with shape or mass content. Rightly termed as shadowy planets, their movement is interrelated and as parts of one body they are at all times just opposite to each other. Greater significance has been attached to the role of Rahu influencing human affairs in various dimensions, especially in Kaliyug

The author of Lal Kitab describes Saturn as a serpent and Rahu and Ketu as its head and tail respectively. As a node of moon, Rahu shall not provide adverse results so long as 4th house or moon is not afflicted. He gives good results when Mars occupies houses 3 and 12, or when Sun and Mercury are in house 3, or when he himself is posited in 4th house. Rahu further provides good results if placed together with Mercury or expected by him.

Rahu offers highly beneficial effects if placed in houses earlier than Saturn. But if it is otherwise, Saturn becomes stronger and Rahu acts as his agent. Sun provides very good results when Rahu is expected by Saturn, but Rahu gives the effects of a debilitated planet when Saturn is expected by Rahu.

Rahu gets exalted in houses 3 and 6, whereas he gets debilitated in houses 8, 9 and 11. 12th house is his 'Pakka Ghar' and he proves highly auspicious in houses 3,4 and 6. Saturn, Mercury and Ketu are his friends, whereas Sun, Mars and Venus are his enemies. Jupiter and moon are neutral to him.

If Sun and Venus are placed together in a horoscope, Rahu will generally provide adverse results. Similarly, Rahu will provide bad results if Saturn and Sun are also combined in a horoscope.

Here Mars will also become Mars negative. If Ketu is placed in houses earlier than Rahu, Rahu will provide adverse results, whereas Ketu's effect would be zeroed.

Rahu in 1st House

1st house is influenced by Mars and Sun, which is like a throne. The planet in 1st house is considered to be the king of all planets.

The native will achieve a position higher than indicated by his qualification and will obtain good results from government. Rahu in this house would give the result of exalted Sun, but it will spoil the fruits of the house in which Sun is placed. If Mars, Saturn and Ketu are weak only then Rahu would give bad results, otherwise it will give good results in 1st house. If Rahu is malefic the native should never take any electric equipments or blue/black clothes from his in-laws, else his son could be affected adversely. Its malefic result too could last till the age of 42 years.

Remedies

1. Offer 400 gm lead in running water.
2. Wear silver in the neck.
3. Mix barley in milk in ratio of 1:4 and offer in running water.
4. Offer coconut in running water.

Rahu in 2nd House

If Rahu is in benefic form in 2nd house one gets money, prestige and lives like a king. He will have a long life. 2nd house is influenced by Jupiter and Venus. If Jupiter is benefic then the native will live the early years of his life in wealth and comfort. If Rahu is malefic the native will be poor and have a bad family life, suffer from intestinal disorders. The native is killed by a weapon and is unable to save money. In the 10th, 21st to 42nd years of his life, he loses wealth by theft etc.

Remedies

1. Keep a solid silver ball in the pocket.
2. Wear things associated with Jupiter, like gold, yellow cloth, saffron etc.
3. Keep cordial relations with ones mother.
4. After marriage do not take any electric equipment from in-laws.

Rahu in 3rd House

It is the 'Pukka Ghar' of Rahu. 3rd house belongs to Mercury and is influenced by Mars. When Rahu is benefic the native will enjoy great wealth and a long life. He will be fearless and a loyal friend. He would be a clairvoyant for seeing future in his dreams. He will never be issueless. He will be victorious over his enemies; can never be a debtor. He would leave behind property. 22nd year of his life would be of progress. However if Rahu is malefic in 3rd house then his brothers and relatives would waste his money. His money once borrowed would never be returned. He would have defective speech and would be an atheist. If Sun and Mercury are also there (in 3rd house) with Rahu then his sister would become a widow in 22nd or 32nd year of his life.

Remedies

1. Never keep ivory or things of ivory in the house.

Rahu in 4th House

This house belongs to moon, which is an enemy of Rahu. When Rahu is benefic in this house the native would be intelligent, wealthy and will spend money on good things. Going on pilgrimage would be beneficial for him. If Venus is also benefic then after marriage the native's in-laws could also become rich and the native would also benefit from them.

When Moon is exalted the native would become very rich and would benefit from the works or relatives associated with Mercury. If Rahu is malefic and the Moon is also weak then the native will suffer from poverty and native's mother would also suffer. Collecting charcoal, altering toilet, installing oven in the ground and alteration of the roof in the house would be indicative of malefic.

Remedies

1. Wear silver.
2. Offer 400 gm coriander or almonds, or both in flowing water.

Rahu in 5th House

5th house belongs to Sun, which signifies male offspring. If Rahu is benefic native will be rich, wise, enjoy good health. He would enjoy good income and good progress. The native would be a devout or philosopher. If Rahu is malefic it leads to abortions. After the birth of a son, wife's health will suffer for twelve years. If Jupiter is also in 5th housefather of native will be in trouble.

Remedies

1. Keep an elephant made of silver.
2. Abstain from wine, non-vegetarianism and adultery.
3. Remarry your wife.

Rahu in 6th House (Exalted)

This house is influenced by Mercury or Ketu. Here Rahu is exalted and gives very good results. The native will be free of all botheration or troubles. The native will spend money on clothes. The native will be intelligent and victorious. When Rahu is malefic he will harm his brothers or friends. When mercury or Mars is in 12th house Rahu gives bad result. The native suffers from various ailments or loss of wealth. Sneezing while going to work would give bad results.

Remedies

1. Keep a black dog.
2. Keep a lead nail in your pocket.
3. Never harm ones brothers/sisters.

Rahu in 7th House

Native will be rich, but wife would suffer. He would be victorious over his enemies. If the marriage takes place before twenty one years, it would be inauspicious. He would have good relations with the government. But if he engages in business connected with Rahu, like electrical equipments, then he will have losses.

Native would suffer from headache and if Mercury, Venus or Ketu is in 11th house, then sister, wife or son would destroy the native.

Remedies

1. Never marry before 21st year of age.
2. Offer six coconuts in river.

Rahu in 8th House

8th house is concerned with Saturn and Mars. So Rahu in this house gives malefic effect. The native would spend money uselessly on court cases. Family life would be adversely affected. If Mars is benefic and is placed in 1st or 8th house or Saturn (benefic) is placed in 8th house, the native will be very rich.

Remedies

1. Keep a square piece of silver.
2. While sleeping Saunf should be keep under the pillow.
3. Do not work in electricity or power department.

Rahu in 9th House

9th house is influenced by Jupiter. If the native has good relation with ones brothers and sisters it is fruitful; else it would adversely affect the native. If the native is not religious minded then his progeny would be useless for him. Professions influenced by Saturn would be profitable.

If Jupiter is in 5th or 11th house then it is useless. If Rahu is inauspicious in 9th house then chances of begetting a son are less, especially if native files court cases against one's blood relation. Rahu is in 9th and 1st house is empty then health could be adversely affected and one gets insulted and mental problems, especially from olders.

Remedies

1. Use Tilak of saffron daily.
2. Wear gold.
3. Always keep a dog (it saves ones progeny).
4. Have good relations with your in-laws.

Rahu in 10th House

Keeping ones head uncovered gives the effect of a debilitated Rahu in 10th house. The good or bad result of Rahu would depend upon Saturn's position. If Saturn is auspicious then native would be brave, long-lived and rich and get respect from all quarters. If Rahu in 10th house is with Moon it gives Raja Yoga. The native is lucky for ones father. If Rahu in 10th house is malefic then it would adversely affect ones mother or native's health would also be bad. If Moon is alone in 4th house then native's eyes are adversely affected. He suffers from headaches and there is loss of wealth, because of a dark complexioned person.

Remedies

1. Use blue or black cap.
2. Cover ones head.
3. Offer 4kg. Or 400 Gms of 'khand' in a temple, or in flowing water.
4. Feed blind people.

Rahu in 11th House

11th house is influenced by both Saturn and Jupiter. Native could be rich as long as his father is alive. Alternatively, establishing things of Jupiter would help. Native has wicked friends. He gets money from mean people. After the death of ones father he should wear gold in the neck. If Mars is malefic for a native with Rahu in 11th at time of his birth, there is every thing in his house, but every thing gets destroyed later. If Rahu in 11th house is malefic then the native has bad relations with his father or he may even kill him. Planet in 2nd house would act as enemy. If Jupiter/Saturn is in 3rd or 11th house then wear iron on the body and drink water in a silver glass. If ketu is in 5th house then Ketu gives bad results. There may be diseases of ear, spine, urinary problems etc. There may be losses associated with business concerned with Ketu.

Remedies

1. Wear iron. Use silver glass for drinking water.
2. Never take any electric equipment as a gift.
3. Do not keep blue sapphire, ivory or toys in the shape of an elephant.

Rahu in 12th House

12th house belongs to Jupiter. It signifies bedroom. Rahu here gives mental troubles, insomnia. It also leads to excessive expenditure on sisters and daughters. If Rahu is with its enemies then it becomes next to impossible to make ends meet, despite hard labour. It also leads to false allegations. One may even go to the extreme of contemplating suicide. One has mental worries. Telling lies, deceiving others etc. may make Rahu even more malefic. If some body sneezes at the start of any new work if gives malefic effect. There may be theft, diseases or false allegations. If mars is with Rahu here, then it gives good results.

Remedies

1. Take your meals in the kitchen itself.
2. Keep Saunf and khand under the pillow for good night's sleep.

GEM FOR RAHU

RAHU	GOMED	MAROON

REMEDIES OF PLANETS

PLANET

JUPITER

Effects and Remedies

Jupiter is a fiery, noble, benevolent, masculine, expansive, optimistic, positive and dignified planet. higher attributes of the mind and soul, generosity, joy, jubilation and joviality along with high reasoning ability and the power of right judgments are all governed by Jupiter.

Jupiter rules educational interests, law, religion, philosophy, banking, and economics and indicates the extent of one's love and longing for religion, scriptures, elders and preceptors. He is also a signification of wealth, progress, philosophic nature, good conduct, health and children. Jupiter represents 'Thursday' and the yellow color. He is regarded as 'Karaka' for 2nd, 5th and 9th houses. The sun, mars and moon are his friends, where as Mercury and Venus are enemies to him. Rahu, Ketu and Saturn adopt neutrality to him. He stands exalted in the 4th house and the 10th house is the house of his debilitation.

Jupiter provides good results if placed in houses 1, 5, 8, 9 and 12, but 6th, 7th and the 10th are the bad houses for him. Jupiter gives bad results when Venus or Mercury get placed in the 10th house of a horoscope. However, Jupiter never gives bad results if placed alone in any house. A malefic Jupiter affects the Ketu (son) very adversely. Jupiter offers malefic results if he is placed with Saturn, Rahu or Ketu in a horoscope.

Jupiter in 1st House

Jupiter in the Ist house makes the native necessarily rich, even if he is deprived of learning and education. He will be healthy and never afraid of enemies. He will rise every 8th year of his life through his own efforts and with the help of friends in the government.

If the 7th house is not occupied by any planet success and prosperity will come after the marriage of the native. Marriage or construction of a house with one's own earnings in the 24th or 27th year would prove inauspicious for the longevity of the father's life. Jupiter in Ist house along with the Saturn in the 9th house causes health problems for the native. Jupiter in the Ist house and Rahu in the 8th cause the death of the native's father because of heart attack or asthma.

Remedies

1. Offer the things of mercury, Venus and Saturn to the religious places.
2. Serving cows and helping untouchables.

3. If Saturn is placed in the 5th house, don't build a house.
4. If Saturn is placed in the 9th house, don't buy machinery associated with Saturn.
5. If Saturn is in 11th or 12th house avoid use wine, meat and eggs strictly.
6. Ward-off the evil effects of mercury by putting on silver in the nose

Jupiter in 2nd House

The results of this house are affected by Jupiter and Venus as if they are together in this house, though Venus may be placed anywhere in the chart. Venus and Jupiter are inimical to each other. Hence both will affect each other adversely. Consequently, if the native engages himself in the trade of gold or jewellery, then the things of Venus like wife, wealth and property will get destroyed.

As long as the wife of the native is with him, the native will continue gaining honour and wealth despite the fact that his wife and her family may be suffering because of ill health and other problems. The native is admired by females and inherits the property of his father. He may be benefited by lottery or property of a person having no issues, if the 2nd, 6th and 8th houses are auspicious and Saturn is not placed in the 10th.

Remedies

1. Charity and donations will ensure prosperity.
2. Offer milk to snakes for warding off the evils of Saturn placed in the 10th.
3. Fill up the pits if any on the road side, in front of your house.

Jupiter in 3rd House

The Jupiter in the 3rd house makes the native learned and rich, who receives continuous income from the government all through his life. Saturn in the 9th makes the native live long, whereas if Saturn is placed in the 2nd the native becomes extremely clever and crafty.

However Saturn is the 4th indicates that the native will be robbed of money and wealth by his friends. If Jupiter is accompanied by inimical planets in the 3rd the native is destroyed and becomes a liability on his closer ones.

Remedies

1. Worship of Goddess Durga and offering sweets and fruits to small girls and obtaining their blessing by touching their feet. Avoid sycophants.

Jupiter in 4th House

The 4th house belongs to Moon, a friend of Jupiter, who stands exalted in this house. Hence Jupiter here gives very good results and provides the native the powers of deciding the fate and fortune of others. He will possess money, wealth and large properties along with honour and favours from the government. In times of crisis the native will receive divine help. As he grows old his prosperity and money will increase. How so ever if he has built a temple at home Jupiter will not give the above-mentioned results and the native will have to face poverty and disturbed married life.

Remedies

1. The native should not keep a temple in his house.
2. He should serve his elders.
3. He should offer milk to snake.
4. He should never bare his body before anyone.

Jupiter in 5th House

This house belongs to Jupiter and sun. Native's prosperity will increase after the birth of his son. In fact, more sons a native has, the more prosperous he will become. 5th house is the own house of Surya and in this house Surya, Ketu and Brihaspati will give mixed results. However if Mercury, Venus and Rahu is in 2nd, 9th, 11th or 12th houses then

Jupiter sun and Ketu will give bad results. If the native is honest and laborious then Jupiter will give good results.

Remedies

1. Do not accept any donations or gifts.
2. Offers your services to priests and sadhus.

Jupiter in 6th House

6th house belongs to Mercury and Ketu also has its effect on this house. so this house will give combined effects of Mercury, Jupiter and ketu. If Jupiter is benefic the native will be of pious nature. He will get everything in life without asking. Donations and offerings in the name of elders will prove beneficial. If Jupiter is in 6th and Ketu is benefic then native will become selfish. However, if Ketu is malefic in 6th house and mercury is also malefic the native will be unlucky up to 34 years of age. Here Jupiter causes asthma to the native's father

Remedies

1. Offer things connected with Jupiter in a temple.
2. Feed the cocks.
3. Offer clothes to the priest.

Jupiter in 7th House

7th house belongs to Venus, so it will give mixed results. The native will have rise in luck after marriage and native will be involved in religious works. The good result of the house will depend upon position of moon. The native will never be a debtor and will have good children. And if the sun is also in 1st house the native will be a good astrologer and lover of comforts.

However if Jupiter is malefic in 7th house and Saturn is in the 9th the native will become a thief. If mercury is in the 9th then his married life will be full of problems. If Jupiter is malefic native will never get support from brothers and will be deprived of favours from the government. Jupiter in 7th house causes differences with the father. If so one should never donate clothes to anyone, otherwise one will certainly get reduced to extreme poverty.

Remedies

1. Offer worship to lord Shiva.
2. One should not keep idols of god in ones house.
3. Keep gold tied in a yellow cloth always with you.
4. One should stay away from yellow clad sadhus and faqirs.

Jupiter in 8th House

Jupiter does not give good results in this house, but one will get all the worldly comforts. In the time of distress, one will get help from god. Being religious will increase native's luck. As long as the native is wearing gold he will not be unhappy or ill. If there is Mercury, Venus or Rahu in 2nd, 5th, 9th, 11th and 12th house, native's father will be ill and native himself will face loss of prestige.

Remedies

1. Offer things connected with Rahu, like wheat, barley, coconut into running water.
2. Plant a pipal tree in a cremation ground.
3. Offer ghee and potatoes and camphor in temple.

Jupiter in 9th House

9th house is especially influenced by Jupiter. So the native will be famous, rich and will be born in a rich family. The native will be true to his words and will have long life and have good children. In case Jupiter is malefic the native will have none of these qualities and will be atheistic. If the native has any planet inimical to Jupiter in the 1st, 5th and 4th house then Jupiter will give bad results.

Remedies

1. One should go to temple everyday
2. Abstain from drinking alcohol.
3. Offer rice to running water.

Jupiter in 10th House

This house belongs to Saturn. So the native will have to imbibe the qualities of Saturn only then he will be happy. The good results of Jupiter. If sun is in the 4th house Jupiter will give very good results. Venus and Mars in the 4th house ensure multi-marriages for the native. If friendly planets are placed in the 2nd, 4th and 6th houses, Jupiter provides highly beneficial results in matters of money and wealth. A malefic Jupiter in the 10th makes the native sad and impoverished. He is deprived of ancestral properties, wife and children.

Remedies

1. Clean your nose before beginning any work.
2. Throw copper coins in the running water of a river for 43 days.
3. Offer almonds to religious places.
4. A temple with idols must not be established within the house.
5. Put tilak of saffron on the forehead.

Jupiter in 11th House

Jupiter in this house affects the things and relatives of his enemies Mercury, Venus and Rahu very adversely. Consequently, the wife of the native will remain miserable. Similarly, sisters, daughters and father's sisters will also remain unhappy. The native will be a debtor even if mercury is well placed. The native will be comfortable only as long as his father lives with him in a joint family along with brothers, sisters and mother.

Remedies

1. Always keep gold on your body.
2. Put on a copper bangle.
3. Watering a pipal tree would prove beneficial.

Jupiter in 12th House

The 12th house would provide the combined influences of Jupiter and Rahu, who are inimical to each other. If the native observes good conduct, wishes good for all and observes religious practices he will become happy and enjoy a comfortable sleep at night. He would become wealthy and powerful. Abstaining from evil acts of Saturn will make the business of machinery, motor, trucks and cars highly beneficial to him.

Remedies

1. Avoid furnishing false evidence in any matter.
2. Render services to sadhus, pipal gurus and pipal tree.
3. Place water and Saunf on the head side of your bed during nights.

GEM FOR JUPITER

JUPITER	YELLOW SAPPHIRE/TOPAZ	YELLOW

REMEDIES OF PLANTS

PLANET

SATURN

Effects and Remedies

As the slowest moving planet and the chief signification for longevity, Saturn is a barren, binding, cold, dry, hard, defensive and secretive planet. Its effects and influences are felt with greater intensity and for longer periods than any other planet. Saturn is considered to be very favorable for people born in the signs owned by Venus, whereas Saturn is evil to those born in the signs owned by Mercury.

The astrological thesis describes Saturn as a serpent, whose head or mouth is Rahu and Ketu is its tail. If ketu is posited in earlier houses than Saturn, the latter becomes a great benefic for the native. However, if the position is otherwise, the Saturn throws highest poisonous results on the native. Further, Saturn never gives malefic effects if posited in houses of Jupiter i.e. 2, 5, 9 or 12, whereas Jupiter provides bad results if posited in the house of Saturn.

Saturn is considered good in houses 2nd, 3rd and 7th to 12th, whereas 1st, 4th, 5th and 6th houses are bad for Saturn. Sun, Moon and Mars are its enemies, Venus, Mercury and Rahu are friends and Jupiter and Ketu are neutral to it. Saturn gets exalted in 7th house and the 1st house is the house of its debilitation. Venus and Jupiter placed together act like Saturn in that house. Similarly Mars and Mercury placed in a single house act like Saturn in that house. In the former case Saturn behaves like Ketu, while in the latter case it behaves like Rahu.

Venus gets destroyed if Saturn is being expected by the Sun in any horoscope. The aspect of Venus on Saturn causes loss of money and wealth, but the aspect of Saturn on Venus proves highly beneficial. Collision of Saturn and Moon causes operation of the eyes of the native. Saturn gives good results if posited in house earlier than sun.

Saturn can never give malefic results if posited with Sun or Jupiter in a single house, but highly adverse results would follow if posited with Moon or Mars in any house. Saturn releases its poisonous results on the sign and Mars, if it is posited in 1st house, on Mars only if posited in 3rd house, on moon if posited in 4th house, on sun if posited in 5th house, and on Mars in posited in 3rd house. Saturn in 3rd house deprives the native of the accumulation of cash money and kills the children of the native when posited in 5th house and 10th house is empty. It becomes highly benefic in 12th house if friendly planets are posited in 2nd house. Saturn provides very good results if placed in houses 1 to 7 on the condition that 10th house is empty. Saturn in 1st house and sun in 7th, 10th or 11th houses causes all sorts of troubles for native's wife. Combination of Mars and Saturn gives adverse results al through.

Saturn in IST House

1st house is influenced by Sun and Mars. Saturn in 1st house will give good results only when 3rd, 7th or 10th houses are not inhabited by any planet which is inimical to Saturn. If Mercury or Venus, Rahu or Ketu is in 7th house, Saturn will always give good results. In case Saturn is malefic and the native has a hairy body, the native will remain poor. If native celebrates his birthday it will give very bad results however the native will have a long life.

Remedies

1. Abstinence from alcohol and non-vegetarian meals.
2. Burying Surma in the ground will be beneficial for promotion in service and business.
3. Serving monkey will lead to prosperity.
4. Offering sweet milk to the roots of a banyan tree will give good results as regards education and health.

Saturn in 2nd House

The native will be wise, kind and just. He will enjoy wealth and will be of religious temperament. However, whether Saturn is benefic or malefic in this house, it will be decided by the planets placed in 8th house. The state of finance of the native will be decided by 7th house, the number of male members in the family by 6th house and age by 8th house. When Saturn is malefic in this house, after the native's marriage his in laws will face problems.

Remedies

1. Going barefoot to temple for forty three days.
2. Putting a tilak of curd or milk on the forehead.
3. Offering milk to snake.

Saturn in 3rd House

In this house Saturn gives good results. This house is the pukka Ghar of Mars. When Ketu aspects this house or is placed here Saturn will give very good results. The native will be healthy, wise and very intuitive. If the native is wealthy he will have few male members in the family and vice versa. As long as the native abstains from wine and non-vegetarianism, he will enjoy a long and healthy life.

Remedies

1. Serve three dogs.
2. Distributing medicines for eyes free.
3. Keeping a dark room in the house will prove highly beneficial.

Saturn in 4th House

This house belongs to Moon. So it will give mixed results in this house. The native will be devoted to his parents and will be of loving nature. Whenever the native is suffering from bad health, the use of things associated with Saturn will give good results. In native's family some one will be associated with medical profession.

When Saturn is malefic in this house drinking wine, killing of snakes and laying the foundation of the house at night will give very bad results. Drinking milk in the night will also give bad results.

Remedies

1. Offering milk to snake and offering milk or rice to crow or buffalo.
2. Pouring milk in the well.
3. Pouring rum in running water.

Saturn in 5th House

This house belongs to Sun, which is inimical to Saturn. The native will be proud. He should not construct a house till 48 years, otherwise his son will suffer. He should live in the house bought or constructed by his son. He should keep articles of Jupiter and Mars in his ancestral house for welfare of his children. If the native has hairy body, he will be dishonest.

Remedies

1. Distributing salty things while celebrating son's birthday.
2. Offering almonds in the temple and bringing and keeping half of it in the house.

Saturn in 6th House

If the work related to Saturn is done at night it will always give beneficial results. When marriage takes place after 28 years it will produce good results. When Ketu is well placed the native will enjoy wealth, profitable journey and happiness from children. When Saturn is malefic bringing things associated with Saturn, like leather and things of iron, will give bad results, especially when Saturn is in 6th house in Varsha phal

Remedies

1. Serving a black dog and offering meals to it.
2. Offering coconut and almonds in the running water.
3. Serving snakes will prove advantageous for the welfare of children.

Saturn in 7th House

This house is influenced by Mercury and Venus, both friends of Saturn. So this planet gives very good results in this house. The professions associated with Saturn, like machinery and iron, will be very profitable. If the native maintains good relation with his wife, he will be rich and prosperous; will enjoy a long life and good health. If Jupiter is in 1st house, there will be gain from government.

Saturn becomes malefic if the native commits adultery and drinks wine. If the native gets married after 22 years his eyesight will be affected adversely.

Remedies

1. Bury a flute filled with sugar in a deserted place.
2. Serving black cow.

Saturn in 8th House

In 8th house no planet is considered auspicious. The native has a long life, but his father's life span is short and native's brothers turn out to be his foes. This house is considered headquarter of Saturn, but it will give bad result if Mercury, Rahu and Ketu are malefic in the native's horoscope.

Remedies

1. Keeping a square piece of silver.
2. Putting milk in water and sitting on a stone or wood while taking bath.

Saturn in 9th House

Native will have three houses. He will be a successful tour operator or civil engineer. He will enjoy a long and happy life and parents also will have a happy life. Maintaining three generations will protect from the bad effects of Saturn. if the native is helpful to others Saturn will always give good results. The native will have a son, though he will be born late.

Remedies

1. Offering rice or almonds in running water.
2. Work associated with Jupiter-gold, kesar and Moon (silver cloth) will give good results.

Saturn in 10th House

This is Saturn's own house, where it will give good results. The native will enjoy wealth and property as long as he does not get a house constructed. Native will be ambitious and enjoy favours from government. The native should behave with shrewdness and should do his work while sitting at one place, only then he will enjoy the benefits of Saturn.

Remedies

1. Going to temple.
2. Abstinence from meat, wine and eggs.
3. Offering food to ten blind people.

Saturn in 11th House

Native's fate will be decided at the age of forty eight years. The native will never remain childless. Native will earn money by shrewdness and deceit. Saturn will give good or bad results according to the position of Rahu and Ketu

Remedies

1. Before going for an important work place a vessel filled with water and drop oil or wine on earth for forty three days.
2. Abstinence from drinking and maintain good moral character.

Saturn in 12th House

Saturn gives good results in this house. Native will not have enemies. He will have many houses. His family and business will increase. He will be very rich. However Saturn will become malefic if the native starts drinking wine and becomes non-vegetarian, or if the dark room in the house is illuminated.

Remedies

1. Tying twelve almonds in a black cloth and placing it in a iron pot and keeping it in a dark room will give good results.

GEM FOR SATURN

SATURN	NEELAM / BLUE-SAPPHIRE	BLUE

REMEDIES

SATURN'S

SEVEN AND HALF YEAR'S CYCLE
"Shani's-Sade-Sati"

A horoscope is said to be under

"Sade-Sati" effect when the Saturn transits through the 12th, 1st and 2nd house from natal Moon. It is said to be under "Daiya" effect when Saturn Transits over the 4th and 8th house over the natal Moon. The Effect of "Sade-Sati" remain for seven and a half years and that Of "Daiya" remains for two and a half years.

This generally affects health, mental peace and finance.

Generally "Sade-Sati" comes thrice in a horoscope in the lifetime. First in childhood, second in youth and third in old age. First "Sade-Sati" has effect on education & parents. Second "Sade-Sati" has effect on profession finance & family. The last one affects health than anything else.

Remedies of "Sade-Sati"

Generally the best remedy of "Sade-Sati" is to wear an iron ring made of a horseshoe or of a nail from a boat of a river or lake. Their are many other remedies also according to the individual horoscope of a person. "Sade-Sati" is not malefic for all people it is benefic for those people for whom Saturn is a benefic.

After consultation with an astrologer a "Blue Sapphire or Neelam of can be worn to minimize the effect of Saturn

PLANET

Mercury

Effects and Remedies

In astrological parlance Mercury has been understood as an externally variable, vacillating, convertible, neutral and dualistic planet. Mercury reflects the mentality of an individual, governs the reaction to our senses and impressions and rules over the central nervous system. As an intellectual planet it represents intelligence, genius, analytic power and reproducibility.

Mercury is the smallest planet of the solar system. The author of Lal Kitab has compared mercury with a bat, which keeps hanging upside down and pounces upon the face of a child at the first opportunity. The native fails to understand anything and meanwhile the mysterious and mischievous mercury turns the cycle of fortune in the reverse gear.

Mercury produces the effects of the planet or planets it is associated with. Mercury is considered malefic in the 3rd, 8th, 9th and 12th houses. Rahu gives bad results in 1, 5, 7, 8 and 11th houses. If mercury and Rahu both are in their auspicious houses then Mercury causes havoc in the natives houses and produces disastrous result like putting the native behind the bars or creating troubles of the same sort. Mercury is considered auspicious in the 1, 2, 4, 5, 6 and the 7th houses and gives bad results when placed in the 3, 8, 9, 10, 11 and 12th. Its colour is green and moon is its enemy. Sun Venus and Rahu are friends, whereas mars, Saturn, and Ketu are neutral to him. 7th house is the pukka ghar of mercury. It stands exalted in the 6th house and gets debilitated in the 12th house. Affected Venus causes diseases of tooth and nervous system. If mercury is placed alone in any house the native keeps running and wasting time here and there.

Mercury in 1st House

Mercury in 1st house makes the native kind, humorous and diplomatic with administrative skill. Such a native generally lives long and becomes selfish and mischievous by nature having special attraction for non-vegetarian dishes and drinks.

He receives favour from the government and his daughters have royal and luxurious lives. The relatives represented by the house in which sun is placed gain wealth and riches within a little time and he himself will be having many sources of income. If Sun is placed along with Mercury in the 1st house or if the Mercury is expected by Sun the wife of native will come from a rich and noble family and will be good natured. Such a native will be affected by the evil effects of Mars but Sun will never give bad effects.

Rahu and Ketu will have evil effects, which suggests that the in laws and the offspring of the native will be adverse. If mercury is in the 1st house, the native will be adept in the art of influencing others and he will live like a king. Malefic Mercury in the 1st house along with Moon in the 7th house destroy the native because of intoxication.

Remedies

1. Keep away from the things of green colour and sisters in law.
2. Avoid consumption of meet, eggs and liquor.
3. Business that requires your sitting at one place would be more beneficial than the one that requires running around.

Mercury in 2nd House

Mercury in the 2nd house makes the native intelligent self-centred, destroyer of enemies and cheats. He may be able to provide sufficient happiness to his father. He will be rich. The things represented by mars and Venus will prove beneficial to him.

Remedies

1. Abstain from eggs meat and liquor.
2. Association with your sisters in law is harmful.
3. Keeping sheep, goat and parrots as pets is strictly prohibited.

Mercury in 3rd House

Mercury in the 3rd house is not considered good. Mercury is inimical to Mars.

But Mars does not have enmity with mercury. therefore the native could receive benefits from his brother, but he will not be beneficial to his brother or others. By virtue of its aspects of 9th and 11th houses Mercury affects the income and the condition of the father very adversely.

Remedies

1. Clean your teeth with alum everyday.
2. Feed birds and donate a goat.
3. Don't live in a south-facing house.
4. Distribute medicines of asthma.

Mercury in 4th House

The native in the 4th house is considered fortunate, very dear to his mother, good trader and receives favours from the government. However mercury in this house affects the income and health of another person adversely.

Remedies

1. Putting on silver chain for mental peace and golden chain for gaining wealth and property.
2. Putting kesar tilak regularly for 43 days on fore-head.
3. Serving monkeys by offering jaggery.

Mercury in 5th house

Mercury in this house makes the native happy, wealthy and wise. Spontaneous utterances from the mouth of the native will certainly prove true.

It gives very good results if the moon or any male planet is placed in 3rd, 5th, 9th and 11th houses, but if moon and Jupiter are not placed in good houses mercury would provide malefic effects.

Remedies

1. Wear a copper coin in white thread for obtaining riches.
2. Serving cows for the happiness of wife and good luck.
3. A Gou-mukhi house (narrow at the front and wider at the end) would prove highly auspicious where as Sher-mukhi house (wider at the front and narrower at the end) would prove highly disastrous.

Mercury in 6th House

Mercury becomes exalted in the 6th house. The native will be self-made man and will receive benefits from agricultural land, stationery, printing press and trade. Good or evil words from his mouth will never go waste. North facing house will give bad results. Daughter's marriage in the north direction will make her unhappy in every way.

Remedies

1. Burying a bottle filled with Ganga water into the agricultural land.
2. Putting on a silver ring in the left hand of ones wife.
3. Starting any important work in the presence of a girl or daughters, or with flowers in hand proves auspicious.

Mercury in 7th House

In a male horoscope, mercury in the 7th house proves highly beneficial for others for whom the native wishes well. in a female horoscope it produces good result. The pen of the native wields more power then the sword. The sister of the native's wife will prove highly helpful in every matter. If a Moon is placed in the 1st house, overseas journey will be advantageous. Saturn in the 3rd house will make the wife's family very rich.

Remedies

1. Avoid any business in partnership.
2. Avoid speculation.
3. Do not keep relationship with sister in law of spoilt character.

Mercury in 8th House

Mercury gives very bad results in 8th house, but if it is placed along with a male planet it will give good effects of the associated planet. The native lives a hard life, victimized by diseases and during the age 32-34 his income goes down by half. It is more harmful if some planet is placed in the 2nd house. If Rahu is also placed in the same house the native may have to go to jail, may have to be hospitalised or may have to wander from place to place.

Bad results accrue if mars is also placed therein. Mercury here causes disfavour from the government and diseases like blood disorder, eye problem, tooth and vein troubles, as well as big loss in business.

Remedies

1. Get an earthen pot filled with honey and bury it in the cremation ground or deserted area.
2. Place milk or rain water in a container on the roof of the house.
3. Put a ring in the nose of your daughter.

Mercury in 9th House

Mercury provides very bad results in the 9th house also, because this house belongs to Jupiter and Mercury remains inimical to it. It causes continuous mental restlessness and defamation of various types. If moon, Ketu and Jupiter are placed in 1, 3, 6, 7, 9 and 11th houses, mercury does not give very advantageous results.

Remedies

1. Avoid the use of green color.
2. Get yours nose pricked.
3. Offer mushroom filled in an earthen pot to a religious place.
4. Do not accept any Tabeez from any sadhoo or faqir.

Mercury in 10th House

Mercury in the 10th house provides favor from the government. Gives good sources of livelihood. He manages to get his work done in every way. The business of such a native flourishes in a Shermukhi house, but residency in such a house gives very bad result and can be disastrous.

Remedies

1. Consumption of eggs, meat and liquor are strictly prohibited.
2. Offer rice and milk in religious places.

Mercury in 11th House

Mercury in this house gives bad results, because of enmity to Jupiter. At the age of 34 the native undertakes works of extreme foolishness. Here mercury causes loss of wealth, loss of mental peace and loss of reputation. Even hard work is not awarded. However the children of native will be well educated and get married in very rich and noble families.

Remedies

1. Wear copper coin in neck in a white thread or silver chain.
2. Do not keep a widowed sister or father's sister in your house.
3. Avoid green color and emerald.
4. Do not accept any Tabeez from a sadhoo or faqir.

Mercury in 12th House

Mercury here destroys night's sleep of the native and causes troubles of many sorts. He loses peace of mind and very often suffers from headache. He has a long life but suffers from mercury, although, however, if mercury is accompanied by Saturn in this house very good results follow. Saturn along with sun and Mercury in 12th house also give good result. Daughters, sisters, father's sister and niece will be unhappy as long as they are living in the native's house. Such persons are generally self-praising and have irritable nature. If something right or wrong goes into his mind, he will ensure to stick to it in every manner. If such a native is fond of taking liquor he will be of pretentious nature. Speculation in business will prove harmful. Marriage in the 25th year will prove harmful for the native's wife and father.

Remedies

1. Throwing new empty pitcher in a river.
2. Putting on a ring of stainless steel.
3. Putting kesar tilak on face, head and visiting religious places of worship.
4. Taking advice of another person before starting any new or important work.

GEM FOR MERCURY

MERCURY	EMERALD	GREEN

In astrological parlance Mercury has been understood as an externally variable, vacillating, convertible, neutral and dualistic planet. Mercury re

PLANET

KETU (DRAGON'S TAIL)

Effects and Remedies

Ketu represents son, grandson, ear, spine etc. 6th house is considered to be its 'Pucca Ghar.' It gives its exalted effect when in 5th, 9th or 12th house and its debilitated effect in 6th and 8th house. Dawn is its time and it represents Sunday. Ketu represents the opposite node of Ketu, in the tail of the serpent. Its colours are black and white. Venus and Rahu are its friends, whereas Moon and Mars are its enemies. Forty-two years is the age of Ketu. Ketu is also considered to be the bed. So the bed given by in-laws after marriage is considered to be auspicious for the birth of a son and as long as that bed is in the house, the effect of Ketu can never be inauspicious.

Ketu in 1st House

If Ketu is auspicious or benefic in this house, the native will be laborious, rich and happy, but will always be concerned and troubled because of his progeny. He may fear frequent transfers or travels, but ultimately it would always be postponed.

Whenever Ketu comes in 1st house in Varsha Kundli there may be birth of a son or nephew. There may also be a long journey. The native with Ketu in 1st house will always be beneficial for his father and/or guru and causes exaltation of Sun.

If ketu in 1st house is malefic, the native would suffer from headache. His wife would have health problems and would have worries concerning kids. If 2nd and 7th houses are empty then Mercury and Venus would also give bad results. There would be travels, transfers with no gain. If Saturn is malefic it would destroy father and guru.

If Sun is in 7th or 8th house then after the birth of a grandson the health would suffer. No alms should be given in morning and evening.

Remedies

1. Feed jaggery (gur) to monkeys.
2. Apply saffron as Tilak.
3. If offspring is troubled then donate a black and white blanket to temple.

Ketu in 2nd House

2nd house is affected by Moon, which is an enemy of Ketu. If Ketu in 2nd house is benefic then one gets paternal property. One has to travel a lot and his travels are fruitful. Venus gives good results, irrespective of its position. Moon would give bad results. If Sun is in 12th house then one starts earning his livelihood after twenty-four years and is happy. If Jupiter is exalted along with Ketu in 2nd house, then income would be in lacs of rupees. If Ketu in 2nd house is malefic, then one has to travel to dry areas. One cannot rest at one place and would be wandering from place to place. Income may be good, but so would be the expenditure. Thus net gain would be negligible. If there is Moon or Mars in 8th house then native's life would be short and he would have serious problem at the age of sixteen or twenty years. If 8th house is empty then Ketu would give malefic results.

Remedies

1. Apply turmeric or saffron as tilak.
2. One should not be of loose character.
3. If one religiously visits temples and bows his head there then Ketu in 2nd house would give good results.

Ketu in 3rd House

3rd house is affected by Mercury and Mars, both enemies of Ketu. Number 3 would have an important role in the life of the native. If Ketu in 3rd house were benefic then his children would be good. The native would be god fearing and a gentleman. If Ketu is in 3rd house and Mars is in 12th then the native has a son before 24th year of age. The son would be good for wealth and longevity of the native. The native with Ketu in 3rd house usually gets a job, which entails long travels.

If Ketu in 3rd house is malefic then native loses money in litigation. He gets separated from his wife/sisters-in-law. If such a native lives in a house with its main gate facing south, he will have serious problems regarding children. Such a native cannot say no to any thing and so will always have worries. He will have troubles from his brothers and will have to travel uselessly.

Remedies

1. Use saffron as tilak.
2. Wear gold.
3. Offer jaggery, rice in flowing water.

Ketu in 4th house

4th house belongs to Moon, which is an enemy of Ketu. If Ketu is benefic in 4th house then the native is god fearing and lucky for his father and guru. Son is born to such a native only after getting the blessings of one's guru. The son born lives long. Such a native leaves all his decisions to God. If moon is in 3rd or 4th house the result is benefic. Such a native is a good adviser and will never have shortage of money. If Ketu is malefic in this house then the native is unhealthy, his mother is troubled, there is loss of happiness. One may suffer from diabetes. A son is born after thirty six years of age. Such a native has more daughters than sons.

Remedies

1. Keep a dog.
2. Wear silver for peace of mind.
3. Offer yellow things in flowing water.

Ketu in 5th House

5th house belongs to Sun. It is also affected by Jupiter. If Jupiter, Sun or Moon is in 4th, 6th or 12th house then one's financial condition will be excellent and the native will have five sons. Ketu becomes benefic by itself after twenty four years of age. If Ketu in 5th house is malefic then the native suffers from asthma. Ketu gives malefic results till five years of age. Sons will not survive. Livelihood starts after twenty four years of age. The native is unlucky for ones sons.

Remedies

1. Donate milk and sugar.
2. The remedies of Jupiter would be useful.

Ketu in 6th House

6th house belongs to Mercury. Ketu in 6th house is considered debilitated. This is 'Pucca' house of Ketu. Here again the effect of Ketu depends upon the nature of Jupiter. It gives good result regarding son. The native is a good adviser.

If Jupiter is benefic then the native has a long life and his mother is happy and the life is peaceful. If any two of the male planets viz Sun, Jupiter, Mars are in good position then Ketu is benefic.

If Ketu is malefic in 6th house then maternal uncle suffers. The native has to suffer due to useless travels. People turn into enemies without any reason. The native suffers from skin diseases. If Moon is in 2nd house then mother suffers and even the native's old age is troubled.

Remedies

1. Wear golden ring in the finger of left hand.
2. Drink milk with saffron and wear gold in the ear.
3. Heat up a rod of gold and then dip it in milk. Then drink it.

It would restore mental peace, increase longevity and is good for sons.

4. Keep a dog.

Ketu in 7th House

7th house belongs to Mercury and Venus. If Ketu in 7th house is benefic then the native gets the wealth of forty years in twenty-four years of age. The wealth increases in proportion to the children one has. The native's enemies are frightened of the native. If one has the help of Mercury, Jupiter or Venus then the native is never disappointed.

If Ketu in 7th house is malefic then the native is usually ill, makes false promises and is troubled by enemies till thirty-four years of age. If there is more than one planet in Lagna then ones children are destroyed. If one abuses then the native is destroyed. If Ketu is with Mercury then after thirty-four years of age the native's enemies are destroyed by themselves.

Remedies

1. Never make a false promise, be proud, or abusive.
2. Use saffron as Tilak.
3. In case of serious trouble use the remedies of Jupiter.

Ketu in 8th house

8th house belongs to Mars, which is an enemy of Ketu. If Ketu in 8th house is benefic then the native begets a son at thirty-four years of age, or after the marriage of ones sister or daughter. If Jupiter or Mars are not in 6th and 12th house then Ketu does not give malefic results. Similar effect is there when Moon is in 2nd house. If Ketu in 8th house is malefic then the native's wife has ill health. Son will not be born, or may die. The native may suffer from diabetes or urinary problem. If Saturn or Mars are in 7th then the native is unlucky. In case of malefic Ketu in 8th house the native's character determines the health of his wife. After twenty-six years of age the family life suffers.

Remedies

1. Keep a dog.
2. Donate a black and white blanket in any temple.
3. Worship lord Ganesha.
4. Wear gold in the ear.
5. Use saffron as tilak.

Ketu in 9th House

9th house belongs to Jupiter, which favours Ketu. Ketu in 9th house is considered to be exalted. Such a native is obedient and lucky. It increases ones wealth. If Ketu is benefic then one earns wealth through ones own labour. There will be progress but no transfer. If one keeps gold brick in his house then wealth comes. The son of such a native is able to guess the future. One spends a big part of his life in foreign land. One has at least three sons and if 2nd house is auspicious then Ketu gives excellent results. If Moon is auspicious then the native helps his mother's family. If Ketu in 9th house is malefic then the native suffers from urinary problems, pain in back, and problem in legs. The native's sons keep on dying.

Remedies

1. Keep a dog.
2. Establish a rectangular piece of gold anywhere in the house.
3. Wear gold in the ear.
4. Respect elders, especially father-in-law.

Ketu in 10th house.

10th house belongs to Saturn. The effect of Ketu here depends upon the nature of Saturn. If Ketu is benefic here then the native is lucky, concerned about himself and opportunist. His father dies early. If Saturn is in 6th then one is a famous player. If one keeps on forgiving his brothers for their misdeeds the native will go on progressing. If the character of native is good then he earns a lot of wealth. If Ketu in 10th house is malefic then one suffers from urinary and ear problems. The native has pain in bones. The domestic life is full of worries and troubled if Saturn is in 4th house. Three sons would die.

Remedies

1. Keep silver pot full of honey in the house.
2. Keep a dog, especially after forty-eight years of age.
3. Avoid adultery.
4. Use the remedies of Moon and Jupiter.

Ketu in 11th House

Here Ketu is considered very good. It gives wealth. This house is affected by Jupiter and Saturn. If Ketu is benefic here and Saturn is in 3rd house, it gives enormous wealth. The wealth earned by the native is more than his paternal wealth, but one tends to worry about his future. If Mercury is in 3rd it leads to Raj Yoga. If Ketu is malefic here then the native has problem in his abdomen. The more he worries about future, more troubled he is. Grandmother or mother of the native suffers, if Saturn is also malefic. Then there would be no benefit from son or house.

Remedies

1. Keep black dog.
2. Wear an onyx or emerald.

Ketu in 12th House

Here Ketu is considered to be exalted. The native is wealthy, achieves a big position and spends on good works. If Rahu is in 6th house, along with Mercury, then the effect is even better. One has all the benefits and luxuries of life. If Ketu in 12th house is malefic then one buys land from an issueless person and the native becomes issueless himself. If one kills dogs Ketu gives malefic results. If 2nd house has Moon, Venus or Mars, Ketu gives malefic results.

Remedies

1. Worship Lord Ganesha.
2. Do not have a loose character.
3. Keep a dog.

Saunf and khand under the pillow for good night's sleep.

GEM FOR KETU

KETU	CAT'S EYE	OFF WHITE

PLANET

VENUS

Effects and Remedies

As a feminine planet, Venus has been regarded as the goddess of love, marriage, beauty and all worldly comforts. Venus represents that power of love which leads to the merger of two individual selves into one and rules the gentle and refined attributes of human life.

As a preceptor of demons, Venus stands for the husband in the horoscope of a female and represents the wife in the horoscope of a male. Venus offers good results if placed alone in the birth chart. The 2nd and 7th houses are owned by Venus who gets exalted in the 12th house. Saturn, Mercury and Ketu are friends of Venus, whereas Sun, Moon and Rahu act as enemies.

Venus offers very good results if posited in the 2nd, 3rd, 4th, 7th and 12th houses, but the Ist, 6th and 9th houses are considered bad for Venus. Accordingly, Venus offers very good results in the houses of Mercury, Saturn and Ketu, whereas evil effects will follow if posited in the houses of Sun, Rahu and Moon. When Rahu aspects Venus or vice versa, or when both are placed together in a house, the good results of Venus will be nullified and the native will get deprived of money, wealth and family comforts altogether. The eyes of the native's, mother will become severely defective if Moon and Venus are placed just opposite to each other.

Afflicted Venus causes trouble in the eyes, diseases of the ovaries, gout, anaemia and other complications due to over indulgence in amusements and sex, including gonorrhoea and syphilis.

An afflicted Venus may cause vehicular accidents, faithlessness in love and marriage and will deprive the native of the comforts of vehicles, conveyance etc.

Venus in IST House

Venus in Ist house makes the native highly handsome, long-lived, sweet tongued and popular among the opposite sex. Wife of the native remains ill. Religion, caste or creed is never a bar for having sexual relations with anyone. Such a native is generally highly romantic by nature and longs for love and sex with other women. He gets married before he starts earning his living. Such a native becomes a leader of persons of his age group, but leadership of the family members causes several family troubles. Such a native earns great profits through the trade of clothes. Such a native is generally deprived of interest in religious pursuits. When Venus comes in 7th house in Varsha phal, it causes chronic fever and blood cough.

Remedies

1. Do not marry at the age of 25 years.
2. Always act according to the advice of others.
3. Serving a black cow.
4. Avoid sex during daytime.
5. Take bath with curd.
6. Intake of cow's urine is very useful.

Venus in 2nd House

Doing bad or evil towards others would prove harmful to the native. Money, wealth and property would continue to grow upto sixty years. Shermukhi house (wider at the front than the rear portion) would prove disastrous for the native. Business or trade associated with gold and jewellery will be extremely harmful. Business associated with earthen goods, agriculture and animal will prove highly beneficial. Venus in 2nd second house in a female horoscope renders the native barren or infertile and in a male's horoscope makes the wife incapable of producing a son.

Remedies

1. For getting a son, intake of things associated with mars like honey, Saunf or deshi Khand will be highly effective.
2. Feed two kgs of potatoes colour by yellow turmeric to cows.
3. Offer two kgs. Cow's ghee in a temple.
4. Avoid adultery.

Venus in 3rd House

Here Venus blesses the native with a charming personality and every woman would get attracted to him. He is generally loved by all.

If the native gets involved with other women he will have to live in subservience to his wife, otherwise his wife will always be dominated by him, though she may be dominating everyone else coming into contact with her. She would be courageous, supportive and helpful to the native like second bullock of the cart. He will be saved from deceit, theft and harm from others. Contacts with other women would prove harmful and affect the longevity adversely. If planets placed in 9th and 11th houses are inimical to Venus, highly adverse results will follow. He will have many daughters.

Remedies

1. Respect your wife and never insult her.
2. Avoid flirting with other women.

Venus in 4th House

Venus in 4th house strongly establishes the possibility of two wives and makes the native rich, too, If Jupiter is posited in 10th house and Venus is placed in 4th, the native will face adverse results from all sides if he tries to be religious. Venus in 4th house destroys the possibility of a son to the native if he covers a well by a roof and constructs a room or house over it. The business associated with mercury will also prove harmful. Saturn will give disastrous effects if the native consumes liquor. The business or trade associated with mars will prove advantageous to such a native. Venus in 4th and Jupiter in Ist house will create frequent quarrels with the mother-in-law.

Remedies

1. Change the name of your wife and remarry her formally.
2. Throwing rice, silver and milk in the running water or feeding Kheer or milk to mother like women will ward off the quarrels between mother-in-law and daughter-in-law.
3. Keep the roof of the house clean and well maintained for the health of your wife.
4. Drop things of Jupiter, like gram, pulses and Kesar, in the river.

Venus in 5th house

5th house is the Pukka ghar of the sun, where Venus will get burnt with the heat of the Sun. Consequently the native is a flirt and amorous by nature. He will face big misfortunes in life. However, if the native maintains a good character he will steer through the hardships of life and obtain great riches and promotions in service after five years of his marriage. Such a native is generally learned and destroyer of enemies.

Remedies

1. One should not marry against the wishes of his parents.
2. Serving cows and mother like women.
3. Avoid relationships will other women.
4. Native's wife should wash her private parts with curd or milk.

Venus in 6th House

This house belongs to mercury and Ketu, who are inimical to each other, but Venus is friendly to both. Venus stands, debilitated in this house. However, if the native keeps the opposite sex happy and provides her with all the comforts, his money and wealth will continue to grow. The wife of the native should not get dressed like a male and should not get her hair cut like a male, otherwise poverty will crop up.

Such a native must marry a person who has got a brother or brothers. Further, the native should not leave any work in the midway, i.e., before completion.

Remedies

1. Ensure that your wife puts gold clips in her hair.
2. Your spouse must not remain barefooted.
3. The private parts should be washed with red medicine.

Venus in 7th House

This house belongs to Venus, so Venus gives very good results if it is placed in this house. The planet of Ist house offers the effects of 7th house in such a manner as if it is placed in 7th house itself. If a planet inimical to Venus is placed in Ist house e.g. Rahu, the wife and the household affairs of the native will be adversely affected. The native spends his money largely on women. The native should take up the trade or business which is associated will marriage ceremony, like tent house and beauty parlour. Association with one eyed and black woman will prove useful.

Remedies

1. Domestication of white cows prohibited.
2. Serving red cows.
3. Donate Jawar equal to the weight of your spouse to a temple.
4. Throwing blue flowers in a dirty canal for 43 days.

Venus in 8th House

No planet is considered benefic in this house Even Venus in this house becomes rotten and poisonous. The wife of such a native becomes highly irritable and short tempered. Evil utterances from her mouth will certainly prove to be true. The native will be suffering from the feeling of self-pity. Taking guarantee or surety for someone will prove disastrous. If there is no planet in 2nd house, do not marry before 25 years of age; otherwise the wife will certainly die.

Remedies

1. The native should not accept daan.
2. Bowing head in the place of worship and temples.
3. Copper coin or blue flower to be thrown in gutter or dirty

Nullah continuously for ten days.

4. Wash your private parts with curd.

Venus in 9th House

Venus in this house does not offer good results. The native may have riches, but he will get his bread only after hard labour. His efforts are not properly rewarded. There will be dearth of male members, money, wealth and property. If Venus is accompanied by Mercury or any malefic planet the native will be a victim of intoxication and disease from seventeen years of age.

Remedies

1. In the foundation of the house silver and honey should be buried.
2. Silver bangles to be worn after putting some red color on them.
3. Bury a silver piece under a Neem tree for 43 days.

Venus in 10th House

Venus in this house makes native greedy, suspicious and interested in handicraft. The native would act under the control and guidance of his spouse as long as the spouse is with the native all sorts of troubles will remain warded off. If in a motor car no accident will take place or even if it takes place the native cannot be harmed in any manner. The business and things associated with Saturn will prove advantageous.

Remedies

1. Washing private parts with curd.
2. Western wall of the house should be of mud.
3. Abstinence from wine and non-vegetarian food.
4. At the time of illness, the native should donate a black cow.

Venus in 11th House

Venus in this house is influenced by Saturn and Jupiter, because this house belongs to Jupiter and Saturn. This house is aspect by 3rd house which is influenced by Mars and Mercury. Native's wife, through her brothers, will prove very beneficial.

Remedies

1. Remedies of Mercury will be useful.
2. Oil to be given on Saturday.
3. The native usually suffers from low sperm count in his semen. Native should drink milk in which hot piece of gold has been dipped.

Venus in 12th House

Exalted Venus gives very beneficial results in this house. The native will have a wife, who will act as a shield in the time of trouble. Taking help from women will prove highly advantageous for the native, who receives all favours from the government.

Venus being inimical to Jupiter causes health problems to the wife. Mercury in 2nd or 6th houses makes the native diseased, but bestows literary and poetic talent to the native. Such a native gains high spiritual powers at the age of 59 and generally lives up to about 96 years.

Remedies

1. Blue flowers to be buried by the wife at the time of sunset, for good health.
2. The wife will act as a defense wall for the husband, if she gives things in charity to people.
3. Domesticating and giving cows in charity.
4. Offer love, respect and honor to your wife.

GEM FOR VENUS

VENUS	DIAMOND	COLORLESS

CHAPTER 14

ASTROLOGICAL HINTS MICROSCOPY OF ASTROLOGY

SIGNIFICANCE OF DIFFERENT SIGNS

ZODIAC SIGNS

ARIES (21ˢᵗ March-19ᵗʰ April)

Your Ruling Planet Mars
Your Sign Fiery
Born in Sign Movable

CHARACTERISTIC

Your shall have round eyes, shall be quite talkative and urguementive. Short tempered, angry and bilious in nature. Tend to be the eldest of of the children, shall be popular, stingy and unsteady in behavior, moment of arms, hands and fingers are frequently seen while in conversation with others. Full of vigor, honored by the government, sparingly eating habits and shall have few children in life.

Appearance:

A good physique with large bones. Your features and your teeth tend to be good and even you are of medium height and you tend to develop into a unique punchy personality.

Personality:

You possess forceful, courageous, enterprising and industrious instincts. You refuse to give up until and unless you have not achieved your targets.

Winning or losing is not very important to you, giving a good effort and showing a good account of your abilities is quite something where you are more cautious about. In your approach and speech you are quite confident even though you are not equipped with much knowledge of that subject. You are straightforward in your speech and would often not; hesitate in calling a thief a thief.

Calling a thief a thief doesn't always make you popular and even though you're fully aware of this, you really wont care much about others feeling and shall stick to your comments. You neither like pressures being forced upon you nor would like subordination, but would rather wish to be free in thoughts and action, and would love, free style of functioning. You are best suited for guiding, controlling and governing others. You can be very self-assertive, and well equipped to deal with any situation or emergency when the situation demands. You tend to be over optimistic and too impulsive and later regret your actions or inaction and at times overshoot the mark or over trade in business. Because of your impulsiveness you don't hesitate to get into an argument or pick up a quarrel over petty things. You are not the kind of person who would look before you leap, consistency is also not your virtue. Even if you happen to occupy a humble or subordinate position you will try to be at the head of some branch of your work or assignment. Whether in profession or business you will cross all barriers and speed breakers to attain success.

Profession and Career

You are best suited for a career connected with Metals, Engineering, Metallurgy, Surgery and you often tend to become good trade union leaders. Explorers, Explosives, Teachers, Self-Employed Professionals or the business people. Dealers of firearms, Dentists, Mechanics, and Sportsmen are the other fields where you would excel well.

Business and Finances

Though you have a good head for business but when it comes to making investments or tying up new deals, your become quite impulsive and rash. With the result your profits are cut off or minimized, but your financial position remain quite stable.

As you're prone to overrating your own judgment, it is you're over confidence, which combines with your impulsiveness that cuts off or reduces your profits. However, you're able to pull back yourself from major disasters and you do not remain a debtor for long.

You Match with Aries, Leo Scorpions and Sagittarius

Romance and Marriage

You warm hearted nature will provide you with excellent chance for love and romance. But you must restrain yourself from being rash and impulsive. You expect your loved ones to share your thoughts and to respond to your moods in all situations. Your love life is quite stylish, and your living is luxurious. Romance and Love means a lot to you and you not hesitate in keeping every thing aside until you get your desires fulfilled.

YOUR WEAKNESS

You will be such a bad liar that others can immediately see through you. But however selfish you may be, you will feel the sense of your selfishness if pointed out to you and you will readily accept the fact. Since you are a quick-witted, restless character, you may find it too difficult to be patient in any situation, which you do not like. You will put up with adverse conditions only as long as you are confident about it and you will eventually bring about the changes as per your desire and wishes even though you may have to take unnecessary risks in achieving your goals. Bravery and disregard for danger are inheritance in you. You have the capacity to rapidly grasp the essential of a situation, but you shall also have its drawbacks, for not in seeing the whole shape of a problem, they might appear to be resulting in an argument, and leading to give an offence. You may be quick-tempered, but will be at your worst, extremely selfish, and demanding if such an occasion arises.

Health and Disease

The body parts ruled by your sign are muscles, head, and the eyes, and the face. You are quite prone to headaches, head injuries, brain disorders, and burns, are the other positive pointers. Minor accidents are also not ruled out.

You are person who could be recognized by a fine facial bone structure with a shining healthy head of hair. Definitely you are not weak people. You are mostly in a hurry and often do not get time to eat properly, with the result you tend to suffer from stomach ailments because low diet. At times you are subject to blood pressure, heart-related problems, and headaches including sinus and migraines.

As most conditions apply, plenty of water is essential for your body and you should take regular diet and complete rest, whenever excess stress or strain is promulgated.

Lucky Day Tuesday
Lucky Colors Red and white.
Lucky Stones Red Coral, Ruby, Garnet Blood Stone.
Lucky Numbers 9, 18, 27, 36, 45, 54, 63 and 72

ZODIAC SIGNS

TAURUS (20th April-20th May)

Your Ruling Planet Venus
Your Sign Earth
Born in Sign Fixed

CHARACTERISTIC

Ruled by Venus, the planet of love, you are good and sympathetic, caring and loyal. It is often said that you are a good lover of beauty. Your sense of preservation is far developed. Your strong will power generally carries you to great heights even when you are under severe stress and strain conditions. You have tendency to put on weight even though you are strong and well built. You love to have good food and prefer to take high fat diet and enjoy living in comfortable surroundings. At times when you tend to be lazy, and unwilling to do the job or work assigned to you, with the result that you loss the fruitful gains that are stored for you. You're concerned with gaining material wealth and status and you make a sincere effort in achieving them. You have excellent business sense, the ability to make money. You are generous in entertaining your friends, and you enjoy the company of friends much more than the others do. You shall feel happier living in the big cities rather than in small towns.

Appearance

You are well built and hefty and you tend to put on weight easily.

Your eyes are attractive and your body appearance resembles to a bull.

Your lips are well shaped and your skin is soft and glowing. Your movements are quite graceful and well matched. You have broad face stout shoulders with big belly.

Personality

You are a popular learned and sensuous personality. You are practical, persevering and you have good powers of endurance. You often make faithful and loyal friends. You are very careful about your personal comforts and money matters. You are unreasonably stubborn at times, and you lose other people' sympathy in process. You have great power of endurance and patience, but when provoked to anger, your become wild, volatile and would not mind using abusive language. You have a strong will power and are quite conservative in your thoughts and actions. You are bit slow but steady in actions. You would not to waste surplus energy and talent. You would plodder around a subject for pretty long till you are sure about it. You would only than act fast and wisely and see to it, that the concerned matters go to your advantage and favor. You are fond of ease, comforts and luxuries. You become worldly and take pleasure in the good things of life.

Profession and Careers

You would have a good taste for Arts, Music, Theatre, and Cinema. You would also make good singers, dancers, and art and jewelry dealers. Writers, models, actors are the other fields where you excel pretty well. Architects, financiers, bankers, are optional field, which fancy you.

Business and Finances

You make excellent business people and financiers and are known as the money zone of the zodiac. You manage to find opportunities to increase your profits or expand your business where others see none.

You also tend to instinctively find above average avenues of investment. The best deals that you strike are generally those connected with land or property. You work happily as Florist, in Livestock or Poultry industry or are often seen as heads of Super Markets and wholesale food industrialist.

You Match with Taurus, Gemini Virgo, Capricorn, and Aquarius.

Romance and Marriage

Since Venus, which powers you with physical charm, governs you happen to become a good humorist, thus radiating warmth and vitality around you. You are amorous by nature and you find it difficult to restrain the affections one bestowed upon you. You are also easily influenced by the attraction of the opposite sex. You make friends easily and are quite popular with fairer sex. Its a different matter that your romance begins only after you have satisfied yourself or have observed that your partner has the qualities that appeal to you. You are emotionally attached to their spouse once married, you look for unshakable stability. Your patience in personal relationships ensures you with stability and smoothness. You generally full fill your duties and obligations towards your loved ones.

Health and Disease

Though you are a good eater of delicious foods you would at the same time. Love to exercise and help your self in maintaining good health. Your sign rules, tongue and ears, the neck, throat, vocal chords, tonsils, thyroid gland, chin, lower jaw. You are prone to colds, coughs, sore throats, tonsillitis, obesity, blood pressure and constipation.

YOUR WEAKNESS

You can easily be misled by emotions and affections. You tend to be quite jealous and sentimental with regards to the matter of sex. You are dominating and obstinate with the result you almost lose the ground, which you have gained during your interaction with opposite sex. But once you find that everything around you is smooth and the grass is green and lovely you plunge head long to build a happy home and would like to create a world of your own nature.

Lucky Day Friday
Lucky Colors Blue and violet
Lucky Stones Diamond, white zircon.
Lucky Numbers 6, 15, 24, 33, 42 and 51

ZODIAC SIGNS

GEMINI 21st May to 20th June

Your Ruling Planet MERCURY
Your Sign AIR
Born in Sign Movable

CHARACTERISTIC

You are an airy sign you live mostly in the mind. You will be carefree, joyous and reluctant. Your mind will be strong and positive and strong. You are often versatile. Restless and inclined to changes and make improvements whenever there is necessity. You also appreciate traveling in search of adventure and amusement. Your enjoyment of the use of words enhances your ability to converse. You are quick, perceptive, clever, playful and imaginative, and you express yourself to feel alive. You feel fresh when you can move around mentally and physically unrestricted. Your ability to bluff your way out of tight corners is phenomenal, and you will always be on the go. You will be doing more than one thing at a time. This dual phenomenon is an important part of your nature. You need plenty of variety and change. You can very easily become bored, and your answer to drop whatever is boring to you is quite certain and to take, the next job in hand is one of your charactericts. You should be careful not to overstrain your sensitive nervous system, which can break down under pressure. You enjoy mental recreation, but you also appreciate traveling in search of adventure and amusement.

If you're not interested in something, you can be indifferent to your liking and friendship. You love to be in company and attempt a whole variety of things simultaneously.

Appearance

Describing the Gemini is as mercurial is right on the money, since Gemini is ruled by the Planet Mercury. Moving, restless, seeking, learning—Gemini is constant motion, a torrent of wind which is in keeping with this sign's element of Air. The Twins are highly intellectual and won't hesitate to play mind games with a lover, mere child's play to them. They are also great communicators, so get ready to hear everything from pithy remarks to impassioned pleas. Inventive, quick-witted and fun, the Twins will jump around from one lover to the next until they find one which is almost as smart as they are and able to keep up in this high-spirited race. The reward for those who can lasso a Gemini is a free-spirited lover who shines at parties but is also a devil in the bedroom.

Personality

A fine bone structure and movements that are light often set you apart from others and make you good dancers as well. Your facial expressions are usually baby like in their transparency. Quick to smile, with ears that are a bit larger than normal, your physique tends to remain slim even when your food intake begins to cross the limits. The Gemini is always right and never changes his mind—until the next time the argument comes around, when he will take a totally different stand, and deny ever having given vent to his earlier opinions. This is infuriating for his opponents in argument, especially as he has a considerable talent for dialogue—and a tendency to know a very little about a very great number of things, and to master this knowledge skillfully as to seem well informed.

His ability to bluff his way out of tight corners is phenomenal. There then, are his worst faults—inconsistency and superficiality.

Little wonder, perhaps, that the world's most popular journalists in newspaper, radio, and television are Gemini's. For again, they have an insistent urge to communicate.

Profession and Career

You would make good writers, radio and TV producers or anchor people, lecturers, linguists, teachers, travel agents, sales people.

Business and Finances

Like air, you feel fresh when you can move around mentally and physically unrestricted. But when traveling, you're likely to take along beepers, mobile phones, laptop computers, portable radios and televisions, and remote controls. You like being busy, juggling two or more things at once. Boredom, censure or repression could make you impatient, restless, anxious, snappish, sarcastic, gossipy, cynical or nervously exhausted

You Match with Leo Gemini, Libra and Aquarius

Romance and Marriage

A love affair with a Gemini requires great stamina; so start doing those push-ups now! The Twins are both fun and funny and love to laugh, play and romp. They are possessed of a very active mind, which can sometimes lead to a short attention span. The best way to keep the Twins around, and aroused, is through mental stimulation. A razor-sharp and imaginative lover is a godsend to the terrific Twins. This sign also values adventure and travel, so a certain footloose and fancy free-ness will help this romance bloom.

The duality of the Twins allows them to see both sides of an issue, so in times of stress, they are much likelier to be a lover than a fighter. They will also feel especially connected to those who can help them feel, since they spend so much of their time thinking. It's true that your attentions tend to stray even after marriage but it's also true that responsibilities gradually change your attitude and force you into being steady wives and husbands. And yet, you love your home and family and want the best for them. Resolving contradictions where you want to remain free and yet have a good family life are essential for you.

YOUR WEAKNESS

Someone who can roll with the punches and keep smiling in the face of a multi-faceted onslaught is priceless to the hyperactive Twins. It's an added plus if that person is smart, fun, a good friend and a great sport. Gemini's need someone who can be attentive to them and who will naturally enjoy their sparkle and wit. They also prefer a strong partner who is not necessarily as smart as they are but who can pick them up, emotionally, when necessary. If the Twins can make a marvelous mental match, life will be a dream. The Gemini lover is easygoing and caring, yet daring and a ball of fire at the right moments. Mental fireworks are high on their agenda, their own as well as those they can make with another. Only those with plenty of punch need apply for this celestial light show! The Gemini is always right and never changes his mind—until the next time the argument comes around, when he will take a totally different stand, and deny ever having given vent to his earlier opinions. This is infuriating for his opponents in argument, especially as he has a considerable talent for dialogue—and a tendency to know a very little about a very great number of things, and to master this knowledge skillfully as to seem well informed. His ability to bluff his way out of tight corners is phenomenal.

There, then, are his worst faults—inconsistency and superficiality. Little wonder, perhaps, that the world's most popular journalists in newspaper, radio, and television are Gemini's. For again, they have an insistent urge to communicate.

Health and Disease

You suffer from allergies, asthma and frequent colds and flu. The skin, hair, veins as well as throat, kidneys and lumbar region of Gemini's get easily affected.

Lucky Day Wednesday
Lucky Color Yellow
Lucky Stone s Yellow Carnelian Agate)
Lucky Numbers 3, 12, 21, 30, 48, 57

ZODIAC SIGNS

CANCER (22nd June-22nd July)

Your Ruling Planet Moon
Your sign Water
Born in Sign Movable

CHARACTERISTIC

You are changeable, moody, restless and sensitive. You are emotional, tenacious, honest, intelligent, industrious, and miserly. Though proud, talkative, quite independent in your feelings, you are more attached to your home and family.

Physical Appearance

Usually of medium height, your build is sturdy and stocky. Your complexion is generally smooth and free from pimples and blemishes. Most of you have a strong, muscular physique with largish bones. Even symmetrical teeth and a wide mouth.

Personality

Your sign of water makes your nature moody. You tend to keep your emotions hidden in the innermost of your heart. This watery sign also bestows the powers of intuition. You possess strong pioneering instincts and are generally enterprising and industrious. In crunch situations, you are forceful a courageous and refuse to give up until you have achieved your targets or at least put in your best. Like a true sportsperson, you like to play for the challenge and enjoyment and at one level, winning or losing is not so important, what matters more to you is giving a good account of yourself. You are sensitive and take a fancy to any thing, which comes new to you. In your speech and approach, you are direct and forthright. You are very particular about having good food. You're generally easy to get along with.

Your bad eating habits may often lead you to bad health. You don't like pressures being on you and value an easy going, free style of functioning. You tend to be too impulsive and later regret your actions or inaction. You're often also too outspoken and undiplomatic.

Profession and Career

Being hard working and industrious, you are successful in your own profession and business. You often reach high position in life. You generally make good Engineers, Explorers, Metal Workers, Dentists, Surgeons, Mechanics, Self-employed Professionals or Business People. You do well in teaching, writing, painting, advertising, and selling things and also in trade and commerce, particularly, imports and exports.

Business and Finance

Although you have a good head for business and your financial position is usually stable, you're prone to overrating your own judgment, especially when it comes to making investments or tying up new deals. It's your impulsive nature and you're over confidence, which combine to cut it to your profits. Generally, however, you're able to pull back from major disasters and the saving grace is that you'll never remain a debtor. You are highly ambitious when it comes to amassing wealth, but you have to climb an uphill task in achieving the same. Wealth often eludes you even when you inherit your parental property or wealth. You should avoid betting, speculation and horseracing, as you are more likely to lose, rather than gain.

You Match with

Cancer, Leo, Scorpio, Sagittarius and Pisces

Romance and Marriage

You will enjoy your family life. Home and family are of great importance to you and will manage to keep your spouse quite happy and gay. You have a good style of admiration and you indulge in light flirtations. Many of you, despite your deep-seated desire to set up a home, are averse to marriage.

Part of the reason for this is that you are unable to disclose your inmost emotions and feelings even when your heart beats in tune to a strong love tone. Often, you tend to be attracted to an opposite number. Love means a lot to you and you're generally willing to put everything else aside until it fulfills your desires. Warm and loving, you often shower your through various means which includes paying profuse compliments, showering gifts, making stylish dates. Whether you're a male or a female you are usually very frank and forthright and you like to make it clear at the outset itself whether you're simply flirting or whether you are serious in your love and romantic affairs.

HEALTH AND DISEASE

You are likely to suffer from water born diseases, comprising of gastric trouble, inflammatory troubles of liver, minor boils and infection in stomach. At times mental depression and excitement. Diabetes is one factor, where you need to be beware of.

YOUR WEAKNESS

You are lustful, drunkard and fickle minded. You become irritable and your crooked eyes speak of your lust and greed at several occasions.

Lucky Colors Green, mauve, mountain blue.
Lucky Stones Emerald, pearl, cat's eye.
Your Lucky Numbers 2, 11, 20 29,

ZODIAC SIGNS

LEO (23rd July-22nd August)

Your Planetary Ruler Sun
Your Element Fire
Born in Sign Fixed

CHARACTERISTIC

You are extremely sympathetic, generous, honest, straightforward and authoritative. You are honest, frank, and outspoken. You are enterprising and like to command. In fact, your strongest instinct is to rule and command. You love authority. You are quite proud and lucky in money matters. You possess a strong will power and you achieve your objectives in spite of the difficulties or obstacles that come in your way. You are enterprising, soft but outspoken helpful and righteous personality. You are sincere, reputed, independent, impatient bold, generous and a respectable person. A traveler, obstinate and a happy go lucky person. You are affectionate, enthusiastic, cheerful, and optimistic whom, bring sunshine into other lives.

Appearance

You are tall, physically strong, and attractive and have a fair complexion. You have broad shoulders and have beautiful eyes with abundant energy. Your constitution is generally robust; you appear to have fashioned round face with model looks.

Personality

You are inclined to quick anger. Success comes to you only after much struggle. You would remain devoted to your parents. Your wife would be virtuous and happy lady.

Physically, you are strong and if you happen to fall ill, you will recover soon. You are both courageous and valorous. You never want to giveaway. You shun inferior jobs and are fond of a life of luxury works and jobs. You have a strong desire to travel, and you prefer to have an aristocratic society.

Professions and Career

The career best suited for you are Civil Services, Finance, Politics, Armed Forces, Business of Commanding Nature, You are quite courteous, diplomatic and do well in all professions where you may have to deal with dignified people. You are not generally good in dealing with masses or where laborers are involved. Your life starts to boom and you have the tendency to earn money at much younger age.

Business and Finances

You are magnanimous and are, therefore, unable to save in proportion to your income. Business partnerships lead to litigation, which should be settled out of court. There is a danger of part of your property being destroyed by fire. In financial matters, you may not get a square deal from your brothers and sisters, and this may even lead to litigation.

You Match With Aries, Leo, Sagittarius and Gemini.

Romance and Marriage

You love steadfastly, and usually get married fairly early. However, being stubborn, you do not have a smooth relationship with your partner. You want to be overbearing, and unless the partner is submissive and docile, this leads to frequent clashes.

YOUR WEAKNESS

You tend to have a lot of ego and pride, and you have a certain amount of vanity by which you are easily ruffled. Your inimical feelings continue for a long time. You are pompous and prefer to show off your splendor on many occasions. You at times get suspicious, even when there is no substantial cause. You are inclined towards betting, gambling speculation, and games of chance. The greed of becoming rich at one go often attracts you.

HEALTH AND DISEASE

The heart and the aorta, upper back, spleen and the spinal chord form your major vulnerable health areas and can result in heart diseases, back problems, or spinal meningitis. Your sign rules the heart and back, and your tendency to drive yourself hard, often puts them under pressure. The pressure increases because you enjoy good food and are prone to be overweight. For good health, you've got to respect your body's needs.

Lucky Days Sundays
Lucky Color Red, orange, gold white.
Lucky Stones Ruby, amber, diamonds.
Your Lucky Numbers 1, 10, 28, 37,46, 55

ZODIAC SIGNS

VIRGO (23rd August to 22nd September)

Your Planetary Ruler Mercury
Your Element Earth
Your Sign Movable

Characteristics

You are attractive, modest, reserved, honest, long armed, with drooping shoulders, sweet speech, intelligent, fond of pleasure, music and opposite sex.

Physical Appearance

Often of a small build, you have a large fund bustling energy and are seldom able to sit still for long. Your noses a seldom bulbous, and your lips are generally delicately shaped. Your sky tends to be soft and oily in your younger years.

Personality

You are discriminating, analytical, objective and practical. As a result, you excel in all work in which analysis and critical judgment is required. You have great clarity in your thoughts and strong powers of discerning hidden things. However, although you have a strong love for justice, you are only moderately sympathetic towards others. You are cool-headed and balanced. Happily, you are not vindictive and in fact, quite shy, prefer to work quietly and in seclusion. You are likely to travel a great deal for business or pleasure.

Travel brings good luck and addition to fortune.

By and large, you will rise by dint of your personal efforts and merit. Once aroused, it's difficult for you to cool down. You also tend to live in your imagination far too often.

Profession and Career

You would do well in all occupations connected with higher sciences, mechanics, dietetics, nutrients, health, and labour. Since you go into details, you are industrious, and are devoted to your work. You make good executives, organizers and directors. You are an earthy sign, and if you have an inclination for agriculture and horticulture, you can successful in any occupation connected with land.

Business and Finances

Acquisition of wealth will prove an uphill task. Though the struggle will be hard and beset with many difficulties, you will triumph ultimately due to intelligent handling and hard work. You will, however, have secret enemies, and should be very careful in your investments.

Ideal Match Taurus, Virgo and Capricorn.

Romance and Marriage

Your love life is not smooth as a rule, partly because you have high expectations always. There are, chances of second marriage. Even if there is no second marriage, there may be a long-standing attachment. Many of you have a tendency to fall in love at a comparatively young age, but such a relationship is seldom enduring.

Health and Disease

Your health is, generally, not good in childhood, but as the years pass, and it becomes better. You are likely to have complaints of the bowels and weakness of the sympathetic nervous system, the abdomen and the liver, the gall bladder and gall ducts. Virgos are very fussy food eaters. You are anaemic and suffer from indigestion, gas pains, ulcers, liver upsets, colitis and bowel problems

Lucky Days Wednesday, Saturday.
Lucky Colors Orange, Yellow, Grey, White.
Lucky Stones Emerald, Jade, amethyst, topaz.
Your Lucky Numbers 5, 14, 50, 59 68 and 77

ZODIAC SIGNS

LIBRA (23rd September to 22nd October)

Your ruling planet Venus
Your Element Air
Your sign Movable

CHARACTERISTIC

Libra being the seventh sign of the zodiac and is ruled by the Planet Venus. You are attractive, tall and have a very sharp nose. You are intelligent, learned, religious, lover of beautiful things of nature and fond of pleasures. AS you possess sound judgments you are clever at making schemes. You are quite popular, lover of Art and Music.

Physical Appearance

Physically, you don't appear to be too strong and robust at first glance but you actually have great stamina. Your skin usually has a healthy glow to it and people often envy the texture of your hair.

Personality

You are gentle, compassionate and have an affectionate nature. You are large-hearted, with strong passions. You have a keen sense of honor and justice. In case of a dispute, friends and acquaintances are likely to turn to you as an arbitrator.

If you are appointed as judges, you keep the scales even. You have a keen aesthetic sense as well, and are fond of beauty and symmetry. Your judgments are on the dot but sometimes, you tend to be hesitant and indecisive, preferring to err on the side of diplomacy and tact. You often achieve a good position in life due to unexpected assistance from relatives. In religious matters, you are broad-minded, and want to follow the good and moral tenets of all religions and philosophies. However, you meet serious opposition in life from people in the field of religion and law.

Profession

You succeed in law, art, music, dealing in merchandise, mechanics, or professions connected with wines, spirits and liquors, science and navigation. Advocates, you make good Actors, Judges, Politicians, Diplomats and Salespersons.

Business and Finances

You seldom find yourself in a position where you have to take a loan. You often come into riches through a marriage or by entering into a business partnership. You build up your finances step-by-step for the future, and purchase property by paying regular installments.

You Match with Gemini, Libra or Aquarius.

Romance and Marriage

You are inclined to go through more than one relationship before deciding whom to marry. You are affectionate by nature, and make good friends. Sometimes your friendship is mistaken as love by the opposite sex. You should in fact avoid self-indulgence in matters of sex and affection, and should not enter into bonds of matrimony with the first person you like

Your weakness

You often spend your energy taking care of others instead of yourself. Plenty of water is necessary in a day for you as this keeps you away from toxins. Proper rest is very necessary for your health. So it would be advisable on your part to take proper rest and not to over exhort yourself.

Health and Disease

You are likely to suffer from diseases of the bowels, the bladder, the kidneys, the lumbar region, and the spine. At times, however, you tend to be a bit of a hypochondriac, worrying about your health and that of family members, even when no serious ailments are anywhere on the horizon. You are pretty healthy people but still you are prone to weakness in the lower back when you over exert yourself. You suffer from allergies, asthma and frequent colds and flu. The skin, hair, veins as well as throat, kidneys and lumbar region of you get easily affected.

Lucky Days Fridays, Mondays.
Lucky Colors Blue, green and white.
Lucky Stones Sapphire, Turquoise Opal.
Your Lucky Numbers 6, 15, 42, 51, 60

ZODIAC SIGNS

SCORPIO(24th October to 21st November)

Your Planetary Ruler Mars Pluto
Your Element Water
Your sign Fixed

Characterizes

You have a well-set body and are of middle structure, you have a youthful appearance and are fickle minded fellow. You are clever powerful and dignified at the same time you are cruel, sensual and usually not generous. You are a good conversationalist and you possess equally good writing skills, and are of commanding nature.

Physical Appearance

Generally, you present an attractive and strikingly tidy appearance with not a hair out of place, your nails well cared for and so on. Most of you have a fine skin texture. However, once you have entered your thirties, you tend to put on weights.

Personality

You have a strong and dominating personality, with strong will power. Generally, you never forget a grudge, and take revenge even after a long time. You do not prefer a frontal attack, and opt for indirect means. Subtle strategies and conspiracies hold a special fascination for you.

Therefore, you must be specially beware of who may happen to be your enemies. You are not only subtle, but energetic too. Generally, people around you are quick to note that you have a keen and penetrating

Intellect, combined with great dynamism. You are also analytical, skilful and patient, and have literary abilities and creative talents.

Profession and Career

The most suitable professions for you are those related to music, art and scientific pursuits. You also do well as doctors, particularly, as surgeons in departments of public health. You make good Architects, Executives in Industry, Officers in the Military and Navy, Chemists, Heads of Institutions, Mechanical engineers, Machinists, Sales Managers.

Business and Finances

You are shrewd at business matters, and financially, you generally do well. But you like to make a lot of money all at once. You have to be patient and persevering in building your finances. You should adopt wait and watch policy rather than grabbing all the entire lot at one time.

Ideal Match Cancer, Scorpio and Pisces.

Romance and Marriage

Love and Romance are the basic instincts of your harmful life. You are prone to get attraction of the opposite sex. In spite of your refusal to accept the pure love of the opposite sex you easily get on facial attraction rather than true love. You are considered very sexy and are intense lovers, with the attraction being more of physical craving than pure love. In several cases it has been noticed that probably there may be a tragedy in the first part of your life, and you may marry a second time.

Health and Disease

Your health calls for more care and attention. Since you are a good eater of delicious food you should be more careful in your choice of food. You are also prone to fevers and bruises. The weak parts in your anatomy are the groin and bladder, the pelvis, the stomach and the throat. You are prone to catching infections and contagious diseases.

Your Weakness

You generally put off things till the last moment and you also prepare at the eleventh hour it is because of your fortune that you come out successfully. You have the tendency to start late but again your fortune favors you to finish first. Though on the face it you appear to be frank playful and blunt but actually you would like to keep all secrets in your heart and mind.

Lucky Days Tuesday and Thursday.
Lucky Colors Rust, red, earth brown.
Lucky Stone Bloodstone, Topaz, Garnet, Red Coral.
Your Lucky Numbers 9, 18, 36, 45, 63

ZODIAC SIGNS

SAGITTARIUS (22nd November to 21st December)

Your Planetary Ruler Jupiter
Your Element Fire
Your sign Movable

Charactertics

You are well known for your boldness and dashing approach in relationship and conversations. You are courageous pushy and accommodating. You being a dual sign you believe in that variety is this spice of life. You also insist on your personal freedom and liberty.

Appearance

Generally fine boned with a glowing complexion, large eyes, a pert nose and a charming smile, you tend to walk with a gliding movement. Your bodily actions are usually soft and refined instead of being clumsy and ungainly.

Personality

You are usually quite brilliant, noble and refined. You are swift and sudden in speech and action. Sometimes you speak out your mind even before the other person has finished a sentence. You are truthful, and keep your promises. You are bold, free and dashing. You make friends easily, and are attached to them.

You are socially successful, and many persons of high standing will become your patrons. But some of them will prove to be highly treacherous, and will almost result in your loss of position. Your enemies will prove to be very bitter and persistent. You should take care that your position and prosperity are not threatened by the mischief of your enemies. You have a strong instinct, and are more successful if you work according to your own instincts, rather than on the advice of others. You should avoid betting, speculation and gambling, as this habit may lead to heavy losses.

Profession and Career

You can succeed well in teaching, in the field of religion and law, in politics, administration, and also in business or banking. You are good sports persons, fond of hunting and the outdoor life and would do well in any occupation connected with them. You have a strong dramatic sense as well, and can also do well in occupations connected with the stage.

Business and Finances

Your early years will not be prosperous. You may be subjected to financial stringency on account of losses your parents may have suffered. Success will come to you only after middle age. Up to your thirtieth year, you are likely to have frequent setbacks in your financial career. But success does come to you, as your sun sign is ruled by Jupiter, which stands for honor, riches and position. You do not have a strong inclination towards purchase of real estate and immovable properties. Consequently, very few persons born under this sun sign build large estates.

Ideal Match Aries, Leo, Sagittarius and Pisces.

Romance and Marriage

In choosing your spouse, you are more idealistic than passionate. Consequently, even after the engagement, you break off the relationship if you find that your finance is not up to your mark. You love, but since you are not demonstrative in your affections, others may misunderstand them as lacking in warmth. However, if your spouse fails to keep in pace with you, the marriage may break. At times, there are two marriages, one of which proves detrimental to your progress.

Health and Disease

Your general health is good, but you are likely to suffer from nervous disorders. The sign Sagittarius rules the hips, thighs and the muscular system. It is also connected with the motor impulses. You are likely to suffer from mental tension, Sciatica, Hip Disease or some kind of lameness.

YOUR WEAKNESS

You being a masculine sing, you do not hesitate to think and you speak out and act, as you desire. Though you are truthful in your thoughts people will misunderstand and take you as their enemies because of your harsh and bold talks, you will speak out what you feel is right without considering how the others would value your such statements. You are advice not to be out spoken if you want to maintain your relationship with others.

Lucky Days Monday and Thursday
Lucky Colors Red, Pink, and Purple.
Lucky Stones Topaz, and Turquoise.
Your Lucky Numbers 3, 12, 21, 39, 48

ZODIAC SIGNS

CAPRICORN (22nd December to 19th January)

CAPRICORN (22nd December to 19th January)

Your Planetary Ruler Saturn
Your Element Earth
Your sign Moveable

Characteristics

You will be economical, prudent, reasonable, thoughtful and practical in life. You will be calculative and you will execute any work after taking a thoughtful and careful decision. You will have the required push and confidence and you will not hesitate in bringing through chance in your career, once you take a bold and careful decision you have a study nature, immense tolerance but at times you will lack the required degree of patience. You are serious in disposition, and humility is one of your chief characteristics.

Appearance

You are good looking, with sharp features, well shaped eyebrows and sensual lips. Your eyes are piecing in their intensity at times. You facial outlook is also quite pleasing and attraction.

Personality

You are prudent, cautious and hard working. You are active and vigorous, and, at the same time, plodding. You are endowed with a spirit of service, and have a strong sense of duty. You have initiative that brings you success. You are practical and economical in spending. You are loyal and conscientious in your work. Your practical nature, at times, gives the impression that you lack warmth. But actually, you are loving and devoted. You will meet opposition from persons occupying high or low ranks, but will, ultimately, surmount all obstacles. You will have powerful patronage of a very high personage, particularly, if you are in the armed forces. In service, you will give satisfaction to your superior. You often rise high in politics too.

Profession and Career

You succeed well in all occupations where hard work and plodding are the main features. You do well in work connected with Agriculture, Forestry, Education, Biology, in Factories and large organizations.

Business and Finances

You are versatile and shrewd in business. You earn money on your own and not due to any windfall, legacy or inheritance. Money also comes to you late in life. You have to toil pretty hard to get to the highest position in life. Money does not come to you that easily.

Ideal Match Taurus, Virgo, Libra and Capricorn.

Romance and Marriage

You do not marry in a hurry, and do so only when you are assured that the other party reciprocates your love. However, you do not prove stable in your affections.

This is not due to an inborn unfaithful disposition but due to the influence of others. Your spouse may be fickle, and bring about a break in your marital relationship. Often, you prefer to marry a homebody who can provide home comforts and good companionship.

Health and Disease

You are likely to suffer from rheumatism or gout. You are liable to get liver trouble nervous tension should be avoided. Your stomach is weak spot. Your health gets better with your age. You tend to suffer from joint problems, arthritis, neuralgia and rheumatism. You are prone to skin diseases and have problems with bones, gall bladder, teeth and spleen.

Your Weakness

You often tend to become desperate, broken hearted and test yourself to a greater height where you feel the burden of physical strain. Therefore you should correct yourselves and you should be aware of others as well as your fault and deficiency you should avoid nervousness at all cost.

Lucky Days Saturday
Lucky Colors Grey, black, blue, brown.
Lucky Stones Blue Sapphire, Amethyst, Onyx.
Lucky Numbers 1, 10, 4, 22, 35, 44

ZODIAC SIGNS

AQUARIUS (20th January to 18th February)

Your Ruling Planet Saturn, Uranus
Your Element Air
Born in Sign: Fixed

CHARACTERISTIC

Being the eleventh sign of the zodiac, you have a broad outlook and human understanding. You are outspoken, social, intelligent, and you possess good retentive power. You are also shrewd, clever headed you have your own way of thinking and doing things and you carry out your works according to your own discretion. You will not hesitate to do any unusual or irregular thing even if you consider tobe morally upright. Your sense of dressing and the taste of clothing would be something different and you not like to imitate others. You have your individuality, mannerism peculiarity and your own specialty. You are often far ahead with fresh ideas and schemes. You generate new ideas and at times act in a way which shows that the laws are not made for you which means you over act and your actions are beyond anything body's imagination. You develop good intuition and mental will prefer to go for deep meditation and good concentration.

Appearance

You are middle stature strong person and have broad shoulder and large bones with a little amount of grace and your physical appearance is quite striking. Quite of you possess high cheeks and a peculiar winning smile.

Personality

You have an alert mind, and are keen to acquire more knowledge. You have striking intuitive and psychic powers. You possess a strong will power, and are hard working. You are fond of solitude, and are patient and persevering in your efforts. You are religious and philosophical. You see religion and philosophy as a manifestation of beauty and harmony, a means of universal love and service to mankind. You have a logical mind, and would do well to be guided by your own intuition and reasoning rather than that of others in arriving at decisions. You are kind hearted, original, simple, energetic and systematic. You are honest to your friends and enjoy enormous respect in your group. Your friends and contacts will range from many influential and eminent people yet you will feel melancholy and lonely at times. You will be ready to help others at the moment's notice but will always remain personally detached. You are an idealist independent, inventive thinker, quick witted, positive, excitable and, when need be you are also aggressive and combative.

Profession and Career

Since you a scientific bent of mind the profession and career best suited for you are Finance Marketing, Administration, Writing, Physiologists, Acting and you excel well when you are given the chance to handle most difficult situation or posts. You are also excellent when it comes to public dealing and can speak well in public Meetings. You do well as Leaders, Managers and Bosses.

Business and Finances

You are not so keen on building your bank balance, yet you do save money, which you are inclined to use for the benefit of the public at large. You have a strong desire to possess a second house, such as a country home.

You are fond of traveling, but one of these journeys will be the cause of financial reverses or loss in social position. You have very good relations with your servants and employees. But you should be careful that the latter do not cause you any financial harm.

You match with Gemini, Libra or Aquarius.

Romance and Marriage

Your domestic life is usually gets disturbed when you tend to lose your mental balance. Your love affairs will have a strong intellectual and artistic bias. Since you are very idealistic, you will have to be adaptable in your matrimonial relationship, even if you find that your partner does not come up to your standard. Your spouse will have an artistic temperament but is likely to be proud and imperious.

Health and Disease

You suffer from high blood pressure, hardening of arteries and Circulatory problems. Your sign rules nervous and lymphatic systems the ankles, calves of the legs, and throat, lungs, heart. You have a strong constitution, but are liable to fall ill suddenly, and such illnesses affect your nervous system. Precautions should also be taken against infectious diseases. You have a tendency to put on weight if you are not careful. You are also prone to sinus and bladder infections, varicose veins and cramps in lower legs.

YOUR WEAKNESS

Since you are over sensitive, your feelings are easily hurt. You often tend to loose control of yourself and do undesirable acts or things which you regret later. Though you are quite social yet you suffer from loneliness at times. In personal life you often indulge in lovely romantic affairs or extra marital affairs, which make your married life unhappy.

Lucky Days Sunday, Saturday
Lucky Colors Purple, Grey, black, blue, bluish green.
Lucky Stone Sapphire, aquamarine, opal, onyx.
Your Lucky Numbers 4, 13, 22, 31, 40, 49.

ZODIAC SIGNS

PISCES (19th February to 20th March)

Your Planetary Ruler Jupiter, Neptune
Your Element Water
Your sign Fixed

Characteristics

You will be philosophical, restless, contemplating, imagining, honest, outspoken and helpful. You will be sweet tempered and socially inclined towards others. You being a common and famine sign your expression and thoughts will be modified and even thoroughly changed when you are in front of the audience you will have the desire to study the occult science and the divine life of god.

Appearance

You are generally of short stature with a tendency to be plump, short limbs, a full face, pale complexion, a tendency to develop a double chin, muscular and spherical shoulders. You have big and protruding eyes, soft and silky hair and a wide mouth.

Personality

You have a kind, loving, truthful and sympathetic nature. Usually, you are courteous and hospitable, helpful and humane, and you cannot harm any one even if you try. Being a dual sign, you are a puzzle to others and even to yourself. By and large, you are sweet tempered and social.

Professions and Career

You can be successful as accountants, bankers, as performers in music and opera houses, cinema, practitioners of occult sciences, actors, liaison officers, personnel in medical and education departments.

Business and Finances

You have good business ability. You are end owed with skills, which will bring you wealth and power. You do not relish the idea of being dependent on your children in old age so you keep the money safe for that period. You are helpful to needy people but mostly make advances of money to those who can repay on demand. You have plurality of interests.

Romance and Marriage

You are strongly attracted to romance and look for a combination of good looks and intellect in your partner. However, you tend to be suspicious by nature towards your partner, which can kill your love. You are easily taken in by flattery, and should not select a partner who sets too much store on socialization.

Ideal Match Virgo, Cancer and Pisces.

Health and Diseases

Your mostly inclined to suffer from Nervous, Depression, Insomnia Anemia and Eye trouble.

Your Weakness

You are have the quality to speak and understand the domestic difficulties of the poor and will go about to assist them in the need of their hour but without considering your own financial position. The main weakness in you that you will rely upon all your friends and you will realize late in your life that your friends have not withstood to your expectation.

You are advised not to keep contemplating and daydreaming.

Lucky Days Monday, Tuesday and Thursday
Lucky Colors Yellow, and Orange
Lucky Stones Yellow Sapphire, Opal and Ruby
Lucky Numbers 2, 11, 22, 31,40

CHAPTER 15

ASTROLOGICAL HINTS MICROSCOPY OF ASTROLOGY

COMPATABILITY OF ZODIAC SIGNS

ZODIAC SIGNS

ARIES WITH OTHER ZODIAC SIGNS

ARIES WITH ARIES	ARIES WITH TAURUS
ARIES WITH GEMINI	ARIES WITH CANCER
ARIES WITH LEO	ARIES WITH VIRGO
ARIES WITH LIBRA	ARIES WITH SCORPIO
ARIES WITH SAGATTARIUS	ARIES WITH CAPRICORN
ARIES WITH AQUARIUS	ARIES WITH PISCES

ARIES WITH ARIES

An Aries female tends to dominate and if one person will submit to the other there should be much compatibility between two persons born in this fire sign. If both Arians have dominant and forceful aspects in their horoscopes, conflict will arise, as both partners desire to be head of the family. The situation dictates that both shall go for their own careers or directions independently. What starts out so promisingly ends in disharmony? A divorce can be rather be violent and heart breaking.

There in order to lead a happy and peaceful life they both have to submit to each other their likes and dislikes.

ARIES WITH TAURUS

Aries is impulsive, but Taurus is steady. Both are highly sensual, but the deliberate teasing and unpredictable lovemaking of Taurus can annoy Aries. Taurus is possessive and views Aries's need to be an individual desire rather than individual demand. Taurus is good at earning money but Aries is more spend thrift. This match may not make a fine combination as Venus, the goddess of love, rules Taurus nature and Mars the fiery planet rules Aries. Taurus being slow moving may find the going a bit hectic, though excitement may help to stimulate the friendship but this friendship may not be a lasting affair. Arians tend to omit their temperamental outbursts. Taurus is not highly emotional on the surface, but they can become furious as a bull, as and when they see red in Aries.

ARIES WITH GEMINI

They won't bore each other because as both love to talk more. Gemini is versatile and ingenious and Aries is dynamic and intelligent. They share a special compatibility, for Gemini is as restless and anxious to try new things as Aries is. Gemini is clever enough to counter Aries's needs. The signals are definitely go. Aries is likely to be the leader sexually, and Gemini delights in thinking up variations to keep Aries's interest at a peak. Gemini being a mercurial sign, where the mind plays an important part in all love making, and the emotional Arian may be too much for the conventional nature of the Gemini. This combination sometimes has a great deal of hankering because of strong differences in their personalities. It is not a great match up.

ARIES WITH CANCER

These two are fascinated with each other. Cancer is cautious. Cancer loves heart and home and Aries hates to be tied down. Resentments often build up and they argue over petty mattes. Aries has a sharp tongue that wounds the Cancerians. This combination is usually hard to match. The moon rules Cancerians, making them moody, sentimental and secretive. Their tendency is to live in the past, and they have a difficult time forgetting serious quarrels or disagreement that may occur occasionally this is quite true of this couple.

ARIES WITH LEO

This is usually a great combination. But both have got egos problems and both like to lead. Aries wouldn't dream of taking second place, and Leo needs constant watch. They can work it out properly if neither tries to defame the other. Though it's a fine sexual match, as both are fiery and romantic. Aries is optimistic and open to life; Leo is generous and good-hearted. They could find room to compromise easily as with both sides being emotional in their make up, Leo will fascinate an Arian mate if Aries will allow Leo to hold the centre of the floor on occasions. Their sex life could be legendary and infidelity kept to a minimum, or eliminated all together if each of them find what they want from each other, and not have a physical compulsion to stray. Leo admires the aggressive tendencies of fiery signs. That is why Arians make this an ideal union.

ARIES WITH VIRGO

Mercury rules Virgo and Aries is ruled by Mars. But they have totally different ideas. Aries's passions are impulsive and direct. Virgo's sexuality is more enigmatic and takes time to be revealed. In other areas Aries is full of exciting new plans and ideas, and insists on being boss. Virgo is critical and fussy, and likes things to be done the way he wants. They end up making war, not love and do not blend well astrologically. Virgos desire a well-ordered existence and won't be happy under Arian leadership. If the Arian allows Virgo space, and acknowledges the virtues of Virgo, the two can make for a dynamic relationship.

ARIES WITH LIBRA

Libra wants peace, quiet, and harmony while Aries wants action and adventure. Both like social life, entertaining, and pleasure, but both are restless in their ways. There is a powerful initial attraction between these two but their love life may be bit unconventional. Libra will look for someone less demanding, and Aries will bind someone for more dictating.

Marvellous affair but poor marriage shows. Libra's refined and artistic temperament wishes for reciprocal attachments. And this is something Aries cannot provide. There is a wider the ordinary margin for error though, and most of these combinations will go at the distance and nonreciprocal.

ARIES WITH SCORPIO

With Mars dominating both signs it makes for very positive temperaments unless there are some bad natal planetary aspects. Since Aries won't take orders from Scorpions and Scorpio will never take a back seat. Love cannot be a bonfire between these two. Though they've physical, energetic, and passionate in their sexual nature and each has a forceful personality and wants to control the other there is no room for these two. This combination is can make an ideal match if one ignores to dominate the other.

ARIES WITH SAGITTARIUS

The Mars-Jupiter duo is usually an ideal match for each other. Sagittarius is a perfect ideal and temperamental match for Aries. They both are active, spontaneous people. There may be a little conflict because both are impulsive and brutally frank. However, they have wonderful senses of humour and enjoy each other's company. If they make it in the bedroom, they'll make it everywhere else. Most people of these matches are in it for life. The Sagittarius means liberty, and the pursuit of happiness while Aries is subscribes to this theory. And for this reason, that makes them a good match

ARIES WITH CAPRICORN

Capricorns are usually patient and are traditionally easygoing. Arians are too impatient to cope with the slowness attitude. Saturn represents the Capricorn and Mars governs the Aries. Aries's taste for innovation and experiment may not please Capricorns. Aries is restless, fiery, and impulsive; Capricorn is ordered, settled, and practical. Capricorn needs to dominate and so does Aries. Problems often crops up over moneymaking schemes. Not a hopeful combination. Capricorn will nod against the Arian will and a disagreement is bound to occur. In the matter of sex there is an affinity; however, their inherent personalities clash. The combination of a fire sign with an earth sign. Aries is a fiery in nature while Capricorn is earth, cautious and reserved. Aries prefers to take action while Capricorn would rather plan and wait. Without a great deal of tolerance and patience, there is not much hope for this union.

ARIES WITH AQUARIUS

Both signs are of independent nature but at times Aquarius will do things without notice with which Aries may become impatient. Since both are active, ambitious, enjoy a wide range of interests, and are equally eager for sexual adventure. As both are independent Aquarius energies more than Aries and Aries may at times feel neglected. Aries finds the Aquarian unpredictability exciting, but feels entirely insecure. However, with a bit of tact and understanding on both sides, this is a great affair that could turn into something even better. This could possibly be a good relationship, but will require a positive attitude on both parts.

ARIES WITH PISCES

Pisceans are romantic and they desire the delicate approach that which the Arian lacks. Aries will draw Pisces out of their shell, and in turn will be appealed by Pisces mysterious nature in terms of sexuality. The boldness and confidence of Aries adding to the Pisces's intuitions and fantasies end in an eventful union. Pisces is somewhat shy and Aries likes to be dominant, Pisces likes having someone to be looked upon. For a happy coupling thus requires only a little more tact on Arian part.

COMPATABILITY

ZODIAC SIGNS

TAURUS WITH OTHER ZODIAC SIGNS

TAURUS WITH ARIES	TAURUS WITH TAURUS
TAURUS WITH GEMINI	TAURUS WITH CANCER
TAURUS WITH LEO	TAURUS WITH VIRGO
TAURUS WITH LIBRA	TAURUS WITH SCORPIO
TAURUS WITH SAGITTARIUS	TAURUS WITH CAPRICORN
TAURUS WITH AQUARIUS	TAURUS WITH PISCES

TAURUS WITH ARIES

Taurus is possessive and views Aries's need to be an individual desire rather than individual demand. Aries is an impatient, energetic sign, rather domineering the slower-moving Taurus may find the going a bit hectic, but the excitement may help stimulate courtship since Taurus is a highly emotional sign, though very obstinate when dictated to. Taurean nature is ruled by Venus, the goddess of love, and Aries is ruled by Mars the fiery planet. Aries is impulsive, but Taurus is steady. Both are highly sensual, but the deliberate teasing and unpredictable lovemaking of Taurus can annoy Aries. This match may not make a fine combination as Taurus being slow moving may find the going a bit hectic, though excitement may help to stimulate the friendship but this friendship may not be a lasting affair.

TAURUS WITH TAURUS

Both are earthy creatures that prefer safety to adventure. From a physical stand point; this appears to be a compatible combination. Both share a fondness for money, and are hardworking, loyal, and affectionate.

The female Taurean tends to be more sentimental than the male Taurean, but each is as possessive than the other, which works out fine. Because they are both earthy and direct about sexual needs, there should be no problem in that department, if one adheres to the will and wishes of the other.

TAURUS WITH GEMINI

The Gemini personality may prove to be too restless for the Taurus nature. The two signs are emotionally at distance. These two are completely unalike in temperament. Taurus is fixed in opinions, resistant to change. Gemini is restless, vacillating. Gemini is attracted to Taurus's passions, but in time Taurus's instinct for security and stability will be offended by Gemini volatile nature. Taurus's demands are simply too much for Gemini, who seeks excuses. Taurus with the innate need to possess will never be able to hang on to the unsettled Gemini. Gemini loves change and Taurus resists it so becomes rather difficult for both of them to come to an understanding in the matters of making love.

TAURUS WITH CANCER

Usually this makes a good combination. Cancer likes a good home with much affection. This is what every Taurean hopes to find when undertaking conventional responsibilities. Cancer needs someone like Taurus to depend on as Cancer gives Taurus the loyalty and feedback it needs. Taurus is ambitious for money and security, and Cancer has exactly those same goals. Similar interests and desires make for harmonious meetings. From an emotional point of view, there is nothing in the stars that bars the prospect of a happy married life between these two partners. This is a good combination as both signs are naturally attracted by the others sense for feelings and emotions.

TAURUS WITH LEO

Venus and the Sun make a good combination, especially when each understands the other's faults. Excellent physical qualities and great attraction is there for both partners. Taurus will supply the attention that Leo requires but will expect it to be returned. A strong attraction physically and emotionally but having too many obstacles to cope with.

TAURUS WITH VIRGO

With both being earth signs there will be much common ground for these two. Both Virgo and Taurus desire material success and security. Taurus keeps a careful eye on expenditures, which pleases Virgo. Although they lack what might be called a spontaneous approach to life, neither puts a high value on that. Both share the same intellectual pursuits. Taurus's attraction and Virgo's sharp mind are a good combination for success as a team.

TAURUS WITH LIBRA

Libra an air sign loves to roam and Taurus an earth sign loves to sit and waits patiently. With understanding it could be a harmonic relationship. Taurus balances Libra's indecisiveness. Taurus finds Libra a warm, romantic, partner. Libra is born to charm. The love goddess and it does shine on the two lovebirds that are until one-steps out of line. Both signs are ruled by Venus and have sensual natures, but each expresses this quality differently. However there are common interest and a meeting of the mind and body making this a very good marital combination. They appreciate beauty and the finer things of life.

TAURUS WITH SCORPIO

These two are opposites in the zodiac, but they have more in common than other opposites. Both are determined and ambitious, and neither is much of a lover. These are zodiac opposites, but they are compatible earth and water signs. This usually manifests itself in a strong physical attraction. This combination mutually admires each other. Jealousy however is the big problem with this pair and that seems to be always showing its face. Taurus must be careful to keep faith with the scorpion, or else this combination will fall down without warning.

TAURUS WITH SAGITTARIUS

These are two very different personality types the more reserved Taurus and the outgoing Sagittarius both has an appreciation for the truth. Sagittarius has an easy live and let live attitude this might work if Taurus can tie a string to Sagittarius's.

The Taurus who marries a Sagittarian will find that no amount of arguing or berating is going to change the reckless Sagittarian With some understanding they can find harmony in their characters as long as they allow each other their personalities. With the Taurean being possessive and the Sagittarian being freedom loving, the Sagittarian may find this hard to co-operate with.

TAURUS WITH CAPRICORN

A good combination of the basic earth signs. Both are responsible and practical natures. They even have a mutual desire for success and material things. Capricorn is a strong match for Taurus, for they both have passions that are straightforward and uncomplicated. Capricorn is a bit more secretive than Taurus. With both partners having mutual understanding of each other's personalities this can be a very compatible marriage. Venus and Saturn blend very well from an emotional point of view.

TAURUS WITH AQUARIUS

These two live on opposite sides of the planet, in fact some times, Taurus will wonder if Aquarius is even from this planet. Neither is likely to approve of the other. Taurus is conservative, careful, closemouthed. Aquarius is unconventional, innovative, and vivacious.

Taurus is lusty and passionate while Taurus needs security and comfort. Aquarius, a fancy-free loner who resents ties that bind. This combination heads in for many difficulties. The Aquarian being unpredictable both love ease and comfort but their views on how to obtain them are very different. Another big irritation for the Taurus lover is the unwillingness of the Aquarius to share his secrets. Aquarius will find the Taurus attention somewhat smothering and restrictive.

TAURUS WITH PISCES

These two can share a great deal of their appreciation for beauty, art, and sensuality and just about any of the finer things in life. Pisces may not altogether understand Taurus's materialistic approach to life. Taurus's practical, easygoing nature helps Pisces through its frequent changes of mood.

In love, Taurus is devoted and Pisces adores. This usually is a very happy combination. Pisces being romantic, imaginative, impressionable and flexible is just what the Taurus native is looking for.

COMPARABILITY

ZODIAC SIGNS

GEMINI WITH OTHER ZODIAC SIGNS

GEMINI WITH ARIES	GEMINI WITH TAURUS
GEMINI WITH GEMINI	GEMINI WITH CANCER
GEMINI WITH LEO	GEMINI WITH VIRGO
GEMINI WITH LIBRA	GEMINI WITH SCORPIO

GEMINI WITH SAGITTARIUS	GEMINI WITH CAPRICORN
GEMINI WITH AQUARIUS	GEMINI WITH PISCES

GEMINI WITH ARIES

Gemini respects the refined, intellectual approach to continual bliss. Impatient Arians may find this frustrating, after awhile may try to find a less difficult companion. This lively, energetic pair can be good friends as well as good lovers. Aries will probably make the decisions because Gemini has difficulty in that area. Not a great match up, but can work with understanding and effort. Aries needs to calm down. Don't get me wrong. Gemini is versatile and ingenious and Aries is dynamic and intelligent. They share a special compatibility, for Gemini is as restless and anxious to try new things as Aries is. Gemini is clever enough to counter Aries's needs. Gemini being a mercurial sign, where the mind plays an important part in all love making, and the emotional Arian may be too much for the conventional nature of the Gemini. It is not a great match up.

GEMINI WITH TAURUS

The Gemini personality may prove to be restless for the Taurean nature. Taurus wants life to be stables and ordered, while Gemini is easily bored and looks for new experiences. These two are completely unalike in temperament. Taurus's demands are simply and Gemini seeks excuses. Gemini loves change and Taurus resists it so becomes rather difficult for both of them to come to an understanding in the matters of understanding each other. An unpromising match.

GEMINI WITH GEMINI

As both are of air signs and are ruled by the planet mercury. These two will never bore each other, for they are interested in everything. A compatible combination this should prove to be, at least both would understand each other's changeable nature. The Gemini demands for change and variety will keep this relationship some how moving. Whether it produces a happiness or sadness depends on at least one of the companion paying attention, at least for some time. Discussions will be lively and ever changing life may become restless but again they cannot have it in any other way.

GEMINI WITH CANCER

Cancer needs security and homely atmosphere whereas Gemini dislikes to be being tied down. These two have too little in common for a long-term relationship. Gemini lacks patience with Cancer's moods and Gemini's sharp tongue is too harsh for Cancer's strong ego. While Gemini is constantly on the alert for change, Cancer is satisfied to become a truly homely mate. Cancers are driven by emotion and feelings and generally prefer to be constant. Gemini's unstoppable movement may prove be unsettling to Cancer's needs. They are poised for a downward trend. Gemini makes Cancer feel quite insecure and their affair is likely to result in a volatile behaviour.

GEMINI WITH LEO

On the surface there is great mutual attraction for both signs. While Leo loves with his heart first, Gemini loves with his mind.

Both are naturally attracted to glamour and flattery of the world. Their affair is a chase after variety and amusement. An affectionate pair who really enjoy each other. Leo will probably demand more adoration than Gemini is willing to give. Socially, each tries to upstage the other, but they have a lot of fun together doing it. There is good reason to be optimistic about this pairing; all in all this is a very good combination of air and fire.

GEMINI WITH VIRGO

Both are Mercury-ruled and have a mental approach to life. They are attracted to each other because of a mutual interest in intellectual ideas. Both have active minds. Virgo's analytical approach seems like indifference to Gemini. Virgo looks on Gemini's busy social life as superficial and a waste of time. Virgo is critical; Gemini is tactless. Mercury is calculating and logical; in Virgo it is critical and demanding. Gemini's ever-present desire for change would be much for the realistic Virgo. One point for the two to be compatible would be the desire for good clothes, cleanliness, mutual desire for friends and associates who are engaged in intellectual and artistic pursuits. Gemini can deal with Virgo's critical eye, well, this could work.

GEMINI WITH LIBRA

These two air signs are well suited in every way. Both signs have much in common and enough to make an ideal partnership. Libra being under Venus's influence and Mercury ruling Gemini makes for a very good planetary combination. This will be a very stimulating relationship. One sign compliments the other and brings out the better part of each other's nature. Gemini will find it easy to communicate with Libra who is only too happy to share his information and ideas. They are affectionate, fun loving, entertaining, and travel fond. This is considered to be a great astrological influence for a long and happy marriage.

GEMINI WITH SCORPIO

An air sign with a water sign. Gemini is too changeable and inconstant for intense Scorpio, who needs and demands total commitment. Scorpio is basically a loner; Gemini likes to glitter in social settings.

Gemini has a strong penchant for independence, while Scorpio wants to dominate and possess. Gemini's desire for freedom of action will clash with the jealous and possessive nature of Scorpio. While some Gemini-Scorpio combinations may work out fairly well, the pure Gemini-Scorpio alliance packs as much power as an atomic bomb. These two will have some difficulty rectifying their innate natures. Love conquers all. Then again, too much, stifles some. These two are opposites in the zodiac and are attracted to each other like magnets. They'll especially enjoy each other's minds for both have wide-ranging and varied interests.

GEMINI WITH SAGITTARIUS

Gemini is ruled by Mercury and Sagittarius is ruled by Jupiter the planet of knowledge and wisdom. Both have bright minds, but Sagittarius is outspoken while Gemini likes to enjoy fun. They are usually a compatible combination with both being frank, outspoken, and a certain amount of personal understanding being made. They meet on a common ground, and can plan their lives with equilibrium. They are restless, adventuresome, imaginative, and fun loving. No other opposite signs in the zodiac enjoy each other more than these two. However if Sagittarius forgoes its ego and Gemini restores to concrete planning they can make a good combination otherwise their combination may not last long.

GEMINI WITH CAPRICORN

Capricorn gets worried about security, while Gemini feels about losing its liberty. The Saturn ruled Capricorn will be at differences with the Mercury ruled Gemini. Patience is a virtue with Capricorn, but it is not so with Gemini. Gemini's need for a survival does nothing to make Capricorn feel secure. Gemini's free talks, meets opposition from conservative Capricorn. Capricorn's great drive to execute will prove to be too much for the Gemini. Until they both are ready to minimize their goals. Capricorn will go on hunting until he gains the upper hand. Of course with these two people going together anything is possible and the outcome of the result may not be satisfying to each other.

GEMINI WITH AQUARIUS

Gemini is bit inconstant or unstable, Aquarius understands somewhat Gemini's needs. Gemini is always looking for surprises and the Aquarian can give them. Gemini and Aquarius get along quite easily. They share a taste for new things, travelling, meeting new people and doing new things. Since both are unpredictable, things may always go smoothly with them. But love keeps getting them together, for Aquarius adores Gemini's wit and good cheer. The caring, thoughts of Aquarius will find a smooth home with Gemini. Uranus, the ruling planet of Aquarius, is full of surprises and sudden changes. This will suit the Gemini perfectly. There will be plenty of none stop variety to afford the stimulation that Gemini needs for its dual personality and goal.

GEMINI WITH PISCES

Their passion is quite high, and so are their problems. Pisces get easily hurt by thoughtless Gemini. Gemini is mischievous and playful, but Pisces is sensitive and takes things to heart easily. Each practices in his or her thoughts in their own way: Gemini needs freedom and Pisces needs unending appreciation. Pisces just can't feel secure with talkative moods of Gemini, and he tries to pull the net in his own way. This atmosphere eventually makes it hard for Gemini to breathe his own liberty. The freedom of Gemini is stake if he marries a Piscean. Gemini's should be prepared to change their ways if they want to seek happiness with a loving and possessive Piscean.

COMPARABILITY

ZODIAC SIGNS

CANCER WITH OTHER ZODIAC SIGNS

CANCER WITH ARIES	CANCER WITH TAURUS
CANCER WITH GEMINI	CANCER WITH CANCER
CANCER WITH LEO	CANCER WITH VIRGO
CANCER WITH LIBRA	CANCER WITH SCORPIO
CANCER WITH SAGITTARIUS	CANCER WITH CAPRICORN
CANCER WITH AQUARIUS	CANCER WITH PISCES

CANCER AND ARIES

The moon rules Cancer, making him moody, sentimental and secretive. Aries is ruled by mars and makes him bold and aggressive. Cancer is easily hurt by Aries's aggressiveness and sharp tongue. Cancer likes security and Aries needs freedom to explore new worlds. Both like to accumulate money. Aries wants to spend it and Cancer wants to keep it. Too many problems here. This combination is usually hard to match. Cancer holds on like that of a crab, while Aries cannot part with the things so easily that are with them. The secretive nature of Cancer has the potential of clashing with the openness of Aries. Though Aries can be moody too, it is not quite so bad as Cancer. If they make it through the first year or so the rest may turn out to be an easy affair.

CANCER AND TAURUS

This is a good combination as both signs are naturally attracted to each other. Both need security and both are loving, affectionate, and passionate. Both are moneymakers, and together they enjoy the delights of heart and home. Taurus is good for Cancer's moodiness. What each needs the other supplies?

From an emotional point of view, there is nothing in the stars that bars the prospect of a happy married life between these two partners. One thing is what Tureen should remember is that Cancer is sensitive, and will crawl into a shell if he or she is unhappy emotionally.

CANCER AND GEMINI

Gemini is constantly on the alert for change, Cancer is satisfied to become a true mate. Cancer's nature is emotional and Gemini's nature is openness and that makes it difficult for them to understand each other. Cancer will try to keep Gemini penned in, and Gemini can't abide that. Cancer and moodiness may become too much for Gemini to cope with. There would be better compatibility where the female is a Gemini and the male is a Cancerian, Cancers are driven by emotion and feelings and generally prefer to remain constant while Gemini's unstoppable movement and talkative nature will prove unpleasant to Cancer desire.

CANCER AND CANCER

They understand each other perfectly and can also wound each other without even trying hard or harsh. Both are too sensitive, demanding and dependent. They have a lot in common, and each needs an enormous amount of attention. That's the main drawback and trouble.

This combination can make married life easy going, because each will have a sympathetic understanding for the other's moods, and wishes. Though there are times were they may disagree, with each clinging to their previous experience and teachings each will no doubt understand the other better. Both will give enough consideration to their company and they should have no trouble in finding constant happiness.

CANCER AND LEO

Usually this is a good combination, since the Cancer reflects the light of the Leo. Leo's heart will soon forgive the mood outbursts that Cancer shows from time to time. Leo will appreciate cancer's attention and as long as cancer can forgive and forget that they feel neglected at times. Cancer will feel a bit more enthused around Leo and will probably let Leo run things.

Cancer has to get used to Leo's generous, open heartedness. Leo is just what insecure Cancer is looking for. Cancer's marvellous intuitions tell it exactly how to handle this Leo.

CANCER AND VIRGO

Virgo's demands may be a bit much for Cancer's desire for peace and quiet. Cancer's response is emotive while Virgo's is analytical. Cancer may have to warm up Virgo a little, since there is fire under the ice. This can turn into a comfortable, and affectionate relationship. Cancer's struggle for financial security works perfectly with Virgo. Cancer's dependency neatly complements Virgo's need to protect, and each is anxious to please the other. The full, affectionate feelings of cancer will not be completely satisfied by Virgo's direct approach to the practical matters at hand. Virgo will appreciate the loyalty and sincerity of cancer, but will need to be a little more demonstrative and affectionate with cancer.

CANCER AND LIBRA

Cancer is not temperamentally suited to cope with the freedom loving Libran. This pair operates on entirely different levels. Cancer is too temperamental and possessive for airy Libra. They both love a beautiful home, but Libra also needs parties and people and outside pleasures. When Cancer turns critical, especially about Libra's extravagance, Libra starts looking elsewhere. On the positive side though, they could make it. Ruled by the Moon and Venus respectively, there is common ground here despite the fact that we have a water sign and an air. Libra will appreciate Cancer's loyalty and generosity. Cancer wants love Libra seeks perfect intellectual communion.

CANCER AND SCORPIO

Water signs rule both. Cancer is loyal; Scorpio's jealousy isn't provoked. Cancer admires Scorpio's strength while Scorpio finds a haven in Cancer's emotional commitment. Both are extremely intuitive and sense what will please the other. Together they can build a happy home where they feel safe and loved. This relationship has great intimacy, intensity, and depth. Things just get better all the time. Scorpio should make a good mate for quiet spoken cancer. Scorpio and cancer could well prove the ideal marriage combination.

CANCER AND SAGITTARIUS

A water and fire combination. Sagittarius likes to wander, while Cancer is a prefers to stay at home. Cancer's commitment to total togetherness only makes Sagittarius desperate to get away. In addition, outspoken Sagittarius's bluntness continually wounds sensitive Cancer. They happen to be better friends than lovers. There is a vast difference in natures and the likely hood of being compatible is all but impossible, unless there are some positive aspects in their charts. Cancer is too needy for Sagittarius. On the good side, they are both generous people.

CANCER AND CAPRICORN

Both signs have plenty in common. Capricorn has too many other interests to give Cancer all the attention it needs. Cancer is shy, sensitive, and needs affection, while Capricorn is aloof, and domineering. Capricorn has the ability to make cancer's dream come true, while Cancer is happy wishing for and wanting the success and security that the Capricorn strives for. The elements of water and earth go well together but these are zodiac opposites you can expect both side of the coin. They will have to take the good with the bad and there will be plenty of both. Capricorn lacks the warmth and sentiment that Cancer requires.

CANCER AND AQUARIUS

Cancer has a conservative taste while Aquarius taste is usually the opposite. Aquarius is quick-minded, unpredictable, and apt to be impatient with cautious, hesitant Cancer. Cancer needs to feel close and secure. The social side of the Aquarian may prove to be too much for the Cancer. Aquarian's love to share their life stories with the world while cancer is satisfied to concentrate on personal obligations. Odds against this combination are too great for this combination, unless one will become convergent to the other. Aquarius has a need to be independent and often appears detached in a close relationship with cancer.

CANCER AND PISCES

A harmonious match and quite a perfect match as both are ruled by the water signs.

The sentimental combination of these two signs make for an ideal marriage. Although both will have their moments of gloom and doom, they will soon come out in the sunshine to forgive and forget each other. They are both romantic, need to love and be loved and can probably communicate to each other without speaking or making facial gestures. Both are emotional, intensely devoted, and sensitive to each other's moods.

COMPARABILITY

ZODIAC SIGNS

LEO WITH OTHER ZODIAC SIGNS

LEO WITH ARIES	LEO WITH TAURUS
LEO WITH GEMINI	LEO WITH CANCER
LEO WITH LEO	LEO WITH VIRGO
LEO WITH LIBRA	LEO WITH SCORPIO
LEO WITH SAGITTARIUS	LEO WITH CAPRICORN
LEO WITH AQUARIUS	LEO WITH PISCES

LEO WITH ARIES

This is usually a great combination. But both have got egos problems and both like to lead. Aries wouldn't dream of taking second place, and Leo needs constant watch. They can work it out properly if neither tries to defame the other. Though it's a fine sexual match, as both are fiery and romantic. Aries is optimistic and open to life; Leo is generous and good-hearted. Leo admires the aggressive tendencies of fiery signs. That is why Arians make this an ideal union.

LEO WITH TAURUS

Leo requires but will expect it to be returned. Leo loves to dominate and eventually Taurus being strong willed but more patient.

Venus and the Sun make a good combination, especially when each understands the other's faults. Excellent physical qualities and great attraction is there for both partners. Taurus will supply the attention that Leo requires but will expect it to be returned. A strong attraction physically and emotionally but having too many obstacles to cope with.

LEO WITH GEMINI

On the surface there is great mutual attraction for both signs. While Leo loves with his heart first, Gemini loves with his mind. Both are naturally attracted to glamour and flattery of the world. Their affair is a chase after variety and amusement. An affectionate pair who really enjoy each other. Leo will probably demand more adoration than Gemini is willing to give. Socially, each tries to upstage the other, but they have a lot of fun together doing it. There is good reason to be optimistic about this pairing; all in all this is a very good combination of air and fire. All in all this is a very good combination of air and fire.

LEO WITH CANCER

This is a combination of fire and water. Usually this is a good combination, since the Cancer reflects the light of the Leo. Leo's heart will soon forgive the mood outbursts that Cancer shows from time to time. Leo will appreciate cancer's attention and as long as cancer can forgive and forget that they feel neglected at times. Cancer will feel a bit more enthused around Leo and will probably let Leo run things. Cancer has to get used to Leo's generous, open heartedness. Leo is just what insecure Cancer is looking for. Cancer's marvellous intuitions tell it exactly how to handle this Leo.

LEO WITH LEO

The both being fire signs. Two positive and strong willed individuals. Both are romantic, colourful, and exuberant about life. Each not only wants to sit on the throne, each wants to be the power behind it as well. They want to be the head of their social groups. The two are constantly competing for leadership; unhappy results can result from this. The only hope for a successful partnership is for the female to be content to rule the home and the male to shine in the business and social world.

It's difficult for one Leo to make room for another ego as large as its own, but that's exactly what's needed here.

LEO WITH VIRGO

Leo being a fire sign and Virgo being the earth sign. Here is a good chance for a happy partnership. Virgo is practical Leo is extravagant and a spendthrift. Leo likes to live life in a really big way, but Virgo is conservative. This is one of those relationships that depend on the type of relationship it is. Leo will overwhelm Virgo, whose criticism will irk Leo. In business it is best when Leo leads and Virgo follows and the differences will be tolerated. Both of them should look elsewhere. If Virgo will permit Leo to hold the limelight and refrain from being too critical they should have no real barriers to a happy and successful partnership. But this may be quite hard.

LEO WITH LIBRA

Leo being a fire and Libra being an air sign. The comparability of this two shall be tiring affair. The hale and hearty Leo may prove to be too much for the sensitive Libra nature, though they have a lot in common that could make for a good combination. The sun ruling Leo and Venus ruling Libra usually form a strong and luxurious aspect. Libra is indecisive and Leo will naturally take charge. Both signs love luxuries, are subject to flattery, and are very artistically inclined. The book may not always balance because they're both extravagant and love a beautiful setting in which to shine. Each will also try to outdo the other in order to get attention.

LEO WITH SCORPIO

Leo being a fire sign and Scorpio being water sign. Two very strong willed individuals generally create some rather stormy moments. But Leo finds it hard to cope with Scorpio's jealousy and possessiveness. Scorpio considers Leo a showpiece. Scorpio doesn't understand Leo's need to be continually surrounded by an admiring audience. Scorpio would rather dominate than admire, and that doesn't suit Leo's kingly state. Two shinning personalities join together. Basically this should make for one of the most compatible combinations, but long and happy partnership will be far better a Leo female marries a Scorpio male.

LEO WITH SAGITTARIUS

Both being of fire sign. The pendulum can swing in any body's favour. Together they share a liking for freedom, adventure, and meeting new people. Leo's natural quality of leadership brings out what loyalty Sagittarius can give. Leo is very proud, but self-confident and expansive Sagittarius is quite happy to let Leo go. Both love change and excitement and have a great zest for life.

LEO WITH CAPRICORN

Leo being a fire sign whereas Capricorn is an earth sign. The combination of these two may at time lead to severe complications. The slow Capricorn may prove to be too much for the carefree nature of Leo. Leo will think Capricorn stingy with affection because Capricorn's reserved, undemonstrative nature cannot give Leo the adoration it needs. Neither will take a back seat nor let the other dominate. This affair will be on the rocks before it even leaves the dock. Leo forgives and forgets; Capricorn being the one who is slow to anger and seldom forgets. This pair would not form the ideal basis for mutual understanding. Leo likes to live for the moment and Capricorn prefers to make calculated movements.

LEO WITH AQUARIUS

Leo is a fire sign and Aquarius is an air sign. The comparability of this two in terms of worldly affairs can often become difficult to match. Both like socializing and meeting new people, but Leo always needs to perform on centre stage, which makes Aquarius impatient and irritable. Aquarius is too independent to become Leo's devoted subject. And that's where it ends. Leo views Aquarius's aloof emotions as a personal rejection. Both signs are better when doing things for others. Leo loves the world and Aquarius loves humanity. This makes for an excellent combination for a partnership that deals with or caters to the public. Each has a mutual understanding of the other when it comes to intimate matters, needs and desires.

LEO WITH PISCES

A Fire and water combination. Leo being a fire sign and Pisces being a water sign often makes this a unique combination. Both are more inclined to take than to give. Fiery Leo and watery Pisces. This is the depiction of these two. Generally not expected to work but both have an ability to learn from one another if they can get past their innate differences. The strong and hearty temperament of Leo may be too much for the subtle and sensitive Pisces. Pisces, with resilience, takes on the changing moods of any partnership. While Leo is flattered by the dependency of others, Pisces may be too much for Leo to take over a long period of time.

COMPARABILITY

ZODIAC SIGNS

VIRGO WITH OTHER ZODIAC SIGNS

VIRGO WITH ARIES	VIRGO WITH TAURUS
VIRGO WITH GEMINI	VIRGO WITH CANCER
VIRGO WITH LEO	VIRGO WITH VIRGO
VIRGO WITH LIBRA	VIRGO WITH SCORPIO
VIRGO WITH SAGITTARIUS	VIRGO WITH CAPRICORN
VIRGO WITH AQUARIUS	VIRGO WITH PISCES

VIRGO WITH ARIES

Virgo is ruled by Mercury and Aries is ruled by Mars. But they have totally different ideas. Aries's passions are impulsive and direct. Virgo's sexuality is more enigmatic and takes time to be revealed. In other areas Aries is full of exciting new plans and ideas, and insists on being boss. Virgo is critical and fussy, and likes things to be done the way he wants. They end up making war, not love and do not blend well astrologically. Virgos desire a well-ordered existence and won't be happy under Arian leadership. If the Arian allows Virgo space, and acknowledges the virtues of Virgo, the two can make for a dynamic relationship.

VIRGO WITH TAURUS

With both being earth signs there will be much common ground for these two. Both Virgo and Taurus desire material success and security. Taurus keeps a careful eye on expenditures, which pleases Virgo. Although they lack what might be called a spontaneous approach to life, neither puts a high value on that. Both share the same intellectual pursuits. Taurus's attraction and Virgo's sharp mind are a good combination for success as a team. The one drawback is that Virgo is normally in control of their emotional output while Taurus thrives on deep emotion and could perhaps overwhelm Virgo.

VIRGO WITH GEMINI

Both are Mercury-ruled and have a mental approach to life. They are attracted to each other because of a mutual interest in intellectual ideas. Both have active minds. Virgo's analytical approach seems like indifference to Gemini. Virgo looks on Gemini's busy social life as superficial and a waste of time. Virgo is critical; Gemini is tactless. Mercury is calculating and logical; in Virgo it is critical and demanding. Gemini's ever-present desire for change would be much for the realistic Virgo. One point for the two to be compatible would be the desire for good clothes, cleanliness, mutual desire for friends and associates who are engaged in intellectual and artistic pursuits. Gemini can deal with Virgo's critical eye, well, this could work.

VIRGO WITH CANCER

Virgo's demands may be a bit much for Cancer's desire for peace and quiet. Cancer's response is emotive while Virgo's is analytical. Cancer may have to warm up Virgo a little, since there is fire under the ice. This can turn into a comfortable, and affectionate relationship. Cancer's struggle for financial security works perfectly with Virgo. Cancer's dependency neatly complements Virgo's need to protect, and each is anxious to please the other. The full, affectionate feelings of cancer will not be completely satisfied by Virgo's direct approach to the practical matters at hand. Virgo will appreciate the loyalty and sincerity of cancer, but will need to be a little more demonstrative and affectionate with cancer.

VIRGO WITH LEO

Virgo being the earth sign and Leo being a fire sign. Here is a good chance for a happy partnership. Virgo is practical Leo is extravagant and a spendthrift. Leo likes to live life in a really big way, but Virgo is conservative. This is one of those relationships that depend, n the type of relationship it is. Leo will overwhelm Virgo, whose criticism will irk Leo. In business it is best when Leo leads and Virgo follows and the differences will be tolerated. Both of them should look elsewhere. If Virgo will permit Leo to hold the limelight and refrain from being too critical they should have no real barriers to a happy and successful partnership. But this may be quite hard.

VIRGO WITH VIRGO

Since both being the earth signs their comparability speaks of their ego problems that they may be facing while adhering to each other's view. Each of them has to forgo their egos. All is smooth sailing as long as these perfectionists curb their instincts for finding fault. Actually, they bring out the very best in each other. They are responsible, sensitive, intelligent, and take love seriously. They also share passions of the mind, and will never bore each other. Important things. Finding anything resembling compatibility would be hard for this combination. Both have a tendency to end up with a battle of the wits with both opponents evenly matched. Each would over exaggerate the faults of the other.

VIRGO WITH LIBRA

Virgo is an earth sign and Libra is and air sign. Libra enjoys spending money, going to parties, and being the centre of attention. Virgo will try to curb and dominate Libra's fickle and outer directed nature.

Virgo is reserved and practical, and Libra views this as a personal rebuff. Libra will soon drift away in search of more fun-loving companions. Libra may tap Virgo's hidden sensuality but their personalities are altogether too different for real compatibility. Another combination that would have trouble finding a good marital life. Their understanding and their married life can come to settlement provided each of the other forgoes the individual ego.

VIRGO WITH SCORPIO

Virgo belongs to the earth sign while Scorpio belongs to the water sign. The combination sometimes belongs to the mutual admiration society. If Virgo will keep from hurting Scorpio's pride, this combination will be happy and enduring. Scorpio is also possessive and fiercely loyal, which makes Virgo feel loved and protected. They also admire each other's minds. Virgo is logical, intellectual, and analytical. Scorpio is imaginative, visionary, and perceptive. Scorpio is volatile but secretive, Virgo is self-restrained and reserved. The Virgo mind is very fascinated with the mysterious and intriguing Scorpio. The only problem here is on the emotional side. If each of them keeps their emotion aside there is some hope for a longer lasting friendship.

VIRGO WITH SAGITTARIUS

Virgo is an earth sign and Sagittarius is a fire sign. Their comparability often leads to unwanted and undesired conflicts. Though both are intellectual signs but the way their minds work clashes with each other. Sagittarius is expansive and extravagant, while Virgo prefers a simple, ordered, and unpretentious life. Sagittarius's free spirit has nothing in common with hardworking Virgo. The differences here are like day and night. Not all bad but difficult to reconcile with.

VIRGO WITH CAPRICORN

Since these are two earth signs the mercury and sun combination should find mutual grounds for an agreeable partnership. A harmonious pair. Both are diligent, disciplined, and have a sense of purpose. They admire one another and take great pride in pleasing each other. Both need respect and approval and each intuitively gives the other exactly that. With these two signs there are some similarity and compatibility. They are both very exacting. This stops many areas of disagreement. They both take great pride in appearance and surroundings. They can find a friend in each other.

VIRGO WITH AQUARIUS

Virgo is an earth sign while Aquarius is an air sign. Aquarius has venturesome ideas and thinks Virgo unresponsive or cold.

A lot depends on the cultural and educational levels of the partners. Aquarius is interested in other people, causes and Virgo is cautious about emotional giving. Virgo seeks personal achievement and financial security. Aquarius is outgoing, inventive, a visionary. Virgo is reserved, prudent, and very practical about its ambitions. This couple may not even make it as friends. There is a marked difference between the two; the chances for a happy and enduring marriage are almost nil. Each has a distant quality. There is no happy medium with this combination; it is either very good or very bad.

VIRGO WITH PISCES

Pisces is fascinated by Virgo's incisive, analytical mind. Virgo, love means security and mental compatibility. Pisces is the very opposite of Virgo as opposites often are sentimental and are poles apart. It will take a great deal of patience and understanding on the part of Virgo to cope with the sentimental nature of Pisces. This is another pair of zodiac opposites that can be great at times and horrible at others times. The opposites can learn a lot about themselves from their counterparts. It will go a long way in making this combination happy.

COMPARABILITY

ZODIAC SIGNS

LIBRA WITH OTHER ZODIAC SIGNS

LIBRA WITH ARIES	LIBRA WITH TAURUS
LIBRA WITH GEMINI	LIBRA WITH CANCER
LIBRA WITH LEO	LIBRA WITH VIRGO
LIBRA WITH LIBRA	LIBRA WITH SCORPIO
LIBRA WITH SAGITTARIUS	LIBRA WITH CAPRICORN
LIBRA WITH AQUARIUS	LIBRA WITH PISCES

LIBRA WITH ARIES

Libra being an air sign and is a fire sign. Libra wants peace, quiet, and harmony while Aries wants action and adventure. Both like social life, entertaining, and pleasure, but both are restless in their ways. There is a powerful initial attraction between these two but their love life may be bit unconventional. Libra will look for someone less demanding, and Aries will bind someone for more dictating. Marvellous affair but poor marriage shows. Libra's refined and artistic temperament wishes for reciprocal attachments. And this is something Aries cannot provide. There is a wider the ordinary margin for error though, and most of these combinations will go at the distance and nonreciprocal.

LIBRA WITH TAURUS

Libra an air sign loves to roam and Taurus an earth sign loves to sit and waits patiently. With understanding it could be a harmonic relationship. Taurus balances Libra's indecisiveness. Taurus finds Libra a warm, romantic, partner. Libra is born to charm. The love goddess and it does shine on the two lovebirds that are until one-steps out of line. Both signs are ruled by Venus and have sensual natures, but each expresses this quality differently. However there are common interest and a meeting of the mind and body making this a very good marital combination. They appreciate beauty and the finer things of life.

LIBRA WITH GEMINI

These two air signs are well suited in every way. Both signs have much in common and enough to make an ideal partnership. Libra being under Venus's influence and Mercury ruling Gemini makes for a very good planetary combination. This will be a very stimulating relationship. One sign compliments the other and brings out the better part of each other's nature. Gemini will find it easy to communicate with Libra who is only too happy to share his information and ideas. They are affectionate, fun loving, entertaining, and travel fond. This is considered to be a great astrological influence for a long and happy marriage.

LIBRA WITH CANCER

Cancer is not temperamentally suited to cope with the freedom loving Libran. This pair operates on entirely different levels. Cancer is too temperamental and possessive for airy Libra. They both love a beautiful home, but Libra also needs parties and people and outside pleasures. When Cancer turns critical, especially about Libra's extravagance, Libra starts looking elsewhere. On the positive side though, they could make it. Ruled by the Moon and Venus respectively, there is common ground here despite the fact that we have a water sign and an air. Libra will appreciate Cancer's loyalty and generosity. Cancer wants love Libra seeks perfect intellectual communion.

LIBRA WITH LEO

Leo being a fire and Libra being an air sign. The comparability of this two shall be tiring affair. The hale and hearty Leo may prove to be too much for the sensitive Libra nature, though they have a lot in common that could make for a good combination. The sun ruling Leo and Venus ruling Libra usually form a strong and luxurious aspect. Libra is indecisive and Leo will naturally take charge. Both signs love luxuries, are subject to flattery, and are very artistically inclined. The book may not always balance because they're both extravagant and love a beautiful setting in which to shine. Each will also try to outdo the other in order to get attention.

LIBRA WITH VIRGO

Libra is and air sign and Virgo is an earth sign Libra enjoys spending money, going to parties, and being the centre of attention. Virgo will try to curb and dominate Libra's fickle and outer directed nature. Virgo is reserved and practical, and Libra views this as a personal rebuff. Libra will soon drift away in search of more fun-loving companions. Libra may tap Virgo's hidden sensuality but their personalities are altogether too different for real compatibility. Another combination that would have trouble finding a good marital life. Their understanding and their married life can come to settlement provided each of the other forgoes the individual ego.

LIBRA WITH LIBRA

Whereas both are air signs. They both have basically the same interests and qualities, so there would be great understanding in the relationship. The biggest problem may be unresolved conflicts, as neither wants to stir the pot when differences appear. Equally demonstrative, lively, warm, sociable, in love with beautiful things, a problem is that neither wants to face reality. Though they are charming, peace loving, and adaptable, each needs a stronger balance than the other can provide. Also, because they are so much alike. Here is a match made in heaven, unless one had an incompatible sign rising at birth. While both like to be admired. With this combination there is so much in common and so little negatives

LIBRA WITH SCORPIO

Libra is an air sign where as Scorpio is a water sign. Libra may find Scorpio's intense nature a bit overwhelming. Common goals and shared interests could avert any difficulties. There is much sympathetic magnetism between these two signs. While Scorpio is the more dominating sign of the two. There is much to recommend this union, for they have many sympathies in common. Librans are sentimental and susceptible as lovers. This seems to be appealing to Scorpio's dominant and possessive urges. Scorpio is also touchy, moody, and quick to lash out in anger, which is just the kind of person Libra cannot bear. Scorpio seethes and becomes steadily more jealous and demanding, Libra has either to submit or to leave.

LIBRA WITH SAGITTARIUS

Libra being an air sign while Sagittarius being a fire sign. Their comparability is often marked by ego problems if one is able to forgo his/her ego this match can become a lasting affair. They will do well together, if Sagittarius can manage to be around enough to fulfil Libra's need for togetherness. Libra is stimulated by Sagittarius's eagerness for adventure, and Sagittarius is drawn to Libra's affectionate charm. Both are highly romantic, though this quality is more dominant in Libra. Libra will want to settle down before flighty Sagittarius does, but they can work that out. Charming, clever Libra knows how to appeal to Sagittarius's intellectual side and easily keeps Sagittarius intrigued. Sagittarius hates bondage and cannot be confined, and will not tolerate bondage, whether it be legal or not, and will use all the means at his command to break through bonds.

LIBRA WITH CAPRICORN

Libra is an air sign whereas Capricorn is an earth sign. Capricorn believes in hard work and achievement at any price. Libra is fond of socializing and nightlife, while Capricorn tends to be a loner, comfortable with only a chosen few. Libra needs flattery and attention, but Capricorn keeps its affections buried. Capricorn. And Libra's lazy, easygoing ways will offend. On the surface these two seem to be on the opposite, but the Capricorn is very much influenced by Libra. If Libra does not find the steady Capricorn nature too boring, there is good chance here for a successful marriage. Libra had better screen the social environment to suit Capricorn's views or there may be some embarrassing moments later on. Unless Capricorn can open up a little more there could be problems here. Libra requires affection and Capricorn tends to put it off.

LIBRA WITH AQUARIUS

Since both belongs to the Air signs, their comparability can said to be lasting affair. This could be a good combination for marriage. And these two have all the makings for a beautiful friendship: harmonious vibes in socializing, artistic interests, even in involvement in public affairs. Indecisive Libra is delighted with the fact that quick-minded Aquarius likes to make decisions. Possibility one of the few problems may be a misunderstanding because an Aquarius mate is unpredictable at times, and for no reason at all, may seek seclusion and refuse to communicate. In that event, the best thing to do would be to let them enjoy their solitude. Both of these signs are naturally friendly people, while Libra is best at relationship. There may not be monumental disagreements between these two but Libra will need to understand the Aquarian perfectly.

LIBRA WITH PISCES

Libra is an air sign while Pisces is a water sign. This is a reasonably good combination. There is mutual attraction. This is especially true under intimate circumstances. Pisces will be content with Libra's exclusive company. They start off fine, since both are sentimental and affectionate. Pisces feels neglected, and whines and scolds. Pisces senses that Libra's commitment is often insincere and that Libra's charm is mostly superficial. But Libra's love of social affairs may generate jealousy and disharmony in the intimate life.

Libra can get along will with nice people, but the Pisces is more discriminating, and this is the source of their disagreements. There is a mutual appreciation for art and beauty and all that it entails between these two.

COMPARABILITY

ZODIAC SIGNS

SCORPIO WITH OTHER ZODIAC SIGNS

SCORPIO WITH ARIES	SCORPIO WITH TAURUS
SCORPIO WITH GEMINI	SCORPIO WITH CANCER
SCORPIO WITH LEO	SCORPIO WITH VIRGO
SCORPIO WITH LIBRA	SCORPIO WITH SCORPIO
SCORPIO WITH SAGITTARIUS	SCORPIO WITH CAPRICORN
SCORPIO WITH AQUARIUS	SCORPIO WITH PISCES

SCORPIO WITH ARIES

Whereas Scorpio being a water sign and Aries being a fire sign. With Mars dominating both signs it makes for very positive temperaments unless there are some bad natal planetary aspects. Since Aries won't take orders from Scorpions and Scorpio will never take a back seat. Love cannot be a bonfire between these two. Though they've physical, energetic, and passionate in their sexual nature and each has a forceful personality and wants to control the other there is no room for these two. This combination is can make an ideal match if one ignores to dominate the other.

SCORPIO WITH TAURUS

These two are opposites in the zodiac, but they have more in common than other opposites. Both are determined and ambitious, and neither is much of a lover. These are zodiac opposites, but they are compatible earth and water signs. This usually manifests itself in a strong physical attraction. This combination mutually admires each other.

Jealousy however is the big problem with this pair and that seems to be always showing its face. Taurus must be careful to keep faith with the scorpion, or else this combination will fall down without warning.

SCORPIO WITH GEMINI

An air sign with a water sign. These two will have some difficulty rectifying their innate natures. Gemini is too changeable and inconstant for intense Scorpio, who needs and demands total commitment. Scorpio is basically a loner; Gemini likes to glitter in social settings. Gemini has a strong penchant for independence, while Scorpio wants to dominate and possess. Gemini's desire for freedom of action will clash with the jealous and possessive nature of Scorpio. These two will have some difficulty rectifying their innate natures. Then again, too much, stifles some. These two are opposites in the zodiac and are attracted to each other like magnets.

SCORPIO WITH CANCER

Both are ruled by water signs. Cancer is loyal; Scorpio's jealousy isn't provoked. Cancer admires Scorpio's strength while Scorpio finds a haven in Cancer's emotional commitment. Both are extremely intuitive and sense what will please the other. Together they can build a happy home where they feel safe and loved. This relationship has great intimacy, intensity, and depth. Things just get better all the time. Scorpio should make a good mate for quiet spoken cancer. Scorpio and cancer could well prove the ideal marriage combination.

SCORPIO WITH LEO

Leo being a fire sign and Scorpio being water sign. Two very strong willed individuals generally create some rather stormy moments. But Leo finds it hard to cope with Scorpio's jealousy and possessiveness. Scorpio considers Leo a showpiece. Scorpio doesn't understand Leo's need to be continually surrounded by an admiring audience. Scorpio would rather dominate than admire, and that doesn't suit Leo's kingly state. Two shinning personalities join together. Basically this should make for one of the most compatible combinations, but long and happy partnership will be far better a Leo female marries a Scorpio male.

SCORPIO WITH VIRGO

Virgo belongs to the earth sign while Scorpio belongs to the water sign. The combination sometimes belongs to the mutual admiration society. If Virgo will keep from hurting Scorpio's pride, this combination will be happy and enduring. Scorpio is also possessive and fiercely loyal, which makes Virgo feel loved and protected. They also admire each other's minds. Virgo is logical, intellectual, and analytical. Scorpio is imaginative, visionary, and perceptive. Scorpio is volatile but secretive, Virgo is self-restrained and reserved. The Virgo mind is very fascinated with the mysterious and intriguing Scorpio. The only problem here is on the emotional side. If each of them keeps their emotion aside there is some hope for a longer lasting friendship.

SCORPIO WITH LIBRA

Libra is an air sign where as Scorpio is a water sign. Libra may find Scorpio's intense nature a bit overwhelming. Common goals and shared interests could avert any difficulties. There is much sympathetic magnetism between these two signs. While Scorpio is the more dominating sign of the two. There is much to recommend this union, for they have many sympathies in common. Librans are sentimental and susceptible as lovers. This seems to be appealing to Scorpio's dominant and possessive urges. As long as Libra does not hurt Scorpio's pride, Libran will find what they are looking for when they marry a Scorpio. Scorpio is also touchy, moody, and quick to lash out in anger, which is just the kind of person Libra cannot bear. Scorpio seethes and becomes steadily more jealous and demanding, Libra has either to submit-or to leave.

SCORPIO WITH SCORPIO

Since both belong to the water signs. These two people who are so much alike understand each other very little. They are highly jealous and demanding. Both are sulky, brooding, and possessive. Both are in a continual struggle to force the other to relinquish control. Where is a combination that is confusing in its outcome? If both individuals have a thorough understanding of their inherent traits, they can have deep sympathy for each other.

The dominant, possessive, and jealous temperaments of each are things which both will have to handle with extreme consideration. This can be a very good combination or a very bad one.

SCORPIO WITH SAGITTARIUS

Scorpio is a water sign and Sagittarius is a fire. The combination of these to signs is an affair without proper and secured future. Scorpio is dominant by nature, but Scorpio will have trouble keeping their Sagittarian partner under control. Sagittarius is open, talkative, and casual about relationships. Scorpio wants Sagittarius at home, Sagittarius wants to roam. Mutual distrust is easy here. The Scorpion possessiveness will make life unbearable for Sagittarius. Scorpio is attractive to the Sagittarian lust, but that is where the compatibility ends. Not a recommended combination. Live and learn is about the best thing to expect here. Both can bring out some of the other's better qualities but the chance of anything long lasting is remote.

SCORPIO WITH CAPRICORN

Scorpio belongs to a water sign and Capricorn is of earth sign. This is a very hard combination to analyse. Capricorn even likes Scorpio's jealousy-for that makes Capricorn feel secure. These two share a sense of purpose: they are ambitious, determined, and serious about responsibility-and as a team have good auguries for financial success. The emotional incompatibility usually becomes unbearable for the combination to handle. For practical matters there are common traits, but the stubborn nature of both signs could make them enemies when things get down and dirty.

SCORPIO WITH AQUARIUS

Scorpio being water sign and Aquarius being an air sign. The comparability often leads to a breaking affair. This combination usually ends up getting into unpleasant terms after a little time. Unpredictable Aquarius is too much for the solid Scorpio temperament. Aquarius has many of outside interests and this does not sit well with Scorpio. Aquarius is too reserved for the passionate Scorpio. Humanitarian instincts are what Scorpio admires in an Aquarian, but Scorpio has no interest in sharing them with the world.

Scorpio wants to possess the person and Aquarius want to own the world. Without some extremely mature attitude adjustment it will be difficult to rectify the inherent differences in each other's nature. Scorpio wants to stay at home; Aquarius wants to be free to go.

SCORPIO WITH PISCES

Everything seems fine until Pisces gets tired of the little interests that seem to keep Scorpio occupied outside of the home. Scorpio does not appreciate positive qualities of Pisces. Pisces' imagination sparks Scorpio's creativity. Pisces' intuitive awareness and Scorpio's depth of feeling unite in a special closeness. This kind of mating lasts. This may be a love at first sight combination, however it seldom lasts a long period of time. But, on the positive side there is an intuitive bond here that both will find agreeable. There is attraction and emotion and feelings and all that good stuff that they both like.

COMPARABILITY

ZODIAC SIGNS

SAGITTARIUS WITH OTHER ZODIAC SIGNS

SAGITTARIUS WITH ARIES	SAGITTARIUS WITH TAURUS
SAGITTARIUS WITH GEMINI	SAGITTARIUS WITH CANCER
SAGITTARIUSWITH LEO	SAGITTARIUS WITH VIRGO
SAGITTARIUSWITH LIBRA	SAGITTARIUS WITH SCORPIO
SAGITTARIUS WITH SAGITTARIUS	SAGITTARIUS WITH CAPRICORN
SAGITTARIUS WITH AQUARIUS	SAGITTARIUS WITH PISCES

SAGITTARIUS WITH ARIES

The Mars-Jupiter duo is usually an ideal match for each other. Sagittarius is a perfect ideal and temperamental match for Aries. They both are active, spontaneous people. There may be a little conflict because both are impulsive and brutally frank. However, they have wonderful senses of humour and enjoy each other's company. If they make it in the bedroom, they'll make it everywhere else. Most people of these matches are in it for life. The Sagittarius means liberty, and the pursuit of happiness while Aries is subscribes to this theory. And for this reason, that makes them a good match.

SAGITTARIUS WITH TAURUS

These are two very different personality types the more reserved Taurus and the outgoing Sagittarius both has an appreciation for the truth. Sagittarius has an easy live and let live attitude this might work if Taurus can tie a string to Sagittarius's. The Taurus who marries a Sagittarian will find that no amount of arguing or berating is going to change the reckless Sagittarian With some understanding they can find harmony in their characters as long as they allow each other their personalities. With the Taurean being possessive and the Sagittarian being freedom loving, the Sagittarian may find this hard to co-operate with.

SAGITTARIUS WITH GEMINI

Mercury rules Gemini and Sagittarius are ruled by Jupiter the planet of knowledge and wisdom. Both have bright minds, but Sagittarius is outspoken while Gemini likes to enjoy fun. They are usually a compatible combination with both being frank, outspoken, and a certain amount of personal understanding being made. They meet on a common ground, and can plan their lives with equilibrium. They are restless, adventuresome, imaginative, and fun loving. No other opposite signs in the zodiac enjoy each other more than these two. However if Sagittarius forgoes its ego and Gemini restores to concrete planning they can make a good combination otherwise their combination may not last long.

SAGITTARIUS WITH CANCER

A water and fire combination. Sagittarius likes to wander, while Cancer is a prefers to stay at home. Cancer's commitment to total togetherness only makes Sagittarius desperate to get away. In addition, outspoken Sagittarius's bluntness continually wounds sensitive Cancer. They happen to be better friends than lovers. There is a vast difference in natures and the likely hood of being compatible is all but impossible, unless there are some positive aspects in their charts. Cancer is too needy for Sagittarius. On the good side, they are both generous people.

SAGITTARIUS WITH LEO

Both being of fire sign. The pendulum can swing in any body's favour. Together they share a liking for freedom, adventure, and meeting new people. Leo's natural quality of leadership brings out what loyalty Sagittarius can give. Leo is very proud, but self-confident and expansive Sagittarius is quite happy to let Leo go. Both love change and excitement and have a great zest for life. This is an excellent combination for the most part unless Sagittarius is in need of too much freedom and Leo becomes too bossy.

SAGITTARIUS WITH VIRGO

Virgo is an earth sign and Sagittarius is a fire sign. Their comparability often leads to unwanted and undesired conflicts. Though both are intellectual signs but the way their minds work clashes with each other. Sagittarius is expansive and extravagant, while Virgo prefers a simple, ordered, and unpretentious life. Sagittarius's free spirit has nothing in common with hardworking Virgo. The differences here are like day and night. Not all bad but difficult to reconcile with.

SAGITTARIUS WITH LIBRA

Libra being an air signs while Sagittarius being a fire sign. Their comparability is often marked by ego problems if one is able to forgo his/her ego this match can become a lasting affair. They will do well together, if Sagittarius can manage to be around enough to fulfil Libra's need for togetherness. Libra is stimulated by Sagittarius's eagerness for adventure, and Sagittarius is drawn to Libra's affectionate charm.

Both are highly romantic, though this quality is more dominant in Libra. Libra will want to settle down before flighty Sagittarius does, but they can work that out. Charming, clever Libra knows how to appeal to Sagittarius's intellectual side and easily keeps Sagittarius intrigued. Sagittarius hates bondage and cannot be confined, and will not tolerate bondage, whether it be legal or not, and will use all the means at his command to break through bonds.

SAGITTARIUS WITH SCORPIO

Scorpio is a water sign and Sagittarius is a fire. The combination of these to signs is an affair without proper and secured future. Scorpio is dominant by nature, but Scorpio will have trouble keeping their Sagittarian partner under control. Sagittarius is open, talkative, and casual about relationships. Scorpio wants Sagittarius at home, Sagittarius wants to roam. Mutual distrust is easy here. The Scorpion possessiveness will make life unbearable for Sagittarius. Scorpio is attractive to the Sagittarian lust, but that is where the compatibility ends. Not a recommended combination. Live and learn is about the best thing to expect here. Both can bring out some of the other's better qualities but the chance of anything long lasting is remote.

SAGITTARIUS WITH SAGITTARIUS

Since both belong to fire signs. Their combination would be a sweet-sour affair. Two lively, optimistic people on the go all the time. But this exciting, chaotic, eventful relationship is too unpredictable to suit either of them. They have a tendency to bring out the worst in each other. Each remains uncommitted and has so many outside interests that this pair inevitably drifts apart. If this combination is not on the same intellectual and social plane, there is little hope for this couple to have a long happy relationship. They will have to do everything together or nothing at all. All interests being social and business must be the same. May work better as friends or partners.

SAGITTARIUS WITH CAPRICORN

Sagittarius belongs to a fire sign whereas Capricorn attributes to earth sign. Sagittarius is venturesome, sociable, and expansive.

Capricorn is cautious with money and concerned with appearances and Sagittarius is neither. Both should look elsewhere. Capricorn and the outgoing, risk taking Sagittarius. Not much in the way of compatibility but as with most combinations they can learn from each other. Sagittarius may prove to be too much for the sombre and restrictive temperament of Capricorn. Their temperament is entirely different, one is optimistic, and the other is pessimistic. Here again we see the difference between them may not be a lasting affair.

SAGITTARIUS WITH AQUARIUS

Sagittarius is a fire sign whereas Aquarius is an air sign. Their comparability often results in a powerful combination. Each of the other has to forgo his or her own ego. Aquarius is innovative. Sagittarius loves to experiment. These two share a great zest for living and a forward-looking viewpoint. Neither will try to tie down the other. Both seek to explore possibilities to the fullest, and they share idealism about love and life. They'll like each other too. The combination usually has a great chance for success. Both temperaments are very much alike. This is a purely social combination that will revel in a large group of friends and public-spirited associates. Sagittarius readily understands the moods and peculiarities of the Aquarius. There is a very good chance for a successful relationship.

SAGITTARIUS WITH PISCES

Sagittarius is a fire sign and Pisces is water. There is much here for an interesting and sincere relationship. Sagittarius is attracted to Pisces's spirituality. Sagittarius being free and easy will find Pisces too much of a heavy load to haul around. Though, Sagittarius may find that the marriage to Pisces is too confining. There will be a lot of confusion and wonder between these two. At times it will be good and at other times not good at all. Your natures are somewhat opposite to one another and the ability to understand the other's intent and actions will be evident. This combination quite hard to match.

COMPARABILITY

ZODIAC SIGNS

CAPRICORN WITH OTHER ZODIAC SIGNS

CAPRICORN WITH ARIES	CAPRICORN WITH TAURUS
CAPRICORN WITH GEMINI	CAPRICORN WITH CANCER
CAPRICORN WITH LEO	CAPRICORN WITH VIRGO
CAPRICORN WITH LIBRA	CAPRICORN WITH SCORPIO
CAPRICORN WITH SAGITTARIUS	CAPRICORN WITH CAPRICORN
CAPRICORN WITH AQUARIUS	CAPRICORN WITH PISCES

CAPRICORN WITH ARIES

Capricorns are usually patient and are traditionally easygoing. Arians are too impatient to cope with the slowness attitude. Saturn represents the Capricorn and Mars governs the Aries. Aries's taste for innovation and experiment may not please Capricorns. Aries is restless, fiery, and impulsive; Capricorn is ordered, settled, and practical. Capricorn needs to dominate and so does Aries. Problems often crops up over moneymaking schemes. Not a hopeful combination. Capricorn will nod against the Arian will and a disagreement is bound to occur. In the matter of sex there is an affinity; however, their inherent personalities clash. The combination of a fire sign with an earth sign. Aries is a fiery in nature while Capricorn is earth, cautious and reserved. Aries prefers to take action while Capricorn would rather plan and wait. Without a great deal of tolerance and patience, there is not much hope for this union.

CAPRICORN WITH TAURUS

A good combination of the basic earth signs. Both are responsible and practical natures. They even have a mutual desire for success and material things. Capricorn is a strong match for Taurus, for they both have passions that are straightforward and uncomplicated. Capricorn is a bit more secretive than Taurus.

With both partners having mutual understanding of each other's personalities this can be a very compatible marriage. Venus and Saturn blend very well from an emotional point of view.

CAPRICORN WITH GEMINI

Capricorn gets worried about security, while Gemini feels about losing its liberty. The Saturn ruled Capricorn will be at differences with the Mercury ruled Gemini. Patience is a virtue with Capricorn, but it is not so with Gemini. Gemini's need for a survival does nothing to make Capricorn feel secure. Gemini's free talks, meets opposition from conservative Capricorn. Capricorn's great drive to execute will prove to be too much for the Gemini. Until they both are ready to minimize their goals. Capricorn will go on hunting until he gains the upper hand. Of course with these two people going together anything is possible and the outcome of the result may not be satisfying to each other.

CAPRICORN WITH CANCER

Both signs have plenty in common. Capricorn has too many other interests to give Cancer all the attention it needs. Cancer is shy, sensitive, and needs affection, while Capricorn is aloof, and domineering. Capricorn has the ability to make cancer's dream come true, while Cancer is happy wishing for and wanting the success and security that the Capricorn strives for. The elements of water and earth go well together but these are zodiac opposites you can expect both side of the coin. They will have to take the good with the bad and there will be plenty of both. Capricorn lacks the warmth and sentiment that Cancer requires.

CAPRICORN WITH LEO

Leo being a fire signs whereas Capricorn is an earth sign. The combination of these two may at time lead to severe complications. The slow Capricorn may prove to be too much for the carefree nature of Leo. Leo will think Capricorn stingy with affection because Capricorn's reserved, undemonstrative nature cannot give Leo the adoration it needs. Neither will take a back seat nor let the other dominate.

This affair will be on the rocks before it even leaves the dock. Leo forgives and forgets; Capricorn being the one who is slow to anger and seldom forgets. This pair would not form the ideal basis for mutual understanding. Leo likes to live for the moment and Capricorn prefers to make calculated movements.

CAPRICORN WITH VIRGO

Since these are two earth signs the mercury and sun combination should find mutual grounds for an agreeable partnership. A harmonious pair. Both are diligent, disciplined, and have a sense of purpose. They admire one another and take great pride in pleasing each other. Both need respect and approval and each intuitively gives the other exactly that. With these two signs there are some similarity and compatibility. They are both very exacting. This stops many areas of disagreement. They both take great pride in appearance and surroundings.

CAPRICORN WITH LIBRA

Libra is an air sign whereas Capricorn is an earth sign. Capricorn believes in hard work and achievement at any price. Libra is fond of socializing and nightlife, while Capricorn tends to be a loner, comfortable with only a chosen few. Libra needs flattery and attention, but Capricorn keeps its affections buried. Capricorn. And Libra's lazy, easygoing ways will offend. On the surface these two seem to be on the opposite, but the Capricorn is very much influenced by Libra. If Libra does not find the steady Capricorn nature too boring, there is good chance here for a successful marriage. Libra had better screen the social environment to suit Capricorn's views or there may be some embarrassing moments later on. Unless Capricorn can open up a little more there could be problems here. Libra requires affection and Capricorn tends to put it off.

CAPRICORN WITH SCORPIO

Scorpio belongs to a water sign and Capricorn is of earth sign. This is a very hard combination to analyse. Capricorn even likes Scorpio's jealousy-for that makes Capricorn feel secure. These two share a sense of purpose: they are ambitious, determined, and serious about responsibility-and as a team have good auguries for financial success.
The emotional incompatibility usually becomes unbearable for the combination to handle. For practical matters there are common traits, but the stubborn nature of both signs could make them enemies when things get down and dirty.

CAPRICORN WITH SAGITTARIUS

Sagittarius belongs to a fire sign whereas Capricorn attributes to earth sign. Sagittarius is venturesome, sociable, and expansive. Capricorn is cautious with money and concerned with appearances and Sagittarius is neither. Both should look elsewhere. Capricorn and the outgoing, risk taking Sagittarius. Not much in the way of compatibility but as with most combinations they can learn from each other. Sagittarius may prove to be too much for the sombre and restrictive temperament of Capricorn. Their temperament is entirely different, one is optimistic, and the other is pessimistic. Here again we see the difference between them may not be a lasting affair.

CAPRICORN WITH CAPRICORN

Both belong to earth sign. They both have the same faults, which may keep fault finding down to a minimum. With important issues, they would both have what it takes to over come any hardship. Capricorns approve of people like themselves, so with these two there's no lack of mutual respect and regard. Neither one can relax or let down its hair. Both have the same long-range aspirations and the basic qualities to attain them. Great mixture for a happy relationship. The biggest problem here will be keeping things lively and new.

CAPRICORN WITH AQUARIUS

Since Capricorn being an earth sign and Aquarius being an air sign Capricorn believes in self-discipline and Aquarius believes in self-expression. Capricorn finds Aquarius too unpredictable, and Aquarius's impersonal attitude makes Capricorn uneasy. However, they should like each other and love can turn into friendship. This is a very hard combination to analyse. Capricorn wants all effort and anything else Aquarius has to give—to be cantered at home for their mutual good. Capricorn does not like the interest that Aquarius shows to other people. A very doubtful combination.

Too many other differences as well and unless you have other compatible aspects in your birth charts, don't expect a long lasting affair.

CAPRICORN WITH PISCES

As Capricorn being an earth sign and Pisces being a water sign. This is a good combination with complimentary values. And there's nothing Capricorn likes better than being admired. Pisces generous affections and Capricorn's strong sense of loyalty combine to make each feel safe and protected. These very different people meet each other's needs. One of the things that Pisces will admire about Capricorn is his very practical ways. This combination seems to work very well, provided each other admires the other's values first.

COMPATABILITY

ZODIAC SIGNS

AQUARIUS WITH OTHER ZODIAC SIGNS

AQUARIUS WITH ARIES	AQUARIUS WITH TAURUS
AQUARIUS WITH GEMINI	AQUARIUS WITH CANCER
AQUARIUS WITH LEO	AQUARIUS WITH VIRGO
AQUARIUS WITH LIBRA	AQUARIUS WITH SCORPIO
AQUARIUS WITH SAGITTARIUS	AQUARIUS WITH CAPRICORN
AQUARIUS WITH AQUARIUS	AQUARIUS WITH PISCES

AQUARIUS WITH ARIES

Aquarius belongs to an air sign whereas Aries belongs to fire sign. Both signs are of independent nature but at times Aquarius will do things without notice with which Aries may become impatient. Since both are active, ambitious, enjoy a wide range of interests, and are equally eager for sexual adventure. As both are independent Aquarius energies more than Aries and Aries may at times feel neglected. Aries finds the Aquarian unpredictability exciting, but feels entirely insecure. However, with a bit of tact and understanding on both sides, this is a great affair that could turn into something even better. This could possibly be a good relationship, but will require a positive attitude on both parts.

AQUARIUS WITH TAURUS

These two live on opposite sides of the planet, in fact some times, Taurus will wonder if Aquarius is even from this planet. Neither is likely to approve of the other. Taurus is conservative, careful, closemouthed. Aquarius is unconventional, innovative, and vivacious. Taurus is lusty and passionate while Taurus needs security and comfort. Aquarius, a fancy-free loner who resents ties that bind.

This combination heads in for many difficulties. The Aquarian being unpredictable. Both love ease and comfort but their views on how to obtain them are very different. Another big irritation for the Taurus lover is the unwillingness of the Aquarius to share his secrets. Aquarius will find the Taurus attention somewhat smothering and restrictive

AQUARIUS WITH GEMINI

Gemini is bit inconstant or unstable, Aquarius understands somewhat Gemini's needs. Gemini is always looking for surprises and the Aquarian can give them. Gemini and Aquarius get along quite easily. They share a taste for new things, travelling, meeting new people and doing new things. Since both are unpredictable, things may always go smoothly with them. But love keeps getting them together, for Aquarius adores Gemini's wit and good cheer. The caring, thoughts of Aquarius will find a smooth home with Gemini. Uranus, the ruling planet of Aquarius, is full of surprises and sudden changes. This will suit the Gemini perfectly.

There will be plenty of none stop variety to afford the stimulation that Gemini needs for its dual personality and goal.

AQUARIUS WITH CANCER

Aquarius is quick-minded, unpredictable, and apt to be impatient with cautious, hesitant Cancer. Cancer has a conservative taste while Aquarius taste is usually the opposite. Cancer needs to feel close and secure. The social side of the Aquarian may prove to be too much for the Cancer. Aquarian's love to share their life stories with the world while cancer is satisfied to concentrate on personal obligations. Odds against this combination are too great for this combination, unless one will become convergent to the other. Aquarius has a need to be independent and often appears detached in a close relationship with cancer.

AQUARIUS WITH LEO

Aquarius is an air sign and Leo is a fire sign. The comparability of this two in terms of worldly affairs can often become difficult to match. Both like socializing and meeting new people, but Leo always needs to perform on centre stage, which makes Aquarius impatient and irritable. Aquarius is too independent to become Leo's devoted subject. And that's where it ends. Leo views Aquarius's aloof emotions as a personal rejection. Both signs are better when doing things for others. Leo loves the world and Aquarius loves humanity. This makes for an excellent combination for a partnership that deals with or caters to the public. Each has a mutual understanding of the other when it comes to intimate matters, needs and desires.

AQUARIUS WITH VIRGO

Aquarius is an air sign while Virgo is an earth sign. Aquarius has venturesome ideas and thinks Virgo unresponsive or cold. A lot depends on the cultural and educational levels of the partners. Aquarius is interested in other people, causes and Virgo is cautious about emotional giving. Virgo seeks personal achievement and financial security. Aquarius is outgoing, inventive, a visionary. Virgo is reserved, prudent, and very practical about its ambitions. This couple may not even make it as friends. There is a marked difference between the two; the chances for a happy and enduring marriage are almost nil.

Each has a distant quality. There is no happy medium with this combination; it is either very good or very bad.

AQUARIUS WITH LIBRA

Whereas both are air signs. They both have basically the same interests and qualities, so there would be great understanding in the relationship. The biggest problem may be unresolved conflicts, as neither wants to stir the pot when differences appear. Equally demonstrative, lively, warm, sociable, in love with beautiful things, a problem is that neither wants to face reality. Though they are charming, peace loving, and adaptable, each needs a stronger balance than the other can provide. Also, because they are so much alike. Here is a match made in heaven, unless one had an incompatible sign rising at birth. While both likes to be admired. With this combination there is so much in common and so little negatives

AQUARIUS WITH SCORPIO

Aquarius being an air sign and Scorpio being water sign. The comparability often leads to a breaking affair. This combination usually ends up getting into unpleasant terms after a little time. Unpredictable Aquarius is too much for the solid Scorpio temperament. Aquarius has many of outside interests and this does not sit well with Scorpio. Aquarius is too reserved for the passionate Scorpio. Humanitarian instincts are what Scorpio admires in an Aquarian, but Scorpio has no interest in sharing them with the world. Scorpio wants to possess the person and Aquarius want to own the world. Without some extremely mature attitude adjustment it will be difficult to rectify the inherent differences in each other's nature. Scorpio wants to stay at home; Aquarius wants to be free to go.

AQUARIUS WITH SAGITTARIUS

Aquarius is an air sign where as Sagittarius is a fire sign. Their comparability often results in a powerful combination. Each of the other has to forgo his or her own ego. Aquarius is innovative. Sagittarius loves to experiment. These two share a great zest for living and a forward-looking viewpoint. Neither will try to tie down the other. Both seek to explore possibilities to the fullest, and they share idealism about love and life. They'll like each other too.

The combination usually has a great chance for success. Both temperaments are very much alike. This is a purely social combination that will revel in a large group of friends and public-spirited associates. Sagittarius readily understands the moods and peculiarities of the Aquarius. There is a very good chance for a successful relationship.

AQUARIUS WITH CAPRICORN

Aquarius being an air sign and Capricorn being an earth sign. Capricorn believes in self-discipline and Aquarius believes in self-expression. Capricorn finds Aquarius too unpredictable, and Aquarius's impersonal attitude makes Capricorn uneasy. However, they should like each other and love can turn into friendship. This is a very hard combination to analyse. Capricorn wants all effort and anything else Aquarius has to give—to be cantered at home for their mutual good. Capricorn does not like the interest that Aquarius shows to other people. A very doubtful combination. Too many other differences as well and unless you have other compatible aspects in your birth charts, don't expect a long lasting affair.

AQUARIUS WITH AQUARIUS

Both being an air signs. This combination is more compatible then any other combination. One Aquarius finally finds just the right mate in the other Aquarian. They admire and like each other, and especially enjoy each other's sense of humour. Each is involved in all kinds of projects and friendships. With so many outside activities going, they are likely to be apart as much as they are together and that's fine with them. They haven't a thing to quarrel about since they agree on everything: Both of them are much more rational than emotional.

AQUARIUS WITH PISCES

Aquarius is an air sign where as Pisces is a water sign. Their comparability often leads to an unconventional relationship. Pisces needs someone strong to take control. Aquarius shuns any kind of emotional demands. This can be a dreamy affair as someone should show the reality to these people and that's not to say that they are unaware of reality. Both operate in a different manner than the other signs.

If the Pisces is able give the Aquarius the benefit of the doubt, the marriage should be a lasting one.

COMPATABILITY

ZODIAC SIGNS

PISCES WITH OTHER ZODIAC SIGNS

PISCES WITH ARIES	PISCES WITH TAURUS
PISCES WITH GEMINI	PISCES WITH CANCER
PISCES WITH LEO	PISCES WITH VIRGO
PISCES WITH LIBRA	PISCES WITH SCORPIO
PISCES WITH SAGITTARIUS	PISCES WITH CAPRICORN
PISCES WITH AQUARIUS	PISCES WITH PISCES

PISCES WITH ARIES

Pisceans are romantic and they desire the delicate approach that which the Arian lacks. Aries will draw Pisces out of their shell, and in turn will be appealed by Pisces mysterious nature in terms of sexuality. The boldness and confidence of Aries adding to the Pisces's intuitions and fantasies end in an eventful union. Pisces is somewhat shy and Aries likes to be dominant, Pisces likes having someone to be looked upon. For a happy coupling thus requires only a little more tact on Arian part.

PISCES WITH TAURUS

These two can share a great deal of their appreciation for beauty, art, and sensuality and just about any of the finer things in life. Pisces may not altogether understand Taurus's materialistic approach to life. Taurus's practical, easygoing nature helps Pisces through its frequent changes of mood. In love, Taurus is devoted and Pisces adores. This usually is a very happy combination. Pisces being romantic, imaginative, impressionable and flexible is just what the Taurus native is looking for.

PISCES WITH GEMINI

Their passion is quite high, and so are their problems. Thoughtless Gemini easily hurts Pisces. Gemini is mischievous and playful, but Pisces is sensitive and takes things to heart easily. Each practices in his or her thoughts in their own way: Gemini needs freedom and Pisces needs unending appreciation. Pisces just can't feel secure with talkative moods of Gemini, and he tries to pull the net in his own way. This atmosphere eventually makes it hard for Gemini to breathe his own liberty. The freedom of Gemini is stake if he marries a Piscean. Gemini's should be prepared to change their ways if they want to seek happiness with a loving and possessive Piscean.

PISCES WITH CANCER

The water signs rule a harmonious match and quite a perfect match as both. The sentimental combination of these two signs makes for an ideal marriage. Although both will have their moments of gloom and doom, they will soon come out in the sunshine to forgive and forget each other. They are both romantic, need to love and be loved and can probably communicate to each other without speaking or making facial gestures. Both are emotional, intensely devoted, and sensitive to each other's moods.

PISCES WITH LEO

A fire and water combination. Leo being a fire sign and Pisces being a water sign often makes this a unique combination. Both are more inclined to take than to give. Fiery Leo and watery Pisces.
This is the depiction of these two. Generally not expected to work but both have an ability to learn from one another if they can get past their innate differences. The strong and hearty temperament of Leo may be too much for the subtle and sensitive Pisces. Pisces, with resilience, takes on the changing moods of any partnership. While Leo is flattered by the dependency of others. Pisces may be too much for Leo to take over a long period of time.

PISCES WITH VIRGO

Pisces is fascinated by Virgo's incisive, analytical mind. Virgo, love means security and mental compatibility. Pisces is the very opposite of Virgo as opposites often are sentimental and are poles apart. It will take a great deal of patience and understanding on the part of Virgo to cope with the sentimental nature of Pisces. This is another pair of zodiac opposites that can be great at times and horrible at others times. The opposites can learn a lot about themselves from their counterparts. It will go a long way in making this combination happy

PISCES WITH LIBRA

Libra is an air sign while Pisces is a water sign. This is a reasonably good combination. There is mutual attraction. This is especially true under intimate circumstances. Pisces will be content with Libra's exclusive company. They start off fine, since both are sentimental and affectionate. Pisces feels neglected, and whines and scolds. Pisces senses that Libra's commitment is often insincere and that Libra's charm is mostly superficial. But Libra's love of social affairs may generate jealousy and disharmony in the intimate life. Libra can get along will with nice people, but the Pisces is more discriminating, and this is the source of their disagreements. There is a mutual appreciation for art and beauty and all that it entails between these two.

PISCES WITH SCORPIO

Everything seems fine until Pisces gets tired of the little interests that seem to keep Scorpio occupied outside of the home. Scorpio does not appreciate positive qualities of Pisces. Pisces' imagination sparks Scorpio's creativity.

Pisces' intuitive awareness and Scorpio's depth of feeling unite in a special closeness. This kind of mating lasts. This may be a love at first sight combination, however it seldom lasts a long period of time. But, on the positive side there is an intuitive bond here that both will find agreeable. There is attraction and emotion and feelings and all that good stuff that they both like.

PISCES WITH SAGITTARIUS

Sagittarius is a fire sign and Pisces is a water Sign. There is much here for an interesting and sincere relationship. Sagittarius is attracted to Pisces's spirituality. Sagittarius being free and easy will find Pisces too much of a heavy load to haul around. Though Sagittarius may find that the marriage to Pisces is too confining. There will be a lot of confusion and wonder between these two. At times it will be good and at other times not good at all. Your natures are somewhat opposite to one another and the ability to understand the other's intent and actions will be evident.

PISCES WITH CAPRICORN

As Capricorn being an earth sign and Pisces being Water sign. This is a good combination with complimentary values. And there's nothing Capricorn likes better than being admired. Pisces generous affections and Capricorn's strong sense of loyalty combine to make each feel safe and protected. These very different people meet each other's needs. One of the things that Pisces will admire about Capricorn is his very practical ways. This combination seems to work very well, provided each other admires the other's values first.

PISCES WITH AQUARIUS

Both being an Air Sign. This combination is more compatible then any other combination. One Aquarius finally finds just the right mate in the other Aquarian. They admire and like each other, and especially enjoy each other's sense of humour. Each is involved in all kinds of projects and friendships. With so many outside activities going, they are likely to be apart as much as they are together and that's fine with them. They haven't a thing to quarrel about since they agree on everything. Both of them are much more rational than emotional.

PISCES WITH PISCES

Since both belong to water sign, having the same virtues and vices they should get along well together, at least they will have understanding and sympathy for one another. They find it hard to cope with practical realities, and there's no strong partner around to push either one in the right direction. Both have the same interests and the same love of home and possessions. At least both can be anchored to each other, so that they can put their shoulders to the wheel and face the responsibilities that reality demands. They have the refinement and delicacy that each desires. This should be a good combination.

CHAPTER 16

ASTROLOGICAL HINTS MICROSCOPY OF ASTROLOGY

EFFECT OF VARIOUS PLANETS AND THEIR TABLES

EFFECTIVE TABLES OF THE VARIOUS PLANETS WHICH SHALL REDUCE THE ILL EFFECTS OF THE PLANETS

TABLE OF SUN

6	1	8
7	5	3
2	9	4

TABLE OF 15

TABLE OF MOON

7	2	9
8	6	4
3	10	5

TABLE OF 18

TABLE OF MARS

11	6	13
12	10	8
7	14	9

TABLE OF 21

TABLE OF MERCURY

9	4	11
10	8	6
5	12	7

TABLE OF 24

TABLE OF RAHU

13	8	15
14	12	10
9	16	11

TABLE OF 36

TABLE OF KETU

14	9	16
15	13	11
10	17	12

TABLE OF 39

TABLE OF JUITER

10	5	12
11	9	7
6	13	8

TABLE OF 27

TABLE OF VENUS

11	6	13
12	10	8
7	14	9

TABLE OF 30

TABLE OF SATURN

12	7	14
13	11	9
8	15	10

TABLE OF 33

CHAPTER 17

ASTROLOGICAL HINTS MICROSCOPY OF ASTROLOGY

REMEDIES ACCORDING TO LAL KITAB

The general remedies for different planets according to Lal Kitab are following:

Remedies for Sun

1. Fast on Sunday.
2. Reciting or listening to Harivansha Purana.
3. Wheat, jaggery and copper etc, to be given in charity.
4. Maintaining good moral characters.
5. Wearing Ruby or in place of Ruby copper can be used.
6. Throwing copper coins in the flowing water.
7. Keep main entrance from east.
8. Keeping away from black marketing and black marketers.
9. Do not give in alms the article pertaining to Sun if Sun is exalted.
10 Service of Government officials.

Remedies for Moon

1. Keep fast on Monday.
2. Worship Lord Shiva or go on pilgrimage to Amaranth.
3. Milk, rice or silver to be given in alms.
4. Wear a white milky pearl or alternatively silver can be substituted.

5. Blessings of mother (grand mother, mother-in-law, mother's mother, mother's sister).
6. Silver nails in the feet of the bed.
7. Silver or rice to be dropped in the Crematorium.
8. Taking bath in the Ganges or running water.
9. water tank overheads should be cleaned in 5 to 6 months.
10. No water pump or well under the roof.
11. Giving things pertaining to Moon in charity if Moon is in debility but not when she is in exaltation.

Remedies for Venus

1. Fast on Friday.
2. Desi ghee, curd, camphor etc. to be given to places of worship.
3. Wear diamond or the pearl.
4. Perfuming the clothes and using cream & face powder etc.
5. Clothes should be clean and ironed.
6. Worn out clothes or burnt clothes should never be worn.

Remedies for Mars

1. Fast on Tuesday.
2. Sindoor to Lord Hanuman.
3. Throw in the running water pulse of masoor, or honey or sindoor.
4. Service of brother.
5. Sleeping on deerskin.
6. Pure silver to be used.

Remedies for Mercury

1. fasting on Wednesday.
2. Green things in alms or dropped in the running water.
3. Copper coin with a hole to be dropped in the running water.
4. Service of domesticating goat and parrot.
5. Belt to be used.
6. Bangles and clothes of green colour to be given to eunuchs.

7. If Mercury is in debility the things of Mercury should be given in alms, but never should this be done when Mercury is in exaltation.

8. Blessing of daughter, sister, and father's sister, mother's sister and wife's sister. They should also be helped to the extent possible.

Remedies for Saturn:

1. Fastings on Saturdays.
2. Bhairon worship and giving wine to him in temple of Bhairon.
3. Milk for the serpents.
4. Oil and wine to be distributed free.
5. Loaf of bread with mustard oil on it to be given to dogs and cows.

Remedies for Rahu:

1 Sarawati Poojan.
2 Never accept electrical items, steel vessels or blue clothes.
3 Kanya dan.
4 Wearing Gomed.
5 live in joint family.
6 Never use tobacco.

Remedies for Ketu:

1 Fasting on Ganesha Chaturthi and Ganesha Poojan.
2 Til, lime and Bananas etc. to be given in charity.
3 White and black pet dog in the house or feeding such a dog daily.
4 Good moral character and conduct.
5 Sour things to be given to female children below the age of nine years.
6 Black and white till to be dropped in running water.

"MAY THE HEAVENS SHOWER PEACE PROSPERITY AND HAPPINESS TO ALL"

THE FOLLOWING ASTROLOGY SITES

HTTP://WWW.ASTROLOGYBB.COM
HTTP://WWW.BBASTROLOGY.COM
HTTP://WWW.BALDEVBHATIA.COM
HTTP://WWW.BALDEVBHATIA.NET
HTTP://WWW.BALDEVBHATIA.US
HTTP://WWW.BALDEVBHATIA.ORG
HTTP://WWW.BALDEVBHATIA.INFO
HTTP://WWW.BALDEVBHATA.IN
HTTP://WWW.BALDEVBHATIA.BIZ

ARE BEING MANAGED AND MAINTAINED
BY
BALDEV BHATIA
(CONSULTANT-ASTROLOGY)
WORLD FAMOUS

PLEASE NOTE:

FOR CONSULTATION OF ANY PROBLEM REGARDING

1. BUSINESS	2. EDUCATION
3. LOVE, MARRIAGE	4. PROFESSION
5. JOB/SERVICE	6. HEALTH
7. DISEASE	8. FINANCE
9. PROPERTIES/VEHICLES	10. REMEDIES
11. VASTU	12. MEDITATION

ADVICE WITH REMEDY IS GIVEN

E-MAIL YOUR QUERIES TO: baldevbhatia@yahoo.com
PHONE BALDEV BHATIA: 919810075249
: 91 11 26686856

ADDRESS

BALDEV BHATIA
C-63, FIRST FLOOR, MALVIYA NAGAR
NEW DELH-110017, INDIA

SPECIAL NOTE

FROM THE AUTHOR BALDEV BHATIA
THANK YOU FOR READING MY BOOK
MY SINCERE PRAYERS
FOR ALL MY READERS
"GOD BLESS YOU ALL"

"ANY ONE WHO READS AND KEEPS THIS BOOK AS HOLY
MANUSCRIPT, GOD IS SURE TO BLESS HIM, WITH ALL THE
PEACE, HAPPINESS, WEALTH, HEALTH AND PROSPERITY
OF THIS UNIVERSE"

.... Baldev Bhatia